The Cinema of
Ermanno Olmi

The Cinema of
Ermanno Olmi

IAN PETTIGREW

McFarland & Company, Inc., Publishers
Jefferson, North Carolina

This book has undergone peer review.

LIBRARY OF CONGRESS CATALOGUING-IN-PUBLICATION DATA

Names: Pettigrew, Ian, author.
Title: The cinema of Ermanno Olmi / Ian Pettigrew.
Description: Jefferson, North Carolina : McFarland & Company, Inc., Publishers, 2020 | Includes bibliographical references and index.
Identifiers: LCCN 2020041392 | ISBN 9781476665894 (paperback : acid free paper) ∞
ISBN 9781476641225 (ebook)
Subjects: LCSH: Olmi, Ermanno, 1931-2018—Criticism and interpretation.
Classification: LCC PN1998.3.O46 P48 2020 | DDC 791.43023/3092—dc23
LC record available at https://lccn.loc.gov/2020041392

BRITISH LIBRARY CATALOGUING DATA ARE AVAILABLE

ISBN (print) 978-1-4766-6589-4
ISBN (ebook) 978-1-4766-4122-5

© 2020 Ian Pettigrew. All rights reserved

No part of this book may be reproduced or transmitted in any form or by any means, electronic or mechanical, including photocopying or recording, or by any information storage and retrieval system, without permission in writing from the publisher.

Front cover: A scene from the 1978 Ermanno Olmi film
The Tree of Wooden Clogs (New Yorker Films/Photofest)

Printed in the United States of America

McFarland & Company, Inc., Publishers
Box 611, Jefferson, North Carolina 28640
www.mcfarlandpub.com

For my mother, Maribeth Powers, and my wife, Cici

Table of Contents

Acknowledgments   ix
Preface   1
Introduction   3
A Brief Biography   13

1. In the Beginning, There Was … Edisonvolta   21
2. Time Standing Still and Moving Freely: Olmi's Boom Trilogy and the Evolution of His Time-Shifting Style   38
3. Disillusionment with Success During *gli anni di piombo* in Olmi's Post-Boom Trilogy   61
4. Revisiting the Past to Contemplate Our Freedom in the Present: Olmi's History Films   83
5. Exemplary Realities: Olmi's Fables and Parables   113
6. Christ and Religion According to an Aspiring Christian   148

Chapter Notes   181
Bibliography   195
Index   203

Acknowledgments

During this book's long life, it has become indebted to many people. Many of my colleagues, mentors, and friends, have offered insights along the way that have contributed to this book. I hope that I have not forgotten to acknowledge anyone here.

Brigham Young University has one of the best media arts programs in the United States and I am grateful that I was fortunate enough to study under such wonderful professors there. I would like to thank Darl Larsen, Dean Duncan, Jeff Parkin, Amy Jensen, and Randy Astle for contributing to my understanding of film as an art form. Special thanks to Sharon Swenson for being the best theory teacher in the world, her encouragement to pursue graduate studies, and being a tremendous support since I was at BYU.

A day does not pass without my thoughts returning to my friends and mentors in England and the wonderful experience I had studying at the University of Bristol. Alex Clayton, Jacqueline Maingard, Helen Piper, Angela Piccini, Sarah Street, and Cathy Poole all assisted me in various ways as I wrote my master's thesis on *Il posto* and *I fidanzati*. Kristian Moen is one of the best mentors anyone could hope for and helped shape the approach to Olmi's films that I have taken here.

Eduardo Abella and Alvaro Charro at the University of Miami library greatly assisted me in accessing many of the Italian language materials that I have used. They were always patient and willing to help me find exactly what I needed. Many thanks are also due to Christina Lane and Grace Barnes for their feedback on the very early stages of portions of this book when they read my PhD dissertation. When I initially wrote to William Rothman to enquire if anyone at the University of Miami would be interested in supervising a dissertation on Olmi, he was immediately supportive. A very special thanks to him and John Paul Russo, who have both been extremely generous in their willingness to read different parts of this book. They have done everything they could to help me in my career and in completing this project. I hope I have never asked too much of them.

I would also like to offer heartfelt thanks to my family, friends, and colleagues that have made the completion of this book possible. My mother, Maribeth Powers, and my brother, Joel Pettigrew, encouraged me through rough patches all along the way. Gary Allred, Meg Brainard, Eric Browning, Sophia Chen, The Choctaw Nation of Oklahoma, Mark Daniel, Jane Duffus, Steve Freebairn, Christina Freiberg, Jeff Glazier, Michele Greco, Deborah Hall, Zach Hilton, Antonio Iannotta, Warren Jamis, Grace Ji, Brad Justesen, Sergio Kelsor, Khaled Khorshid, Zongchao Li, Joe Lingle, Jiangmeng Liu, Lu Liu, Yu Liu, Peter Magpantay, Andrew Marshall, Charles Marshall, Michael Marshall, Leighton McKeen, Dan Melville, Tony Mendez, Gary Mitchem, James Moore, Ben Mudge, Hans Novelus, Ryan Oberg, Adam O'Brien, Cesar Odio, Carlos Odio, Craig Pacini, Julie Pacini, Linda Parker, Peer Reviewer no. 2, Ellis Pettigrew, Brian Phillips, Jasmine Phillips, Sarah Phillips, Matthew Pink, James Powers, Michael Powers, Marian Prio, Peter Quinn, Jyotika Ramaprasad, Christian Ricks, Cory Schulthies, Sean Sibley, Cylor Spaulding, Nathanael Spencer, Dustin Street, Funing Tang, Amy Toiaivao, Courtney Toiaivao, Lydia Vaughn, Martin Vaughn, Femke Whittaker-Treffers, Qinghua Yang and Yale Yang all offered their faith, love, and support. The Odio and Khorshid families fostered me as I made my way through graduate school. Oscar Jubis and I spent many late nights discussing Olmi and other film-related topics at the University of Miami's Cosford Cinema. Oscar also read through several portions of this book in its early stages. And lastly, I would like to thank my wife, Ciyun Peng. She understood what finishing this book has meant to me and has been patient during the last few years as I have spent so many hours huddled over a computer in libraries and offices and not with her.

Fragments of my discussion of *The Tree of Wooden Clogs* in Chapter 4 appeared as "The Politics of Spectatorship in *The Tree of Wooden Clogs*" in *CINEJ, Cinema Journal* 6, no. 1 (2017): 26–50.

Preface

The roots of this book go back to my undergraduate years at Brigham Young University. In an effort to maintain my Italian language skills, I thumbed through my copy of *The Oxford History of World Cinema* from my film history courses looking for titles from Italy to add to my Netflix DVD Queue. This led to many cinematic misadventures such as viewings of Marco Ferreri's *Non toccare la donna bianca* (*Don't Touch the White Woman*, 1974) and the sword and sandal film *Maciste, l'uomo più forte del mondo* (*Mole Men Against the Son of Hercules*, 1961). But I was also exposed to many of the wonderful works of post–World War II Italian cinema. I found myself particularly affected by Ermanno Olmi's *I fidanzati* (*The Fiances*, 1963) and *L'albero degli zoccoli* (*The Tree of Wooden Clogs*, 1978). I loved the films of his more well-known contemporaries—Fellini, Antonioni, Bertolucci, and Pasolini—but none of them impacted me as Olmi's did. There was something about them that ignited an introspection of my life and also an invitation to consider the way I thought about people who are on the peripheries of my social sphere, provoking me to reflect on other lives.

Eager to see more of Olmi's films, I watched everything of his that I could find that was available in the U.S. through rental, which was, and still is (even in the age of streaming), mostly limited to a handful of prominent festival winners between the 1960s and the late 1970s. I also went to the university library and hunted for any books or articles I could unearth on him. I was perplexed by the lack of English language scholarship his work has received. As I searched deeper, I found some books and articles in Italian, but nothing I could access without interlibrary loan. Already thinking about going to graduate school, this was the exact moment when I decided what I would do for my PhD dissertation, which would later transform into this, the first English language book on Olmi's cinema.

The first draft of this manuscript was submitted a few weeks prior to Olmi's death in May 2018. When I read of his passing, I felt like a friend had died even though we had never met. Reviewing his films closely, I have felt that I have come to know him or at least his *Weltanschauung*. Maybe some would consider that naïve, but I would argue that understanding these films together enriches all of them and reveals a philosophy expressed by their author.

As I have watched Olmi's films and thought about them over the last sixteen years, I remain puzzled as to why his works have not earned him more recognition. Since the success of his second feature, *Il posto* [*The Job*, a.k.a. *The Sound of Trumpets*, 1961], he had drifted in and out of the international film festival spotlight, with decades of relative obscurity in between winning major awards, such as the Palme d'Or (for *The Tree of Wooden Clogs*) and the Golden Lion (for *La leggenda del santo bevitore* [*The Legend of the Holy Drinker*, 1988]). Olmi's films are important because they seek to reveal what has been lost as the concept of work in developed nations has completely transformed over the last few centuries. But in order to appreciate what makes Olmi's cinema valuable, it is necessary to look closely at it. In this book, my methodology is to use close readings of his Edisonvolta shorts and all nineteen of his fictional features. I will detail his style, specifically the time-shifting technique he used throughout his career, and how he designed his films to be viewed experientially.

As I will discuss further in the introduction, some critics and scholars have denounced auteurism for various reasons since its introduction in the 1950s. But the study of directors as auteurs remains a useful approach in studying film and understanding it as an art form. And although I take an auteurist approach to Olmi and his films, it is the thread of humanity's loss of its fundamental relationship with nature, and a hope that humanity can regain this bond, that ties most of Olmi's work together and that will also serve as the link between the chapters of this book.

Introduction

Admired, Yet Neglected

Among the entries of Federico Fellini's *The Book of Dreams*, a collection of illustrated dream diaries the director kept as part of his analytical psychotherapy, there is a vision of four brothers who deactivate a radioactive fish that has been filled with dynamite. Following their heroic efforts, the public thanks the brothers at an award ceremony. Fellini then concludes his recollection of the dream with the hope that "Ermanno Olmi can make a very beautiful film of it."[1] Fellini recorded the dream in 1961, a year after seeing Olmi's first feature *Il tempo si è fermato* (*Time Stood Still*, 1959). Olmi did not know of the dream until the diaries' publication in 2007, long after Fellini's death in 1993, and was never able to ask Fellini why he was specifically selected to make a film about the world being saved.[2] Maybe Fellini's dream perceived something from the younger director's debut feature that indicated Olmi's films would progress from records of Italy's mid-twentieth century economic transformation to his late works' proposal that perhaps there is something valuable to be gained from looking back to agriculturally based lifestyles, something which could be applied to many of the global problems (climate change, dwindling natural resources, social disharmony, etc.) currently faced by humanity. If so, Fellini's dream correctly foretold the career of one of cinema's most undervalued figures.

However, the action-based story implied in Fellini's dream seems as if it would be more fitting for another director. Olmi's films typically call for a patient consideration of normal, everyday people and their relatively uneventful lives. His demanding style may be one of the reasons that he remains such a neglected filmmaker. Outside of Italy, even among film studies academics, Olmi's name is scarcely known. In the United States, very few have seen any of his nineteen feature films beyond the three (*Il posto*, *I fidanzati*, and *The Tree of Wooden Clogs*) now distributed on home video by the Criterion Collection. But even in Italy, where Olmi has received some consideration through book-length interviews, his autobiography, and several books dedicated to analyzing his work, he remains a minor figure, rarely included in the pantheon of great Italian filmmakers such as Fellini, Roberto Rossellini, Vittorio De Sica, Luchino Visconti, Michelangelo Antonioni, Bernardo Bertolucci, and Pier Paolo Pasolini.

We cannot point to any one reason for the indifference most of Olmi's work has received in English language scholarship. Most of his films require active viewership but so do those of Jean-Luc Godard, Fellini, and Andrei Tarkovsky, each of whom has had several English language books dedicated to their work. It could also be argued that the common misconception about Olmi being a religious filmmaker has detracted from his reputation. However, Rossellini, Pasolini, Luis Buñuel, Robert Bresson, and Terrence Malick have all made films exploring religious subjects, or religiosity, which seemingly contributed to their prestige. One practical reason that Olmi's work has not garnered much attention in English language film studies is that his films have only been granted a handful of retrospectives and most of his work continues to be unavailable on DVD or Blu-ray in English speaking countries. Additionally, some of his films that can be obtained from Italy lack English subtitles, rendering them mostly useless unless the viewer speaks Italian.

And yet, many of the critics and scholars who have made the effort to seek out Olmi exclaim their amazement that he continues to be so unappreciated. *Guardian* film critic Derek Malcolm declares, "No other Italian filmmaker of world stature has been as neglected as Ermanno Olmi."[3] Likewise, many acclaimed international filmmakers have shared their admiration for Olmi, citing his work as an inspiration for their own films. Jack Nicholson, who Olmi would have cast as Leo Tolstoy in a film that never materialized, went to the Cannes Film Festival one year just to watch a screening of a restored print of *Il posto*.[4] Xie Xiaojing and Tian Zhuangzhuang, members of the Beijing Film Academy's famed Fifth Generation, British filmmaker Mike Leigh, and the American director Charles Burnett, all indicate that *The Tree of Wooden Clogs* has been a major influence on their own work.[5] Works as diverse as *Hong xiang* (*The Red Elephant*, 1982), *Dao ma zei* (*The Horse Thief*, 1986), *High Hopes* (1988), and *Killer of Sheep* (1977) all seek to emulate Olmi's ability to reflect on quotidian realities.

Olmi's Style and Olmi as an Auteur

In this book, I aim to define how Olmi's films instigate this kind of reflection by giving close readings of his Edisonvolta shorts and all nineteen of his fictional feature films. An extended analysis of each of these works will allow me to illustrate how Olmi's style functions and its requirements of the viewer. Although in Chapter 1 I will discuss other major, perhaps more significant, influences on Olmi's style, Olmi was certainly inspired by the Neo-Realists and their method of confronting reality and encouraging meditative responses from audiences. The Neo-Realists style was defined by their preferences for location shooting, the use of non-professional actors, natural lighting, and long takes, all of which were frequently employed by Olmi. Mark Shiel notes that the Neo-Realists style "is characterized by a disposition to the ontological truth of the physical, visible world."[6] This dedication to the truth arose out of a resistance to fascism. As David Overbey writes in an introduction to a collection of Italian essays on the Neo-Realist movement, "The ethical and moral position of Neo-Realism was, in part, born in the 'war of liberation' and was dedicated to exploring and exposing the rhetorical lies of the Fascist period and to confronting the social reality of the present."[7] Although each had their own variation of this style, De Sica, Rossellini, and Visconti created an aesthetic that sought to present truth and reality, reflecting cinema's ultimate goal as described by French film theorist and critic André Bazin in articles like "The Myth of Total Cinema."[8] For Bazin, these films serve as a conduit to the audience, allowing them to perceive truth through a thoughtful deliberation as they carefully consider the films.

Olmi took this style further and adapted it to the Italy that was reconstructing itself in the 1950s and 60s. While still at Edisonvolta, he tested film's language and form, exercising his editing methods. The most distinctive element of Olmi's style is his use of time-shifting editing, which he experimented with in *Il posto* and then fully implemented in *I fidanzati*. By time-shifting editing I mean fluidly cutting between the present, past, future, and a character's imagination. This technique fragments the narrative and the psyche of the characters. The time-shifting is most often motivated by characters' feelings of responsibility and concern for family members and loved ones, many of whom they have become distanced from (either physically or emotionally), and the absence of the natural world. Olmi's style embodies these separations. Discussing how film replicated perspectives of the twentieth century, Francesco Casetti argues, "If film reconquered and recast our manner of seeing, it was not only because it embodied the gaze of the human eye, but because it embodied the gaze of the twentieth century. The camera captured what lay before it in forms that revealed the attitudes and orientations with which people were compelled to look at the world around them. On the screen, more than a reality objectively recorded, we saw reality in the spirit of the time."[9] Olmi's style evolved from the specific world of his characters and the resetting of their visions of their changing lives and the world surrounding them, "the spirit of [their] time." Although Olmi formed his time-shifting editing technique during the boom, he continued to use it afterward. Then and now this technique also operates as a reframing lens to how we see the world and others.

Although many of Olmi's films utilize a time-shifting editing style, this is not a uniform feature of his work. However, all of Olmi's feature films challenge conventional film forms through time-shifting editing, mediator characters, peripheral figures or through the use of observational long takes that dominate a film, as in *The Tree of Wooden Clogs* and *Time Stood Still*. Olmi's style operates as transformative art, art that requires our participation and the application of our experiences and reasoning to communicate values and meaning. And in transformative art, as Stephen Prince argues, "The reconfiguration of form … permits not just the grasping of new social realities, or of old realities seen anew, but a reshaping of the spectator's relationship with the artwork as well."[10]

Olmi gives us the responsibility of interpreting reality after showing us new ways of viewing it. He expresses the wish that when we learn how to view his films, they will assist us in reshaping how we see reality, aiding us to look at the world as with the "eyes of a child."[11] He does not lead us to an interpretation of reality, but removes obstacles from our vision of city life, nature, and family and romantic relationships to facilitate our own reconceptualization of the world. This strategy conforms with his proposal that cinema be educational, not in the "didactic sense," but in a manner in "which other people participate."[12] He sees his films as a merging of his own experience with that of the viewer. "If I communicate to you an experience of mine which I have taken possession of to the point of being able to communicate it to you, you participate in my experience in an equal measure by adding your own experience to mine."[13] His style constructs a space for an exchange of ideas and experience, posing questions that we must address to assign meaning to his films.

To some, studying the work of a single filmmaker and their style is an outdated form of scholarship. The auteur theory, the idea that there can be a strong authorial presence behind a film, has gone in and out of favor many times since its introduction in film studies during the 1950s and 1960s, partly because, as James Naremore notes, "in many cases the study of authors is an exclusionary, conservative activity, bound up with the perpetuation of traditions and the manufacture of commodities."[14] Auteur criticism can also obscure the work of many contributors to a film in its focus on a single artist. These are certainly valid concerns with the theory's shortcomings. However, it remains true that some filmmakers can make their films into their own personal, artistic expressions, just as novelists, painters, poets, and musicians can create art that bears their imprints. Discussing and critiquing an auteur's body of work can reveal how his or her films function as art, explicating the philosophies of their work and what they have of value to offer audiences.

Olmi is undoubtedly an auteur, both in the sense that he has consistent themes and stylistic features that can be found throughout his oeuvre and also because he has had an unusual amount of control over his films. In nearly all of his films (with the exception of his sole major studio project, *E venne un uomo* [*A Man Named John*, 1965] about Pope John XXIII), Olmi has succeeded in making films on his terms, without the interference of producers and others pushing for changes to meet box-office expectations. Italian state-funded television and film programs financially backed many of his films of the 1960s and 1970s, which were distributed chiefly via Italian TV (although they were also usually given a minor theatrical release and shown at international festivals).[15] With this type of funding, Olmi had a relatively free hand to make films as he wished and has maintained this autonomy throughout the rest of his career.

Olmi's Cinema and Nature

Through my close readings I aim to demonstrate the essential role the natural world holds in much of Olmi's films. The relatively new subfield of film studies known as environmental film studies (and/or ecocinema studies) explores cinema's relationship with the natural environment.[16] According to Paula Willoquet-Maricondi, ecocinema "overtly strives to inspire personal and political action on the part of viewers, stimulating our thinking so as to bring about concrete changes in the choices we make" in relation to the environment.[17] An aspect of Olmi's cinema that even the few critics and scholars who have written on the director have often overlooked is his veneration of nature and his mourning of humanity's broken ties to the environment. The workers in Olmi's Edisonvolta films of the 1950s still possess a close rapport with nature. However, by the time of *I fidanzati* in 1963, Olmi's films began to express a sense of humanity's existential loss as the progress of the industrialized world continued to sever attachments to the outdoors. Many of Olmi's films, like *I fidanzati* and *Il segreto del bosco vecchio* (*The Secret of the Old Woods*, 1993), specifically meet Willoquet-Maricondi's definition. And although I cite ecocinema studies in this book, I do not claim that this book is a work of ecocinema studies. I do not want to force several of the films through a lens they do not fit under. But even in Olmi's films that do not directly probe humanity's relationship with the environment, the characters' surroundings always impinge upon their lives. The castle that Libenzio is employed in nearly suffocates him in *Lunga vita alla signora!* (*Long Live the Lady*, 1987) and Bruno in *Un certo giorno* (*One Fine Day*, 1968) longs to escape the tedium of his office for the countryside property he bought from his ancestors. In this regard, all of Olmi's work consistently reflects upon how living in nature, or being absent from it, directly affects our lives. Olmi sought to remove the blinders from our visions of reality because of the importance he believed the natural world holds for humanity's physical, economical and spiritual wellbeing and survival. This is one of the most compelling reasons for a reconsideration of Olmi's work.

In October 2018, the United Nations' Intergovernmental Panel on Climate Change released a report stating that the world had twelve years to reduce global warming or millions of people across the world would face catastrophic consequences.[18] To many this type of news elicits despair. But as we consider Olmi's films, they lead us to contemplate what individual action can be taken to support environmental reforms that combat climate change in our communities, in our countries, and in the world. In reshaping how we see reality, Olmi's films can also reincorporate nature into our vision of reality. His early work closely documents the human effects of Italy's acceptance of widespread corporate industrialization. His feature films progress from expressing grief at our alienation from the environment to proposing a reconnection to nature through our labor to offset the destruction of our planet and to instigate spiritual renewal through stronger local communities. Olmi's work is arguably one of the most important of any artist to consider in regard to cultivating an appreciation for what, in totality, the natural world offers us.

Because Olmi has received so little attention in English language scholarship, I will follow this introduction with a brief biography reviewing the major events of his career and life. In the rest of this book, rather than considering Olmi's films in chronological order, I have grouped them together topically. Structuring the book in this manner permits me to discuss thematic and stylistic connections between related works, revealing Olmi's approach to each topic.

In Chapter 1, I begin by placing the start of Olmi's career in the context of the demise of canonical Italian Neo-Realism and the beginning of Italy's economic boom. Many critics often automatically view Olmi's style and the subjects of his films as continuing in the vein of Neo-Realism without considering other possible inspirations. The Neo-Realist movement certainly did impact Olmi's approach to filmmaking. However, here I also highlight the influences of Robert Flaherty, John Grierson, and Pier Paolo Pasolini on his films. I then review, through brief analyses of many of the films, how Olmi's style matured as he made short films for the Edisonvolta energy company during the 1950s and early 1960s. This was a critical period in Olmi's career in which he was able to fine-tune his filmmaking skills and discover his impressions about the effects of the boom on humanity and on the environment as he documented the establishment of the country's new infrastructure. I examine all but two, *Il grigio* [The grey one, 1958] and *Venezia città moderna* [Venice modern city, 1957] (both of which I have been unable to view), of the nineteen films Olmi directed while at Edisonvolta. I outline many of the developing aspects of Olmi's style, such as the peripheral figure (characters whom the film focuses on in a break from the narrative), which are already manifest at the earliest stages of his career.

Chapter 2 covers the boom trilogy, a group of films made between 1959 and 1963, in which Olmi explores the social disruption caused by the boom. In *Time Stood Still, Il posto*, and *I fidanzati*, Olmi presents many of the widespread problems that were immediately perceivable as the boom reached its apex: generational conflicts, families and romances separated by the demands of jobs requiring workers to move away from home, and the sacrifice of freedom and traditional values for the promise of economic prosperity. These are not the same issues that were at the center of Neo-Realist films, and Olmi adapted his style to engage with the particular national social concerns of the era. In my discussion of the last two of these films, I define how Olmi used peripheral figures as a device to illustrate the loss of a sense of unity among families and communities. *I fidanzati* is Olmi's first film to transition between the past, present, and imagined futures, following a character's consciousness, often pulled toward loved ones, as it reacts to events, other people, and his or her surroundings. In my discussion of the film, I detail what makes Olmi's time-shifting style unique from filmmakers like Alain Resnais.

During the tumultuous years between the late 1960s and the 1970s in Italy, Olmi made another trilogy of films, *One Fine Day, Durante l'estate* (*In the Summertime*, a.k.a. *During the Summer*, 1971), and *La circostanza* (*The Circumstance*, 1973), set in the post-boom era, that depict the pervasive dissatisfaction and unhappiness that have taken hold of everyday life as a result of unfulfilling work, dysfunctional relationships, and a collective absence of purpose. Chapter 3 investigates how these films engage with the underlying troubles at the heart of *gli anni di piombo* (the Years of Lead), a period that progressed from the Western European student protests of the late 1960s into terrorist violence in Italy from groups on the right and the left throughout the 1970s. In my readings of these films, I explore how instead of using stories about these events, Olmi follows the lives of members of the new middle class whose routine existences are interrupted by events or characters that challenge their worldviews and visions of society, revealing fundamental social tensions. In this trilogy, Olmi presents several characters, like *In the Summertime*'s professor and *The Circumstance*'s Francesco, to highlight alternative worldviews to the dominant materialistic values that fuel consumerist societies. However, he does not prescribe their philosophies, leaving it to us to respond to them.

In Chapter 4, I examine Olmi's history films. In these works, Olmi frames the past in a manner that allows us to reevaluate present-day injustices. All of Olmi's history films depict systems of power that infringe upon their characters' abilities to live freely. The first two of these films, *I recuperanti* (*The Scavengers*, 1970), and *The Tree of Wooden Clogs*, reflect upon what has been surrendered as civilization has moved away from outdoor labor, but also simultaneously acknowledge, through their portrayal of the characters' hardships, the need for progress and societal development. In the other two films, *Il mestiere delle armi* (*The Profession of Arms*, 2001), and *Torneranno i prati* (*Greenery Will Bloom Again*, 2014), Olmi denounces the absurdity of war. In both films, he challenges nationalistic celebrations of military heroes (specifically in depicting Giovanni dalle Bande Nere, a popular Italian hero from the Renaissance era, as someone who was betrayed by the institutions he fought for) and questions national allegiances that require the needless sacrifice of citizens.

Beginning in the late 1980s, Olmi pivoted away from films set in contemporary Italy. Following his recovery from Guillain-Barré syndrome, he began making fables and parables that approach reality from fanciful, idealized worlds. The films covered in Chapter 5—*Long Live the Lady*, *The Legend of the Holy Drinker*, *The Secret of the Old Woods*, *Cantando dietro i paraventi* (*Singing Behind Screens*, 2003), and *Il villaggio di cartone* (*The Cardboard Village*, 2011)—feature characters who overcome moral dilemmas, emerging as heroes. As these characters reflect on themselves and their lives before they make these crucial decisions, love often persuades them of the path they should take.

In Chapter 6, I dispute the common mischaracterization of Olmi, made by scholars and critics such as Richard James Havis, as "an unabashedly Christian filmmaker."[19] This type of designation has caused frequent misreadings of Olmi's films and inaccurately implies that he propagated Christianity. With the exception of *A Man Named John*, the rest of Olmi's films on religious subjects, *Camminacammina* (*Keep Walking*, 1983), *Genesi: la creazione e il diluvio* (*Genesis: The Creation and the Flood*, 1994), and *Centochiodi* (*One Hundred Nails*, 2007), and his own statements about his faith, counter the notion that his films disseminate an institutionally Christian ideology. It is true that Jesus Christ fascinated Olmi and that he believed that Christ's teachings and life provide an excellent example of how to live. Rather than providing institutionally derived ideas about faith and religious figures, such as Christ, Noah, and Pope John XXIII, Olmi's religious films offer his own conception of spirituality, based on his own reading of Christ, loving relationships with others, and a connection to mother nature.

I hope that this book will serve as a starting point for further study and re-evaluations of Olmi's work in English language scholarship. My readings aim to demonstrate why many of Olmi's excellent films, such as *One Fine Day*, *The Scavengers*, *The Legend of the Holy Drinker*, and *Genesis*, demand scholarly attention. His cinema's rich complexity and particular capacity to provoke us to question our vision of the world and ponder why humanity should not cut itself off from mother nature has been overlooked for far too long.

* * *

A Few General Notes

I have not included extended analyses of Olmi's feature-length documentaries and his several dozen non–Edisonvolta short films. However, when appropriate I have integrated some of them into my discussion of his fictional feature films.

Throughout the book, after initially presenting their original Italian titles, I refer to the majority of the feature films by their official English titles. Olmi's Edisonvolta titles have no official English translation, and so I use their Italian titles when discussing them. In the case of *Il posto* and *I fidanzati*, I use their Italian titles because that is how they are commonly known abroad.

When mentioning a character for the first time, I have strived to remain stylistically consistent and add all of the actors' names in parentheses next to their characters. However, in many of Olmi's films some characters have no names and sometimes only a few cast members have been credited. For this reason, I have been unable to credit every actor when I discuss the films.

Lastly, foreign titles which I was able to confirm have a published English title are followed by that title in italics within parentheses. Those titles which I was not able to confirm have a published English title are followed by my own translations, within parentheses, of the original titles, which are capitalized sentence-style without italics.

A Brief Biography

CHARLES THOMAS SAMUELS: What interested you in becoming a director?
OLMI: I wanted to communicate my love of the ordinary things in life. I began by taking pictures of objects and people sheerly for the love of them. Shooting these pictures also was a way of coming closer to the world of work that I shared with my colleagues.[1]

Olmi's cinema defines itself through its fascination with the ordinary: the quotidian activities of everyday people, their relationships, and the way their work and their contact with the natural world informs every facet of their lives. From the short films that initiated his filmmaking career at the Edisonvolta energy company until his final feature, *Greenery Will Bloom Again*, Olmi's films are singular in the degree to which they venerate the lives and humanity of the men and women they depict. In one of the earliest Edisonvolta films, *La pattuglia del passo San Giacomo* (The patrol of the San Giacomo passage, 1954), the narrator introduces the story of a group of laborers replacing a broken electric cable in the mountains with a statement that pithily describes all of Olmi's cinema: "This is a story of the everyday with everyday heroes."

The roots of Olmi's captivation with the beauty of common people, their lives and their existential and theological attachments to the non-human world unquestionably formed during the director's working-class childhood. Olmi was born on July 24, 1931, in Bergamo, a small city around twenty-five miles northeast of Milan. His father, Giambattista Olmi (of Tuscan origins), was a train driver and his mother, Maddalena Teresa, came from a family of local farmers. In his autobiography, Ermanno records that his parents literally fell in love at first sight one day as Giambattista was waiting inside of a train at the station and looked out and saw his future wife. "This is my true date of birth and it is not written on any document. My life began in that first flash of glances."[2] Olmi envisions his parents' first encounter, and many other stories and memories in his autobiography, through a series of impressions that amplify common, daily events into moments of great personal significance in a manner that evokes the time-shifting editing style he adopted as a filmmaker. To relate his first actual memory from when he was around two years old, Olmi initially introduces what the memory recalls, a thunderstorm that he watched with his older brother, Luciano, and then segues into a story about how his grandmother explained his red hair by telling him he arose from the ground under a tomato plant before he returns to his childhood memory. He then describes his first memory of the thunderstorm by how it made him feel, rather than telling a story that directly ties into his personal development.[3] Olmi's narrative progression often mimics the mind's, focusing on brief sensory impressions or fluctuating between events without regard for chronological order.

Olmi remembered his father as a silent, tender man, a veteran of World War I, who would communicate his feelings with expressions rather than words. In the mid-1930s, he was fired from his job as a train conductor for refusing to align himself with, or submit to the dictates and demands of, the rising fascist party and struggled to find work for two years because of his socialist political leanings.[4] He finally landed a position at Edisonvolta, an electric and gas energy company.[5] Olmi believes the stress of trying to survive an Allied bombing raid in 1944 triggered a blood clot in his father, which caused an embolism and then his death a few days later.[6] Edisonvolta, who Olmi praised for never failing to take care of their employees, hired Maddalena so she could support the family following the death of her husband.[7] Around the same time, Ermanno dropped out of school at fourteen, first working as a baker's assistant, and then he also found a position at Edisonvolta as an errand boy (a period that would later directly inspire *Il posto*). Olmi's mother died when he was eighteen and shortly thereafter he moved in with his maternal grandmother, with whom he shared a very close relationship. He lived with her until he was twenty-five when she also passed away.[8]

Luciano proved a more capable student than his younger brother and went on to study at university and eventually became a surgical doctor at San Raffaele di Milano Hospital.[9] Although Ermanno would return to finish school sporadically, he largely gained his education and appreciation for the arts, literature, and the great works of cinema, through his own penchant for learning about topics of specific interest to him. By the time he commenced working at Edisonvolta, he had developed a growing passion for theater, even considering a career with traveling companies to the great dismay of his mother and grandmother. Olmi referred to the theater as his "road to Damascus." He recalled a specific evening when he was five years old and his parents brought him along to the theater because they could not afford a babysitter.[10] The experience of that evening filled him with an excitement that he describes as "near to palpitations of love" and he took advantage of every opportunity that presented itself during his youth to immerse himself in his newfound passion.[11] The memory and feelings aroused by the gilded theater and its spectacle accompanied him into adulthood. He directed a number of professional theatrical productions and operas during the last forty years of his life, including Giuseppe Verdi's *Othello* and Thornton Wilder's *Our Town*.[12]

The theater enraptured Olmi, but he also appreciated the cinema from an early age. The first film that he remembers attending was a German film, *Siegfried* (most likely the first half of Fritz Lang's *Die Nibelungen* [*The Nibelungs*, 1924] epic), also when he was five years old. Like the ambience of the theater, the environment of the cinema itself thrilled the young boy.[13] While a teenager, he remembered seeing the flood of American films to which Italy reopened its doors following the conclusion of World War II. But more consequentially, he also vividly recalled his first viewing of Rossellini's *Roma: città aperta* (*Rome: Open City*, 1945), which awakened him to the possibility of a completely different purpose for films.

> *Rome: Open City* was the discovery of a cinema that was life, that did not separate the screen from the street, but proposed a continuity through the ideal mediator, or at least what it should be, the poet. Therefore, cinema was my second love.... The slap I received from *Rome: Open City* put me in a different kind of relationship with all of the films that, as a spectator, I went to see. My first infatuation with Grierson began, the great discovery of Flaherty. I realized that I went to the cinema no longer to dream, but to understand something more about life.[14]

Besides Pier Paolo Pasolini (whose brief, but inspirational, working relationship on Olmi will be discussed in Chapter 1), one could imagine no other trio of filmmakers who could have held a greater formative influence on Olmi. Rossellini would not only later form a working relationship with Olmi, but he shared with the younger director a faith in a type of cinema that could broaden an audiences' perspective of reality and humanity. Robert Flaherty, considered by many the father of the documentary film, and John Grierson, who produced pioneering institutional documentary works for the General Post Office of Great Britain, would have distinct influences on how Olmi filmed work and displayed the lives of the individuals in both his fiction and non-fiction films. As would be demonstrated by his first works with Edisonvolta, Olmi would fashion his own aesthetic sensibility as a filmmaker after the styles that he came to appreciate as a young man.

Despite her disapproval of her youngest son's desire to pursue a career in the arts when she was still alive, it was Olmi's mother who introduced him to the extracurricular theater group at Edisonvolta that would completely transform his life. Olmi quickly displayed a talent for acting with the group. After his debut performance, the company news bulletin featured a review that applauded his role as an old servant.[15] A few years later, following another well-received performance, he was approached by a company head who asked Olmi if he could use his artistic talents to benefit the company in some fashion. Olmi responded by asking Edisonvolta to buy him a 16-millimeter camera with which he could make films. Now, with camera in hand, Olmi was on the verge of forming a film division at the energy company.[16]

Olmi had absolutely no technical experience with filmmaking when he received the camera and other filmmaking equipment. He was exceptional among the Italian filmmakers who started their careers during the Neo-Realist and immediate post–Neo-Realist periods in that he received no formal training and did not attend film school or any university at all. He learned simply through trial and error, experimenting at first by making films after work and then spending his evenings at the Donato media press where he was permitted to use the company's 16-millimeter Moviola editing machine.[17] In 1953, Edisonvolta officially launched its film division, headed by Olmi. Between its launch and 1961, Olmi had directed nineteen short films and supervised many others.[18] His first fictional feature, *Time Stood Still*, which effectively was the beginning of the end of his time at Edisonvolta, was slyly made under the pretenses of being just another of these short films.

Other large companies in Italy also maintained film divisions, including Fiat and the manufacturing corporation Olivetti. However, many of the films at Edisonvolta's film division (*Sezione Cinema Edisonvolta*) [Edisonvolta Cinema Division] during the 1950s were directly influenced by Olmi's budding political perspective and developing cinematic style. Paola Bonifazio writes, "Whereas Cinefiat narratives focused mostly on Fiat and its workers ... the SCE spoke of the company only marginally, and the paternalism of its managers went beyond the cohort of employees."[19] She adds that one of Olmi's first Edisonvolta films, *Piccoli calabresi sul Lago Maggiore: nuovi ospiti alla colonia di Suna* (Little Calabrians on lake Maggiore: new guests at Suna's summer camp, 1953) "described Edisonvolta's involvement in national social problems" and that several of Olmi's other short films for the company "conveyed some attention and concerns about how rural environments and their social groups were transformed by the arrival of the electric company."[20] As he filmed these transformations, Olmi witnessed first-hand how Italian society remodeled itself following World War II, documenting the building of dams and the development of the country's energy infrastructure.

Time Stood Still was shown out of competition at the 20th Venice International Film Festival, which would also premiere many of his other works. The film won several awards at minor festivals and gained Olmi favorable reviews and notices within Italy. Olmi continued to work at Edisonvolta for the next two years following *Time Stood Still*'s release. It was *Il posto* that truly made a name for him internationally and initially placed him alongside other acclaimed Italian filmmakers, such as Pasolini, Francesco Rosi, and Antonioni, that were promising new directions for Italian cinema after Fellini's *La dolce vita* (The sweet life, 1960) seemingly sounded the death knell for canonical Neo-Realism. Not only did the film win several prizes at Venice, it also went on to win the Sunderland Trophy from the British Film Institute and later was rewarded with the New York Film Critics' Circle Award for best foreign film when it was released in America in 1963.

There was another event surrounding *Il posto* that had greater personal significance for the young director than being recognized by major international film organizations. Despite a charmingly sweet and lauded performance, *Il posto*'s leading actress, Loredana Detto, would never act again.[21] A year following the film's release she went to Olmi in tears because she had no desire to go to Rome to continue the promising start she had made to her film career. Shortly thereafter, they formed a romantic relationship and married in 1963.[22] They have three children: Elisabetta, Fabio, and Andrea. Elisabetta became a film producer and production manager, working on several of her father's films as well as other major Italian productions. Her brother Fabio has also worked in film production, primarily as a cinematographer on several of his father's works and other Italian films. Andrea teaches horse riding.

Olmi's international reputation continued with *I fidanzati*, which was nominated for the Palme d'Or at the Cannes Film Festival. He also began to occasionally make short films for Italy's national television station, RAI (Radiotelevisione Italiana), throughout the decade. Later, the television station would fund his feature films (such as *The Scavengers* and *The Circumstance*) that were often shown first at film festivals and then on television. His fourth feature, *A Man Named John*, an untraditional biopic on Pope John XXIII, was his first internationally co-produced film and also was the first time Olmi worked with a major film star, Rod Steiger, of any nationality. The film was financed by Harry Saltzman, known chiefly as one of the original producers of the James Bond film series. The film was not well received and seems to have been one of the major factors that led to a decline in Olmi's international reputation until the unexpected acclaim that greeted *The Tree of Wooden Clogs*.

When *The Tree of Wooden Clogs* won the Palme d'Or in 1978, Olmi was suddenly placed once again in the international spotlight as one of the premier filmmakers of Italy. Indeed, this was in many ways the apex of Olmi's career. He was never able to consistently retain the unwavering admiration of foreign film scholars and critics that has been granted perennially to compatriots such as Fellini, Antonioni, or Rossellini. In June 1984, he was gripped by a very serious and rare neurological disease, Guillain-Barré syndrome (a disease that leads the immune system to attack nerves), which briefly rendered him completely unable to move and put a stop to almost all film work for two full years.[23] It was during his recovery from the illness that he wrote a short autobiographical novel, *Il ragazzo della Bovisa* (The boy from Bovisa), chronicling many of the events of his own adolescence in Bovisa, a borough in northern Milan where he spent much of his youth.

Beginning in the 1980s, Olmi committed himself to a personal project that has influenced several generations of Italian filmmakers. Following the success of *The Tree of Wooden Clogs*, Olmi was repeatedly approached by students and amateur filmmakers who wanted to build their careers by serving as assistant directors on his films. These requests spurred the idea for a non-traditional film school. In 1982, he founded *Ipotesi Cinema* (Hypothesis cinema) together with RAI president Paolo Valmarana, a program with no tuition, no set instructors, and no homework. In a letter addressed to candidates considering attending the school, the program's emphasis on experiential education is made clear. "We don't want you to come to *Ipotesi Cinema* to learn who can teach you to make cinema, but to create, yourself, the opportunities to learn it. It depends on you."[24] *Ipotesi Cinema* allows its pupils to gain valuable experience while creating works for television and feature length films, several of which, (e.g., *Terra madre* [2009] and *Greenery Will Bloom Again*), Olmi has directed himself. Elisabetta Olmi currently runs the program as the school's CEO. The school has produced filmmakers such as Alice Rohrwacher, whose most recent film *Lazzaro felice* (*Happy as Lazzaro*, 2018) not only pays tribute to *The Tree of Wooden Clogs*, but also to *In the Summertime* and Olmi's fables.

During the 1990s, Olmi started speaking openly about his environmentalist convictions. Many of Olmi's statements correspond with ideas and themes that his films have frequently reflected upon. In hindsight, Olmi's environmentalism was always apparent in his films. His Edisonvolta shorts bear a reverence for the earth and humanity's relationship with the natural world that carried over into many of his fictional features. The director's unequivocal commitment to environmentalist causes was confirmed in 2009 with the release of *Terra madre*, a documentary made in collaboration with the Slow Food movement. The organization gathers biannually at Slow Food meetings to champion biodiversity and build networks of local food producers. Slow Food describes itself as a society that was founded "to prevent the disappearance of local food cultures and traditions, counteract the rise of fast life and combat people's dwindling interest in the food they eat, where it comes from and how our food choices affect the world around us," all principles which appealed to Olmi's environmental ethos.[25] Olmi remained actively involved with the organization, including the curation of an event with Slow Food at the World Expo 2015 in Milan that featured his short documentary, *Il pianeta che ci ospita* (*Our Host Planet*, 2015), until his death in May 2018.

Repeatedly, especially in cursory summations of the director and his most well-known films by critics, Olmi has been labeled a "Christian" or "Catholic" filmmaker. Such classifications are understandable. His body of work includes works on Pope John XXIII, the three wise men, and the book of Genesis. Many of his other films also exhibit a sensitivity to the Christian beliefs held sacred by his characters. However, as is the case with many individuals' faith, Olmi's Christianity was complex and upon close inspection many of his films openly display his religious doubts. At times, he made his disagreements with contemporary Catholicism public. Spurred by his outrage with the Catholic Church during the papacy of Pope Benedict XVI, in 2013 he wrote an enraged book-length open letter to the church, entitled *Lettera a una chiesa che ha dimenticato Gesù* (Letter to a church that has forgotten Jesus). Additionally, in interviews during the latter years of his life, Olmi referred to himself only as an "aspiring Christian" and answers he provided about his religiosity suggest that he had agnostic or atheist streaks in his beliefs. For example, in a conversation with Marco Manzoni, Olmi admitted, "I know that I will never cease to be water and light. I will certainly lose my individuality, but I hold onto the hope that all those components that are life will not be scattered from me."[26]

Although this statement evidences that Olmi held no hope in a traditional Christian conception of the afterlife, the director could be considered a Christian solely on his acceptance of Christ as one of the ultimate role models for how one should live. One can imagine how Olmi would have identified with the carpenter Christ, envisaging a figure whose work with Joseph and others led him to conceive and teach a philosophy of love and peace. Indeed, what seems to appeal to Olmi most about Christ are his human qualities, which the director felt are what makes Jesus, and all of humanity, divine. "I love Christ more than I love God, I love men more than I love God, because I believe that, if he is somewhere out there in the cosmos, this is what he would want."[27] For Olmi, with or without a God, life's ultimate purpose, and the purpose of his cinema, was to learn to recognize and love humanity.

1

In the Beginning, There Was ... Edisonvolta

By the end of the 1950s, the era of canonical Neo-Realism had decidedly concluded. Even prior to *La dolce vita*'s oft-cited ushering in of a new era in Italian art cinema, films such as Fellini's *Le notti di Cabiria* (*Nights of Cabiria*, 1957) and Rossellini's *Viaggio in Italia* (*Journey to Italy*, 1954) demonstrated that filmmakers associated with Neo-Realism were breaking away from the movement. Their styles became more experimental and the stories no longer focused solely on poverty and society's forgotten souls. Italy was entering a new era of unprecedented economic success, a period known as the boom, or sometimes referred to as "the economic miracle." The shifts occurring in Italian cinema were adapting in response to the nation's culture as the country modernized, became increasingly active in globalization, and its citizens prospered financially. Despite these changes, the shadow of Neo-Realism hung heavily over those involved in the movement and those who would emerge in its wake. Time has proven that Neo-Realism was one of the most pivotal moments in film history, influencing all of international cinema, and supporting arguments to include film among recognized major art forms. Since Neo-Realism, Italian filmmakers attempting to make a name for themselves internationally have wrestled with comparisons measuring how their works can be traced back to these films.

Olmi's career at Edisonvolta began in 1953, a year after the last unequivocal work of Neo-Realism, *Umberto D.* (1952), was released. Naturally, critics generally view his approach to filmmaking as descending directly from the styles of De Sica, Rossellini, and Visconti. These links are strengthened when we consider Giuliana Minghelli's observation that for many Neo-Realist filmmakers, landscape represented "...unclaimed, primitive, politically virgin ground from which to discover new stories and storytelling techniques and a new human subject—a space that can accommodate a truly new Italian cinema."[1] As this chapter will demonstrate, Olmi merged this tendency with other inspirations and landscape imagery would become a dominant feature of his aesthetic.

Considering other affinities beyond the Neo-Realists' turn to landscapes for inspiration, Peter Bondanella, the author of the seminal English language survey of Italian Cinema, describes Olmi as being more aligned with his cinematic predecessors than other Italian filmmakers who were also at the dawn of their careers in the 1950s. "Olmi is unusual because his ideology has obvious links to the Christian humanism found in the Neo-Realist works of both Rossellini and De Sica, rather than to Marxist ideology."[2] Bondanella specifically links Olmi's style directly to De Sica's, underscoring the younger director's use of deep focus shots and his "genius for expressively employing the simple and seemingly meaningless gestures, glances and actions gathered from the daily routine of his rather insignificant characters."[3] While the description of Olmi's focus on the everyday is accurate, like most critics (especially in English language scholarship) Bondanella routinely links Olmi with the Neo-Realists without considering the director's Edisonvolta films and the traces they bear of three major influences that perhaps had a more significant impact on Olmi and the development of his filmmaking voice.[4] This chapter has two parts. The first considers the aspects of Robert Flaherty, John Grierson, and Pier Paolo Pasolini's films and philosophies that Olmi incorporated into his own style and artistic interests. The latter portion of this chapter briefly examines the films themselves and how they demonstrate the evolution of Olmi's cinematic voice.

Flaherty, Grierson and Pasolini's Influence on Olmi

After impressing his bosses with his artistic ability, Olmi was given *carte blanche* to form his own cinema division, the Sezione Cinema Edisonvolta, at the energy company and make films. As he developed his technical and storytelling capabilities at Edisonvolta, Olmi broke the boundaries of institutional cinema in his subtle responses (that would become much more direct in his fictional feature work) to the incredible lifestyle changes wrought by Italy's industrialization. As quoted in the biography section, Olmi had himself declared his admiration for Grierson and Flaherty, both pioneering documentarians who had tackled modernization's arrival elsewhere. Their role in shaping Olmi's vision of how to express an intertwined sense of loss for a bygone world and an esteem for rewarding work is essential to identifying the origin of Olmi's interests, the long takes in his style and his framing of nature. Furthermore, Olmi's dynamic early work with Pier Paolo Pasolini evinces that their brief collaboration brought Olmi to the realization that he could use the cinema as a tool to render the ordinary sacred and compelled him to explore the medium's spiritual capacity.

Although several other major Italian filmmakers (Pasolini, Fellini, and Rossellini) are regularly identified as spiritually minded filmmakers, only Olmi's works have uncovered the inextricable ties between labor, nature, and an individual's understanding of his or her place in the cosmos. Italy's development in the 1950s severed these bonds for many when thousands of Italians left the fields and entered offices. Not until *Il posto* would the director fully explore the societal costs of abandoning agricultural labor for the promise of more comfortable and assured livelihoods. But his sponsored documentaries convey a growing awareness of the fundamental differences between the world of progress and the rustic, nature-centered world of his beloved maternal grandmother. In Olmi's budding style at Edisonvolta, we can trace this romanticist longing for a world disappearing, the inspiration for the style to conserve it, and the sense of preservational responsibility that would become a major focus of his later work, directly to Flaherty.

Cinema, with its singular capabilities to visually document the world and its subjects' perceived movements, was bound to produce a figure devoted to preserving traditions threatened by extinction. Some have perceived Flaherty as an opportunist, taking advantage of the people, he claimed to aid. In her assessment of his most famous film, Sue Matheson remarks that "*Nanook of the North* ... capitalized on public nostalgia for a lost frontier and the atavistic desire to experience one's own distant aboriginal beginnings."[5] Whatever his motivations were, Flaherty was determined to travel far and wide to warn of the impending loss of cultures formed over millennia and the natural world that bred them. Aidan Arrowsmith writes that Flaherty was on a mission to assist endangered peoples by "flagging the threat posed to them from the spread of modernity and capitalism."[6] In 1922, Flaherty's re-creation and documentation of Inuit life in *Nanook of the North* established a new form of cinema. But his work transcended simple preservation. Keith Beattie observes that what made *Nanook of the North* so radical was in its "construction of a narrative which transcended a mere series of travelogue scenes in a way which did not impose a predetermined structure upon its content." He continues, "Specifically, Flaherty's significant contribution to documentary cinema was the recognition that scenes from reality could be edited into a narrative that relied on the dramatic effects of fictional cinema."[7]

Flaherty's documentary style earned him critical appraisal from Bazin, who found in the infamous seal hunting scene from *Nanook of the North* a method of filming that captures something ineffable, something beyond the visible. "What matters to Flaherty, confronted with Nanook hunting the seal, is the relation between Nanook and the animal; the actual length of the waiting period. Montage could suggest the time involved. Flaherty however confines himself to showing the actual waiting period; the length of the hunt is the very substance of the image, its true object."[8] As Bazin notes, editing the scene through various cinematic codes (e.g., the inclusion of interspersed clocks sped up to demonstrate the time taken by the hunt or shots of the position of the sun at the beginning and end of the hunt) would have been adequate to suggest the time involved. But the decision to edit sparingly and allow the hunt to be completed in most of its entirety in view of the camera allows Flaherty to make the length of the hunt into an experience that we can share. We receive a sense of the skills and diligence required to complete the task that Nanook is recreating for the camera.[9] In scenes from Olmi's later work, such as the pig slaughtering scene in *The Tree of Wooden Clogs*, the effect of this aesthetic strategy on Olmi is clear. But even at the tail-end of Olmi's Edisonvolta career, he incorporates this style as he films miners, dam builders, and electricians at work in a manner that also respectfully retains the proficiency required by their jobs.

Flaherty also elevated the workers in his films, perhaps most significantly in *Louisiana Story* (1948), and did not hold them accountable for the destruction of nature. Like Olmi, Flaherty had some experience making institutionally sponsored films that gave him a free hand. Sponsored by Standard Oil when he made *Louisiana Story*, with the condition that he make something about oil exploration, Flaherty faced a challenging dilemma: he could make a film on his terms celebrating cultures living in undisturbed harmony with nature, as he had done in his previous feature films, but this might lead to overt criticism of his sponsor. Flaherty found a way to negotiate his conflicting interests by portraying the potential harm that an oil company could unleash upon a local area, and then depicting the oil company's workers resolving the damage created by the company and befriending the local populace. As Erik Barnouw writes, Flaherty portrayed the workers as "friendly, modest, magnificent in action," all words that we could also apply to Olmi's workers.[10]

Ostensibly, it is Grierson more than Flaherty who would have provided a more straightforward example of how to excel in institutional filmmaking for Olmi. Grierson, who championed Flaherty's style of filmmaking and viewed him "as one of the five great innovators in the history of film," produced many institutional films for organizations like the UK's Empire Marketing Board and General Post Office in the same vein as his American colleague.[11] In these documentaries, the filmmakers, working under Grierson's supervision, never overlook the human faces and hands behind seemingly mechanical and soulless operations such as the transportation of mail or coal mining. A fervent Labour Party supporter, Grierson produced films that managed to ingrain these jobs with dignity and a lively beauty that was motivated by his renowned beliefs about the political possibilities of the cinema.[12] Patricia Aufderheide notes that Grierson "celebrated the power of documentary to observe 'life itself,' using real people who could help others interpret the world and real stories."[13] When embedded in Grierson's films, this socially minded philosophy reclaims the human lives that society can abandon due to barriers erected by civilization's progress.

However, Grierson stood at an opposite pole of thought with Flaherty regarding the evolution of society. He did not share his colleague's proclivity toward nostalgia, nor Flaherty's desire to construct heroes from cultures resisting the attraction of the industrialized world and its promised material benefits. Grierson, influenced by Vertov, Pudovkin, and Eisenstein, in his desire to use film as a tool to drive society forward, held obvious stylistic and philosophical differences regarding the purpose of the cinema. Andrew Sarris observed that the Soviet theories and aesthetic principles prized by Grierson compelled him and his colleagues to display a "romanticism of machinery."[14] As an example of the clear distinction in the positions between the two filmmakers, one need look no further than Grierson's sole directorial effort, *The Drifters* (1929), which begins with intertitles proudly proclaiming "herring fishing has changed. Its story was once an idyll of brown sails and village harbors,—its story is now an epic of steam and steel." Through its images of men happily working together interspersed with shots celebrating the ship machinery's capabilities to assist fishermen with their work, *The Drifters* categorically diverges from Flaherty's romanticist idealization of earlier ways of working and living.

While Olmi did not celebrate mass industrialization as Grierson did, he did inherit the Scottish filmmaker's emphasis in exposing the human side of labor. Work's role in providing meaning to life is one of the central tenets of Olmi's cinema, where the lower classes and the poor feel fulfilled if they enjoy their work. It cannot be a coincidence that the first of Olmi's works to completely express this philosophy also happened to be one of two collaborations with Pasolini. Labor itself never became a revisited theme in Pasolini's films, but his works do possess an earthy spirituality that was molded by his political commitment to working class people. As Sam Rohdie observes, "Pasolini's reworking of Marxism with his sense of the sacred and his reformulation of Catholicism by his sense of social commitment was a theme in all of his work.... Marxism and Christianity became for him not opposed but analogous."[15] Olmi's work with Pasolini alerted him to the potential of cinema to express the spiritual in ordinary lives and events. He did not share Pasolini's Marxist allegiance, but his works repeatedly reflect the belief that the moral guidance received from Christianity, especially regarding the treatment of the poor and needy, is essential to guiding one's political decisions.

Olmi's Edisonvolta Films

Now we will turn to the Edisonvolta films themselves to demonstrate how these influences unfolded as Olmi's style matured. Even though it would not be until *I fidanzati* that he would acquire the time-shifting film language that is a central feature of his style, many of the short works (*Dialogo, Manon finestra 2, Il pensionato, Tre fili fino a Milano, Il grande paese d'acciaio*) are excellent and markedly reveal Olmi's cinematic inspirations and point to the themes that would define his work. I feel it is important to give many of these films some attention as only a few of them have been discussed in detail before in English language scholarship, and introductions to these films may serve non–Italian speaking scholars who wish to explore Olmi's work further.[16]

A pair of the films are only worth mentioning in passing. *Costruzioni meccaniche Riva* (Mechanical constructions Riva, 1956) idealizes machinery, lacking almost any acknowledgment of the workers behind the scenes. *Le grand barrage* (The great barrier, 1961) is a tedious travelogue of two tourists visiting many of the company's dams across northern Italy. It contains very little of interest beyond tranquil, alpine winter scenery. Thankfully these two are rare exceptions. Though a handful of the other films are not especially impressive, there are important details within them worth discussing.

There is some disagreement on whether *Piccoli calabresi sul Lago Maggiore: nuovi ospiti alla colonia di Suna* or *La diga del ghiacciaio* (The glacier's dam, 1954) was Olmi's first film following the formation of the Sezione Cinema Edisonvolta (SCE).[17] *Piccoli calabresi sul Lago Maggiore* was one of four films Olmi made in the SCE's initial year. This nine-minute piece chronicles the relocation of a large group of Calabrian children to summer camp-like accommodations owned by Edisonvolta following wide-scale flooding in the southernmost region of mainland Italy. As noted in the biographical section, the institutional goal of several of these works was to use these films as a form of public relations, presenting Edisonvolta as caring for its customers and promoting values that it wanted associated with its brand.

Piccoli calabresi sul Lago Maggiore has the tone and style of a newsreel film. Olmi manifests none of his aesthetic ambitions here. Close-up shots of boys and girls, as well as voiceovers read by the children as they play, dance, and sing, invite us to reflect both on the charitable nature of Edisonvolta and also ties together a narrative pushing that hope has been restored while the displaced adolescents are away from their families and homes. However, the one item that makes this piece of particular interest is that a little over halfway through the film a young Olmi interviews a boy who has remained at the camp for six months. It is fitting that he appears here as the film's subject had particular significance for the fledgling director. As a boy, he also stayed at Edisonvolta owned camps for three years, between 1941 and 1944, to escape Allied bombing raids of Northern Italy during World War II.[18] Indeed, the extremely personal bonds forged between Olmi's family and Edisonvolta through his parents' employment at the agency and Olmi's activity with the company from a young age were crucial to his career. Edisonvolta increased his ability to discover his cinematic voice while making films for a corporation. The company's genuine benevolence fostered an environment that supported the development of a style progressively transitioning from making routine reportage of dam construction and public relations material to humanist-centered and eco-critical filmmaking.

The other contestant for Olmi's first SCE film, *La diga del ghiacciaio* does venture briefly beyond the dam at its center. The oft unseen lives of the men involved in building these structures bookend the film.[19] The eponymous dam was a new hydro-electric facility that was to be built among the Alps in the Formazza valley near the Italian-Swiss border. The film commences with bucolic images of a small village in the valley and a narrator describing a church in Riale built to memorialize the men who died building the Morasco dam. Following scenes marveling at the dam's construction and a midway sequence of quickly paced shots of different men working, rolling cigarettes, and waiting anxiously for dynamite to explode, the last minute of *La diga del ghiacciaio* focuses on a man sitting alone in the dark. This is the first time in the film that the narrative concentrates on a single person. The narrator describes the workers' loneliness and the time spent reading letters from home over and over again as a cut is made to a medium shot of the same man and then to a shot behind him as he looks at a postcard. Olmi's emphasis on the sacrifices made by these men in constructing the dam at the beginning and the conclusion places a Griersonian touch on the work, providing early traces of the peripheral figures that extend the worlds of his films.

La pattuglia del passo San Giacomo also takes place in the picturesque Formazza valley. Like *Piccoli Calabresi sul Lago Maggiore* it emphasizes Edisonvolta's role in the community and its service to its customers. Once more, the rustic scenery of the valley opens the film with children skiing along paths in a village and men cutting down trees for lumber. Unfortunately, the downing of one tree fells a power line. Immediately following the collapse of the line, a series of shots show us utility workers urgently responding as an alarm rings over the soundtrack. Three subsequent shots show different men calling up the line of authority for repairs, clearly promoting the idea of Italy's growing interconnectivity provided through industry and technology companies like Edisonvolta following the war.

Beyond its institutional goals, *La pattuglia del passo San Giacomo* tells a story, the narrator tells us, of "the everyday with everyday heroes."[20] And the workers we see truly are everyday people. In none of these films do the laborers wear uniforms that separate them from other citizens. When we hear snatches of their conversations, it is typically dialect spoken warmly amidst friends. The film echoes Flaherty's interest in depicting worlds where traditional lifestyles and people could adapt to the changing environment triggered by industrial development. Jack Coogan writes that Flaherty's *Louisiana Story* was "interested in exploring the ways relationships between peoples and environments can be imagined and constructed" and "how technology might be held in a larger framework, in relationship to more comprehensive and inclusive human values."[21] By the time he made *La pattuglia del passo San Giacomo*, Olmi was also investigating the links between the rise of new technologies, people and their environments, as demonstrated through the workers' accustomizations to Italy's rapid development. For example, when the workers climb a snowcapped mountain, they use a horse to pull their tools up to the downed electric line. In the film's closing moments, after the repairs, we see the fruits of these men's labors when the film returns to the village at evening as a young boy looks in a lamp-lit store window. Olmi chooses a small, intimate scene to illuminate the effects of the laborer's work on the audience's daily life, firmly connecting it to the community.

Another 1954 work, *Dialogo di un venditore di almanacchi e di un passeggiere* (Dialogue between an almanac seller and a passerby), began as an experiment by the director in using a new type of camera, the Eclair 300, that ran quietly enough to allow him to record sound directly instead of the common practice at the time in Italian filmmaking of re-recording all dialogue in post-production. Olmi states that he chose this particular work, a short dialogue from a collection entitled *Operette morali* (moral works), by the great Italian writer and philosopher Giacomo Leopardi, to practice recording dialogue during production because he "was interested in its various notions of time: that of the calendar, the time of thought, and aspirations of the future."[22] This work, several of the other shorts, and *Time Stood Still* all reflect Olmi's early curiosity with the nature of time, which would gradually become integrated into the way he experimented with non-linear editing and narrative.

Dialogo di un venditore di almanacchi e di un passeggiere is one of the most significant of Olmi's Edisonvolta shorts not only because of its early representation of his interest in time, but also because it contains an experiment with a device that Olmi would use to expand the world of his films beyond their main narratives. The two characters featured in the first five minutes of the film do not enter into the latter half's adaptation of Leopardi's dialogue at all. These two are prototypes for the peripheral figures that would appear in many of the director's films of the 1960s and 1970s. The first half of the film features shots of the city's surrounding landscapes before following two musicians making their way into Milan to play music on the streets. We hear no dialogue and their journey is displayed through a series of long takes. As they make their way into the city, the two men pass cars, industrial machinery, and a billboard advertisement for a bike: all signs of the growing economy. As suggested by the framing of the musicians walking from their homes in the outskirts of the city against the billboard advertising the bike, these men are venturing into the city because the boom has created surplus income in the city that they can also benefit from. Having arrived at their destination, the two men prepare to play their music when they notice another musician has claimed the spot for himself, forcing them to find a more suitable location to earn their day's wages playing music for Christmas shoppers.

Olmi never clarifies who these characters are and they quickly vanish from the film as it transitions to an arcade where several vendors sell their wares during the holiday season. One conversation becomes the focus in which a poor almanac salesman reveals his continuing unhappiness, year after year, to a potential customer. At this moment, the film's editing tempo shifts and the distance separating these people from one another evaporates during a typical shot reverse-shot conversation sequence. Following the conversation, the film juxtaposes shots of well-lit Milan streets over images of church bells ringing. The structure that ties together these locations, people, and moments demonstrate Olmi's recognition of the typical lack of connection between people occupying and working in this metropolitan space.

In his utilization of the peripheral figures in this adaptation, Olmi concentrates on the moral aspect of Leopardi's dialogue. In an introduction to his translation of the *Operette morali*, Giovanni Cecchetti writes, "The *operette* are 'moral' in the sense that they proclaim the true nature of life itself and ultimately advocate facing it for what it is."[23] By seeking to broaden our conception of city life through the two musicians' extension of the narrative, Olmi successfully experiments with the structure of the film, provoking an awareness of the rapidly changing national environment in a fashion that follows Grierson's commitment to educate the masses about the world.

Grierson's penchant for placing human faces on industrial development was not the only inspiration for these peripheral figures. Several of the Neo-Realist filmmakers had begun using similar characters in their films at around the same time *Dialogo di un venditore di almanacchi e di un passeggiere* was made. An example from Rossellini's *Journey to Italy* in comparison with Olmi's use of the peripheral figure will exhibit how they utilize these extra-narrative characters differently. After a failed attempt at an extra-marital relationship, Alexander Joyce (George Sanders) resorts to picking up a prostitute. During this scene, events unwind chiefly through observational long takes. Alex sees the prostitute and gazes at her, walks toward his car looking back at her, enters and stops in front of the woman, prompting her to get in. In the moments that follow, they pull over in a park and she lays her head on his shoulder and relates to Alex that a friend died who had just given birth to a child seven months beforehand. She tells Alex that if he had not picked her up, she would have committed suicide. She then asks where he wants to go. He responds that now he just wants to go for a drive and that he will take her wherever she wants. During this conversation, there have been awkward pauses which prompt reflection on what is occurring in these characters' minds and what has developed between them in the short time they have known one another. The pauses, created by silence and the stillness of the long takes, invite reflection and personal application. Tag Gallagher writes in his biography and critical study of Rossellini of this moment that "It is improbable that such scenes would occur, but this time they do, like moments in our own lives that didn't have to happen, but do, and sometimes alter our tack."[24] Rossellini's style enables an unlikely situation to become real by our engagement and consideration of these characters with an application of our own experience.

Olmi's use of this kind of extra-narrative character is distinct from Rossellini's, as in *Dialogo di un venditore di almanacchi e di un passeggiere*, through extra-narrative lines that enter the film and provide an extended distance from the main story. In Rossellini's films the extra-narrative characters, such as the prostitute, play into part of the narrative's progression, whereas in Olmi's films, these are figures that are hinted at and that surface to remind us of their existence; improbable encounters that alter our vision but often do not interact with the protagonists or their narratives at all.

In *Dialogo di un venditore di almanacchi e di un passeggiere*, we see the effects of modernization on the city, but more often in the Edisonvolta films we witness how its gradual expansion affects inhabitants of more sparsely populated areas of Italy. Another SCE film observing the evolving rapport between the workers, their homes, and the industrialization of their vicinities, *La mia valle* (My valley, 1955) centers on the unidentified narrator and his shared history with his small hometown. Specifically, he describes the poor condition of his village prior to the arrival of a group of workers who construct a dam. After assembly of the dam commences, the narrator is also hired to work on the development of the structure, and many years later, after it has been completed, he continues to work at the site as a watchman.

La mia valle adopts a Flahertyesque commitment to being entrenched in the lives of its subjects. In an article downplaying the influence of Flaherty on Satyajit Ray's *Pather Panchali* (1955), Chandak Sengoopta writes that Flaherty "believed in living with his subjects and getting fully into their lives while making his films. The 'actors' in his most famous films were recruited from the local populace."[25] Sengoopta provides evidence that the approach adopted in making Ray's film, (despite initial acclaim from Flaherty enthusiasts who felt the Indian filmmaker's debut work carried forward the filmmaking style of *Nanook of the North* and *Louisiana Story*), had very little in common with the methods adopted by the pioneering documentarian. Olmi's description of his pre-production habits mark him as a much more suitable candidate as a torchbearer of Flaherty's filmmaking methods. "I begin work on a film looking for places and people. I search for people in the places where they already live. When I find them, I gather them and begin working with them.... The film gets made through my provocation and their personal involvement, which consists of gathering a series of contributions from, and without the knowledge of, the actors themselves."[26] *La mia valle* demonstrates the effectiveness of this process. Olmi's technique differs from the characteristic commonly attributed to Neo-Realism of utilizing non-professional actors in that he develops the story and the characters out of the performers' lives. As in Flaherty's films, in *La mia valle* we watch non-professional actors recreate their labor, implanting part of themselves on screen. We see women and men spinning wool and herding sheep and we see photographs from the narrator of the construction of the dam, his family and friends. By its conclusion, the film has convinced us of a type of transparency between its characters and their counterparts in reality. In the majority of his fiction films, even in the latter half of his career when he consistently selected major stars for lead roles, Olmi continued the practice of finding many of his actors through their actual professions and backgrounds.

In the same year as *La mia valle*, Olmi directed two works that experiment with collision-style editing. Olmi's adaptation of Gabriele d'Annunzio's poem "L'onda" (The wave, 1955) was originally paired as a short featurette with Nicholas Ray's *Run for Cover* (1955) during its initial Italian run. John Woodhouse argues in his autobiography of d'Annunzio that the poem itself "attempts to capture linguistically and rhythmically the shape, sound, color, size, movement, in short the essence of a wave."[27] Its potential to be realized on film was recognized by Olmi, who also co-edited the piece. This is the first of Olmi's works to apply a complex editing structure, developing an aesthetic based on pacing and visual rhyming. Recitation of the poem does not begin until over three and a half minutes into the seven-minute film. No dialogue runs over the images of boats paired together that open the film, nor the succession of rhyming shots of sea-weathered buildings, city waterfronts, stormy clouds, and finally the ocean itself that follow them. Each shot is visually connected to the images that will follow it. The repetitive rhythm of the shots echoes the motion of the ocean's waves, visually mimicking the poem's short cadence and form.

Another example of Olmi's incipient editing strategy is glimpsed in an early scene of *Il racconto della Stura* (The story of the Stura, 1955). The "Stura" of the title refers to the Stura di Demonte, a river in the Piedmont region of Italy that the film identifies as its protagonist. During a sequence when the narrator personifies the river and its capability to create electricity, characterizing the river through descriptions of its voice, liveliness and energy, various shots of the river flowing collide, oscillating between images of the water from several perspectives and locations to mimic its sense of movement. *Il racconto della Stura* is one of many Edisonvolta films that exhibit Olmi's maturing aptitude for pitting the accomplishments of humanity against nature. This motif does not imply a futility to existence or work. Rather it argues for a veneration of nature as a provider and inspirer. *Il racconto della Stura*'s prelude introduces the river's valley, focusing on a small village in ruins that the narrator tells us was destroyed by the recent World War. These evocations seem out of place, especially in an institutional film, until we recall that Olmi is both emphasizing the location and its recent troubled history and pointing to the nation's rapid recovery following the war. John David Rhodes suggests that specific places like these in film can have a "doubleness" about them, that they "become signs of both the fixity and particularity of identity (cultural, urban, geographic) and symbols of historical violence and its capacity to make and unmake the permanence that place would have seemed to promise."[28] Olmi underscores nature's indifference to the events of World War II, noting the impermanence of war's devastation by setting the stage for the rest of the film's optimistic perspective on how natural resources can fuel the country away from its recent troubled past.

These environmentally conscious works reform the natural world into a holy space, a kind of temple where time disappears. Another short from 1955, *Buongiorno natura* (Hello nature), accompanies three city slicker brothers who take a trip in the Valley of Viù. The film is funded by Edisonvolta but serves no direct institutional purpose. Even though the brothers are unskilled outdoorsmen, they thoroughly enjoy the peace that nature affords them. Similarly evoking the sereneness of the outdoors, *Cantiere d'inverno* (A worksite in winter, 1955) features a three-minute interlude that poetically describes and displays a dam immediately prior to the bulk of its workers returning to their homes in the valley to celebrate the holidays. It offers a significant portion of its running time to the worker's relationship with nature. *Cantiere d'inverno* tonally and aesthetically sets the stage for Natale and Roberto in *Time Stood Still*. Accompanying images of the site and shots of a few workers who have stayed behind to guard the dam, cranes, and buildings covered in snow, the narrator observes, "It seems as if time stands still. Perhaps winter is not the name of a season, but the name of eternity." Olmi's debut feature borrows this short sequence's perception of the season's tranquil character to frame the later film's generational conflict in a seemingly timeless setting.

In 1956, Olmi made his first great work, a film that assimilates his reverence for nature and the spiritual contentment that is received from meaningful labor. While at Edisonvolta, he serendipitously worked with the eminent literary figure Pier Paolo Pasolini, who was also in the initial stages of his filmmaking career. The pairing of Olmi and Pasolini is especially significant since they are two of the only major Italian art cinema filmmakers to hail from working class families to emerge between Neo-Realism and the 1970s. Their relationship seems to have allowed them to test out their artistic ambitions and confirm their social commitments. Olmi recalled that he and Pasolini spent a lot of time talking about the cinema, "Not in a technical sense, but in terms of how an author should position himself in confronting reality."[29]

Debates of how to represent reality in the cinema arose to the artistic and critical frontlines in Europe since Neo-Realism and carried on through the various New Wave movements that spawned around the world in the 1950s and 1960s. Pasolini continued this debate as a theorist, most notably in his wish for a type of "free indirect discourse" in his essay "The Cinema of Poetry." He defines this concept as "the immersion of the filmmaker in the mind of the character and then the adoption on the part of the filmmaker, not only of the psychology of his character, but also of his language."[30] This approach builds on Bazin and his consideration of film's relationship with reality in Italian Neo-Realism. Discussing what De Sica, Rossellini, and Fellini had in common, Bazin states, "The relation between meaning and appearance having been in a sense inverted, appearance is always presented as a unique discovery, an almost documentary revelation that retains its full force of vividness and detail. Whence the director's art lies in the skill with which he compels the event to reveal its meaning—or at least the meaning he lends it—without removing any of its ambiguity."[31] Olmi first achieved this balance when he worked with Pasolini. Although Pasolini felt that no filmmakers had fully assumed their characters' language until the 1960s, the first film he wrote for Olmi, *Manon Finestra 2* (Manon window 2, 1956), is structured in a manner that heralds his later position in its reinforcement of the ambiguous perceptions of the miners at the center of the film.[32]

Manon Finestra 2 is Olmi's first eloquent piece of cinema. It's a work that confidently trusts its mise-en-scène, editing, and its poetic correlation with the story of Saint Barbara. It sets aside an omnipresent narrator after its introduction and allows us to dissect its vivid appreciation and sanctification of a group of miners and their work. Although the narrator still relates occasional facts about the miners and their jobs, viewers of Olmi's preceding Edisonvolta work will be struck at this work's reliance on ambient sounds and relative silence. As with the majority of the Edisonvolta films, *Manon finestra 2* relies on a very loose narrative. Its frame is an evening shift of the miners completing their typical duties.

The workers are filmed with an attitude of reverence as they initiate their climb up to *finestra 2* (window 2), the cave where they will spend the night. In three successive shots of their ascension, lasting over half a minute, the miners resemble pilgrims traveling to a sacred location. Once they have received their orders for the evening, the narrator describes the worship the miners give to a portrait of Saint Barbara by placing flowers underneath it. The film then cuts to one of the workers standing outside reflectively staring up at the sky and viewing the lightning of a brewing storm. Here, *Manon finestra 2* alludes to Saint Barbara's association with lightning, and her function as the patron saint and protector of miners, a reference it continues through the night as the storm opens, concludes, and the workers exit the cave in the morning to a beautiful sunlit valley.

The film's detailed observations of the miners as they prepare dynamite, set it off and clear the resulting debris, justify its solemn attitude toward them. Its meditative study of the minutiae of their routines offers a form of Pasolini's later cinematic ideals through the sanctification and the value given to their labor. This reflects what Naomi Greene sees as Pasolini's "desire to exchange the social and historical world of the Neo-Realists for a universe that opens upon the sacred, the mythic, the epic."[33] For both Olmi and Pasolini, *Manon finestra 2* unquestionably served as a formative experience for their departures from Neo-Realism's vision of labor and the development of their diverging approaches to depicting the sacred and its ties with working class people.

Tre fili fino a Milano (Three cables all the way to Milan, 1958) continues in the vein of *Manon finestra 2* in its quiet, precise monitoring of the laborers at work, both films esteeming the individuals at the heart of the industrialization of Italy. Here the workers are in the Daone Valley of northwestern Italy erecting cable towers that enable the transfer of electricity as far as Milan. Olmi's camera does not rest on its subjects as much as Flaherty's during Nanook's seal hunt, but the cutting does not elide the time required for the workers' tasks. Rather, like Flaherty, Olmi illuminates the links between their traditions, their work, and the land. It lacks *Manon finestra 2*'s poetic allusions, but *Tre fili fino a Milano* does evidence the sense of the sacred that the earlier film possessed and that would appear frequently in the director's works after he left Edisonvolta. Morando Morandini comments that the film has a "fairy-tale like atmosphere, almost magical" in its portrayal of the workers.[34] There is a sense of an enchanting other-worldliness in the workers' genuine jovial and cheerful demeanor as they work and sing in dialect while erecting transmission towers. Perhaps part of this uncanniness springs from the incongruent collision between the two worlds of the film. Although views of Milan are absent, the destination of the power lines remind us of the burgeoning white-collar epicenter of the country's boom, standing in distinct contrast to the idyllic peace pervading the scenes shown here.

This division also permeates *Michelino 1° B* (1956), the longest of the films from this period at forty-four minutes. The novelist Goffredo Parise authored the script and had recently written two books featuring adolescent boys like the film's protagonist, Michelino. However, none of Parise's Jungian-inspired investigations or well-rounded characters were called upon for this work. The film's sole purpose is to exhibit the schools that Edisonvolta developed to train electrical engineers, reviewing the year to year experiences and activities of students. Of interest is Michelino's initial journey to Milan for school, which is exhibited with childlike wonder through the swift cutting and low-angle shots at the city's attractions, trolleys, busy streets and modern buildings. As with *Dialogo di un venditore di almanacchi e di un passeggiere*, and later *Il posto*, Olmi documented in *Michelino 1° B* the cultural phenomenon of the migration of over 300,000 people to Milan during the initial years of the economic miracle.[35] Even though the film does not push for a meditation on the consequences of these events, there is a hint of romanticism in Michelino's fondness for the ocean and boating while he is at home and in his desire to become a fisherman like his grandfather. In becoming an electrical engineer, he will veer away from the occupation of his seafaring, fisherman ancestors and we cannot fail to anticipate how different his life will be from theirs.

Olmi addresses the challenges faced by older Italians in Italy's changing economy in his first work for the RAI television network, *Il pensionato* (The pensioner, 1958), produced in collaboration with the SCE. A grumpy, retired mechanic (Piero Faconti) has problems sleeping at night because two young men have set up a printing press directly below his apartment. When he yells at them to tell them he is trying to sleep, they apologize but respond they have a lot of work to complete. Later, after the narrator informs us of the mechanic's boredom, he sees the pair struggling with a piece of equipment in the courtyard and he brusquely offers to help them. By the film's ending, he also stays occupied late into the evening and keeps his wife awake. Faconti, despite howling and grumbling in dialect, needs no translation to express his cantankerous mood, giving an excellent, nuanced performance that transforms the character's attitude from melancholic resignation to renewed zest after he has found new employment. Several of Olmi's recurring interests (e.g., generational miscommunication) appear for the first time in *Il pensionato* and are convincingly treated despite the moralistic nature of the film. Its focus on the role of the elderly in society during the boom, as Italians began to increasingly live longer, treats a subject that was becoming a growing concern for many Italian families. The pensioner is not only bored because of his lack of work, but because he has been displaced from his hometown and his children. In a voiceover, the mechanic informs us that he would like to return to Brianza, on the outskirts of Milan, but chooses to remain in the city center because he fears he would never see his only child if he moved. *Il pensionato*'s resolution of these problems presents an atypical conclusion in the director's fictional works.

Following the release and success of his first feature in 1959, Olmi made a few more shorts for Edisonvolta before leaving the company. The first, *Il grande paese d'acciaio* (The great land of steel, 1960), is one of only a handful of the Edisonvolta works that was shot outside of northern Italy. A Sicilian tune complements the first four and a half minutes of scenes of Syracuse. Shots of farmers tilling their fields and tending to their animals initially dominate the film, until a gradual encroachment of industrial technology intrudes upon these scenes. The song concludes and gives way to a narrator, explaining Syracuse's ancient history and its eventual return to the world stage as a modern city, evidenced through an imposing chemical plant under construction that monopolizes the film's latter half. However, the narration lasts briefly, the song returns, and a series of tracking shots follow a donkey-pulled cart, transporting construction materials across the building site. The movement of the camera following the cart, supplemented by the buoyant music, has a contemptuousness to it, reflecting the workers' aversion to discarding the working methods that contribute to their culture and character. Moments like these undercut the institutional role of the film, which is forthright in its suspicion at the threats posed by progress. Paola Bonifazio perceives in Olmi's Edisonvolta films "a pathetic commemoration of the human expenditure that the process of modernization costs both in terms of human beings and nature."[36] *Il grande paese d'acciaio* takes this commemoration one step further, striking a tone of irreverent defiance to the industrial invasion taking over the workers' lives and transforming their landscape.

The last of the Edisonvolta films attributed to Olmi as a director, *Un metro lungo cinque* (One meter is as long as five, 1961), chronicles the construction of a reservoir on the border of Switzerland and Italy in the Lei

Valley. The title of the work originates from a saying of the film's workers, marveling at the voluminous mountain-top views that seem to elongate and enlarge everything within sight. The film itself seemed to have a similar effect on its audience, as evidenced by Roberto Rossellini, who remarked after seeing the film, "This way of making cinema means discovering a world."[37] It contains the same revelatory interest in its workers that characterizes *Manon finestra 2* and *Tre fili fino a Milano*, highlighting specifically in this film the presence of migrant workers and their importance to the project's completion.

Tullio Kezich, a journalist and playwright who later became a close friend and screenwriting collaborator of Olmi, wrote the screenplay, which structures the narrative to conclude the film with an aged, rambling head of accommodation making a wistful farewell to the workers and the site. It is noteworthy that the film closes with the heartfelt oration of a common worker, rather than an earlier scene featuring a government representative speaking at the celebration of the dam's completion. Bidding farewell to his companions and recalling their time together, the elderly man foretells that those visiting the dam in the future will know nothing of the sacrifices and labor behind the dam, a fact that he does not complain of but that the film is determined to negate through its appreciative attendance to the men and their digging, mining, drilling, and building. The head of accommodations' words also serve as a fitting goodbye for Olmi to the company that meant a great deal to his personal and professional lives.

To discuss Olmi, his feature films and how he branches off from Neo-Realism, it is important to consider these early works and the impressions that Flaherty, Grierson, and Pasolini left on the director and his style. Additionally, the lack of significant alterations in Olmi's style and interests between his time at Edisonvolta and his boom trilogy attests to the artistic freedom granted him by the company. With no formal training to impede him, Olmi greatly benefited from the bounds of the energy industry's framework to discover a style that befit his germinating filmmaking philosophy on the workers he encountered daily, their professions, on the societal direction of Italy following the war, and more broadly, on the vital role the natural world plays in all of our lives.

2

Time Standing Still and Moving Freely

Olmi's Boom Trilogy and the Evolution of His Time-Shifting Style

For nearly a century prior to Italy's economic miracle, the country lagged significantly behind other major European countries, such as Germany, France, and the United Kingdom, in its development, "[acting] out the role of a great power while lacking the means."[1] Many Italians fortunate enough to have employment worked in low-wage, highly physical labor. As Italian historian Paul Ginsborg states, discussing the country at the end of World War II, "[Italy] was little changed, outside of its major cities, since the time of Garibaldi and Cavour. It was still predominately a peasant country, of great and unspoiled natural beauty, of sleepy provincial cities, of enduring poverty, especially in the South, of rural culture and local dialects."[2] Following World War II, many industries began to prosper as the country recovered, abandoned fascist protectionism, and entered the free trade market.[3] Life all over Italy underwent sudden changes as Italian cities demonstrated signs of new affluence that eventually trickled into more rural areas. As John Foot reports, Italians were eager to enter the consumer market. "With increasing prosperity, many Italians were able to purchase consumer goods for the first time (usually on credit)—televisions (broadcasting began in 1954); cars...; scooters...; fridges and washing machines. The number of private cars in Italy rose from 364,000 in 1950 to 4.67 million in 1964. Fridges produced by Italian companies shot up from 18,500 in 1951 to 370,000 in 1957 and 3.2 million in 1967."[4] The financial success of the boom was unprecedented in Italy and nearly everyone wanted a piece of it. Many Italian migrants drifted to the metropolises of the North, hoping to fill white-collar office jobs that would buy these symbols of success. In later years, workers flocked to opportunities across the peninsula as industrialization spread to more remote areas and the country left behind systems that permitted the exploitation of agricultural workers by wealthy landowners.

Accompanying the growth of the economy, a complete metamorphosis of culture swept over the country. After receiving much needed recovery aid from the United States' Marshall Plan, Italy was firmly on the side of the U.S. as the Cold War broke out. Under America's influence, Italy not only opened its doors to free trade, but it also permitted the world's cultural exports to spread across the nation. Globalization's effects progressively expanded from economic centers to small villages, especially impacting younger people and thereby creating generational divides. This was the first Italian generation that would largely grow-up without expecting to work the fields or the ocean every day. The mental and cultural landscapes shaped by such interactions was bound to shift to more cosmopolitan affairs and interests. Donald Sassoon explains that a new youth condition in Italy was created by the arrival of new cultural forms. "These united young people not only across regional divides, but also across countries. This was made possible by technological and media developments, the production of cheap records, cheap clothes, radio and television broadcasting of new music and new modes of speech."[5] As in many other countries across the world during the middle of the twentieth century, Italy would give birth to a generation of young people whose ideas, philosophies, and goals in life had little resemblance to those of their parents.

Beginning with *Il posto* and continuing through *Un certo giorno,* in the 1960s Olmi continually returned to stories, in major and minor projects, involving youth and unrequited love. Besides his feature films during this period, he made a number of shorts for Italy's public television broadcasting network, RAI. Some of them were collected in the anthology film *Racconti di giovani amori* (Stories of young love, 1967), which was given a brief theatrical release in Italy.[6] The most noted of these shorts was *La cotta* (*The Crush*, 1967), a story about a teenager beset by bouts of puppy love. Several critics, and even colleagues, berated Olmi for making such apolitical work during the unrest that defined the decade. For Olmi, the era was defined by a conformity that demanded total political devotion from young people, an expectation that trod upon their natural inclinations. He recalls that during research he spoke with young men and women who would express their dissatisfaction with their love lives and society's concurrent expectations that they put those feelings aside for politics. He decided to reflect this underlying issue in his films. "I wanted to show that while they spoke of politics, the kids didn't stop falling in love, and they couldn't find fulfillment of those sentiments concerning other realities in politics."[7] As this chapter demonstrates, Olmi's depictions of such aspirations in young lives does intersect with the political through portrayals of lovers adapting to the demands of their increasingly urban-centered nation, narrative detours, his peripheral figures, and his developing time-shifting style.

The generational conflict that erupted at the boom, plays itself out in all three of Olmi's first feature films, receiving the most direct attention in the relationship between the two protagonists of *Time Stood Still*. Its setting at a hydroelectric dam security post in the Italian Alps places the film at a distance from the epicenters of the boom. However, the tensions created through the developments in the cities even penetrate this seemingly isolated location. *Time Stood Still* picks up stylistically and thematically from films such as *Manon finestra 2* and *Cantiere d'inverno* that Olmi had recently made at Edisonvolta. Just like those works, it exposes Olmi's admiration for Flaherty, matching nature against the impending advancement of industrialization and the ways this confrontation transmutes the lives of Italian workers. It was initially proposed to the energy company as another of its institutional short films. Already with a story in mind for his first feature, Olmi had slyly reported to his employers that he wished to make a lengthy documentary, concealing his intentions to make a fictional narrative because he felt they did not understand art cinema and would think that he wanted to make a genre or comedy film.[8] He successfully deceived his employer, partly by meeting his budget constraints with a near skeleton crew of around twenty people on set.[9] He also kept his costs low by utilizing non-professional actors for his two protagonists, Natale (Natale Rossi) and Roberto (Roberto Seveso), the former a laborer from Camonica Valley and the latter a student who worked near the Edisonvolta offices.[10]

Shot in black and white cinemascope with a 2.35:1 ratio at a dam in the Camonica Valley, *Time Stood Still*'s images of the wintry Alps provide the film with a sense of scale and grandeur that minimizes the achievements of the boom. This type of beautiful natural scenery reoccurs throughout Olmi's films but is surprisingly uncommon in cinema. And as Scott MacDonald argues, this type of imagery can confront the viewer with their reality in ways that refocus attention to the environment. "It can model fundamental changes in perception not only in terms of what we see in movie theaters, on television, or online, but in how we function in the 'real world.' And it can do so without announcing any polemical goal."[11] Tapping into the style he developed at Edisonvolta for minimizing industrialization's electric towers by placing them in the shadows of mountains, Olmi deliberately, and quietly, returns our gaze to the breathtaking majesty of nature. Barely visible under the snow, the dam is incongruent with the landscape. The incursion of the hydroelectric dam on the mountains parallels the conflict between Natale and Roberto, the traditional and the neoteric.

At the beginning of the film, Salvetti (Paolo Guadrubbi), Natale's original co-worker, departs for his Christmas holidays and Roberto arrives as a substitute for Salvetti's replacement when its discovered that the original replacement's wife is giving birth.[12] The two men have a number of awkward encounters as they adjust to one another over the course of a day and a half. An avalanche occurs the morning after Roberto's arrival and cold weather forces the pair to stay in a church overnight after the barracks they are based in loses power. At the church, Natale brews up a remedy of milk and brandy when Roberto comes down with a fever. The next morning as Natale carries Roberto back up to the barracks on his back, the film concludes as they enter their re-powered quarters.

The story's simplicity conceals the film's silent, comprehensive attendance to the men, specifically Natale, as they maintain the site and the quiet unfolding of the pair's relationship that we witness mostly through their own curious observations of one another. After Salvetti departs, there is a stretch of seven minutes without any dialogue as the film follows Natale cleaning the watchmen's barracks, making the beds, chopping wood, tracking and setting a trap for an elusive rabbit, digging a hole in the ice to access fresh water, and killing time by making the hot stovetop pop with flicks of water from his finger. We watch all of this in Flahertyesque long takes that impress upon us the skill and craftiness of Natale as he completes his supervisory rounds.[13] In setting the trap for the rabbit Natale reveals himself to be a *bricoleur*. The camera follows him as he gathers string, a hollow cylinder, bait, and assembles the trap outside of a window where the rabbit's tracks lie. The duration of these shots call attention to time and the seeming agelessness, except the presence of the dam, of this setting. It seems that Natale has found an existence outside of time and that he would happily continue his life alone in the Alps, forgetting about the rest of the world and any further progress civilization makes. In a play on the film's title and this ambience, while Natale awaits his new companion a clock in the barracks' kitchen stops ticking and he has to reset it, signaling Roberto's crass interruption of this Eden-like situation.

Even after Roberto arrives, a distinct ambience of silence prevails. The new colleagues do ask each other questions, but they both appear uneasy in one another's presence and rely more on what they can gather from curious glances rather than from conversation. Marc Henri Piault writes, "The film attests to the paradoxical functions of silence in the process of communication: beyond and often despite the spoken word, in the film we sense an elusive encounter masked behind furtive gestures that defy explanation."[14] Others see more pernicious effects in the lack of dialogue. Clodagh Brook rightly contends that silence characterizes all of Olmi's works, but she takes the lack of dialogue out of the films' context when she asserts that it "betrays an ideologically reactionary message: women, the poor, and the weak remain, and ought to remain, locked into positions of powerlessness."[15]

As I will demonstrate here and in the rest of the chapters, this misreading neglects Olmi's strategic use of silence to express the intricacies of characters and their relationships to each other and their environments.

As an example of Olmi's deliberate use of silence in *Time Stood Still*, when Roberto exits the barracks to relieve himself, a one-camera setup creates a wordless comic scene expressing the men's curiosity about one another. After Roberto exits the barracks, a cut is made outside of them looking into the dining room through a window. Natale is framed within the window sitting at the table reading. Once Roberto has walked past, he stands up and peeks into the book the younger man was reading. He sits down again and after Roberto crosses the window in the other direction, he tries to put the book back in its original place. Natale waits until Roberto enters his room and then he also exits the barracks. We remain in the same viewing position, and as Natale walks past the window, Roberto exits his room, gathers his items from the table, and then swiftly sneaks a peek at Natale's book. This sequence exemplifies Olmi's ability to allow the unspoken nuances of a relationship to be given meaning by the viewer and implies nothing about the possession of power. For several minutes preceding this scene, the younger man's attempts to nail a shelf to a wall is unremarked upon, but visibly irritates Natale when the pounding knocks his things out of place. The uneasiness felt during these situations confirms Olmi's effective adaptation of his style at Edisonvolta to quietly observe workers and their labor. The stylistic approach (long takes interspersed with close-ups of the work and the workers) of those films that record the intricacies involved in digging caves and laying electric wires is used here, and in the rest of Olmi's fictional work, to the effect of capturing, in the manner that only cinema can, the indefinable aspects of personalities and their relations to others.

The tension of these scenes is augmented by fragments of conversation that allude to the changes in the cities. Before he leaves, Salvetti informs Natale that he is headed to Gênes (Genoa) where there are so many people "that you don't see time go by." He states that the city has "whites, blacks, all races and at night it's so lit up you'd think its day." When Roberto arrives, he brings the spirit of these transformations with him, including the educational aspirations of a growing middle class. After finishing his dinner during his first night's watch, he opens up a textbook and tells Natale that he wanted to come to the site so that he could spend the next month studying for an economics exam he has in February. Too many of the recent temptations at home, such as going out dancing at night with newly monied tourists, distract him. Natale does not respond to any of his colleague's enthusiastic chatter, but continues to read his book, *Cuore* (*Heart*), which we will discover later is bound up in a traditional approach to love and

2. Time Standing Still and Moving Freely 43

life.[16] The economic miracle opened up career paths, free time and hobbies for young Italians that Natale's generation never would have imagined.

Roberto also brings with him a more palpable example of his generation's break with tradition: rock 'n' roll. The morning after Roberto's arrival, Natale walks to the bottom of the dam whistling a cheerful tune. As he enters a doorway of the building, a thundering noise startles him and he looks back at the barracks in terror, perhaps expecting that an avalanche has occurred. He runs back up the hill with urgency until he realizes that it is only a rock 'n' roll record (sung in poor English). After Natale's fears are assuaged he returns to the area below the dam. Roberto dances inside the kitchen and continues singing along and cavorting around as he prepares his breakfast. A quick cut, from an askew angle, is made to the rotating record player, which then turns to adjust itself to display the player right side up, the shot commenting on the disharmonious air by inverting the mood of earlier scenes where Natale was depicted calmly enjoying radio programs and music.

Natale continues to be annoyed throughout the day but by the end of the night he finally finds the words, in the longest conversation of the film, to express his perplexity with Roberto and the challenges to his worldview brought about by the boom. After dinner, because an avalanche has cut off their electricity and a fierce winter storm rages outside, they decide to bring their bedding into the kitchen next to the stove's fire. They retire to their beds and Natale recommences reading his book, which catches the eye of Roberto. Roberto lets Natale know he has read the book as well by repeatedly stating how beautiful and moving it is. Natale responds by saying that it is full of beautiful things that "could never happen these days. It's another world." Roberto replies that his dad says the same thing too but that he does not agree because he thinks the world is "always the same." As the conversation continues, Natale voices the apprehensions of a generation as it undergoes sudden and tremendous cultural changes. He also expresses Olmi's repeated concern for the loss of the way in which work so often reflected an individual's personality, becoming an organic part of his or her life. But he eventually warms to Roberto and the boom, bringing the film to the most optimistic conclusion of the trilogy.

In the film's closing moments, a small miracle occurs that disproves Natale's suggestion that good things do not happen in the world anymore. Due to the cold, the men agree to move to the site's church where Roberto reveals that he feels ill. In an act of compassion, Natale, trudging through the storm, returns to the barracks to gather materials to prepare some makeshift medicine for his young friend. At the church once again, he builds a fire to boil milk, adding a touch of brandy with some hesitation because he knows Roberto is a teetotaler. After Roberto consumes the drink along with a medicinal tablet, their flashlight loses power. Natale walks over to a candelabrum resting on the altar of the church and lights the first candle. The light reveals a beautiful mural depicting the Madonna holding the infant Jesus in her arms. After looking back at Roberto, he decides to light the rest of the candles of the candelabrum and pauses for a moment to reflect on the painting. As the shot of the mural fades out, the new day's dawn skyline (cloudy but with a beam of sunlight shining through) fades in and the two images are briefly juxtaposed through a dissolve to suggest the birth of a new era. In the graphic match between the fade-out of the shot of the candlelit mural and the fade-in of the dawn's sun rising over the mountains, this moment also continues the link between spirituality and nature that Olmi made in *Manon finestra 2* into Olmi's feature films.

In the morning, Roberto awakes feeling fit, although his breath leads him to suspect that Natale spiked the medicinal concoction. Carrying Roberto piggyback up to the barracks, Natale denies he used alcohol when asked and agrees to not relate the young man's illness to the surveyor so that the boy may remain at the dam. In a final, playful acknowledgment of the cultural collision that occurs in the film, Roberto's rock 'n' roll record interrupts the conclusion's peaceful musical score, and the camera rapidly jerks the shot away from the tranquil scene of the dam against the mountains and pans over to the barracks as if to remind us that even though a friendly bond has been created between the two men, many more adjustments will be needed for them to attune themselves to one another.

Some critics find that the conclusion makes use of the church as a kind of *deus ex machina* to resolve the difficult societal issues that problematize the two men's relationship. For example, in John Gillett's review of the film in *Sight and Sound*, the critic gives a mostly favorable critique, but has some complaints regarding the ending. "Although Olmi makes the most of this setting photographically and emotionally, for me the last scenes are marred by a whiff of Catholic sentimentalism, a hint of that self-consciousness so carefully avoided everywhere else."[17] As already mentioned, similar criticism is frequently leveled at Olmi, assuming that because of his faith his depictions of religious imagery, ideas or stories, immediately diminish the quality of his films. But dismissing this particular scene because of its use of Catholic symbols is a mistake, because in doing so it denies the extra-religious symbolism of the mural and the miracle, the confidence of an alignment between two competing worldviews and the hope that future generations will carry forward the virtues cherished by Natale.

Time Stood Still was shown out of competition at the Venice Film Festival in 1959 and was given limited international distribution that did not garner much consideration for the director and his debut feature. It was *Il posto* (1961) that brought Olmi international attention, winning prizes from Venice, the National Syndicate of Italian Film Journalists, the New York Film Critic's Circle, and the British Film Institute. Bosley Crowther's *New York Times* review typifies the glowing responses Olmi was receiving. "One hesitates, of course, to be too clamorous about Mr. Olmi on the strength of this one film. It is modest in its intentions, limited in its scope. But it clearly reveals a picturemaker who knows how to make a camera see the poetry in life and hint at vain longings and ironies too sad and depressing to tell."[18] Based on their viewing of just this film, other critics, such as *Film Quarterly*'s Ernest Callenbach, were also signaling the arrival of "a first-class filmmaker ... an artist of the last ditch stand being waged, in all the industrialized cities of the world, against the civilization we have created."[19] Although almost all responses to the film are acclamatory, responses to its tone differ. In English language film studies, along with *The Tree of Wooden Clogs*, *Il posto* is one of the director's two most discussed films. Many scholars, echoing the initial reactions of Crowther and Callenbach, have found the film depressing, referring to the Kafkaesque bureaucracy of the tests required by Domenico's future employer and the film's depiction of the soulless office space.[20] Others have found the film to be the most humorous of Olmi's career, likening Domenico's relatively expressionless appearance to the famed stone face of Buster Keaton.[21]

Il posto was not produced by Edisonvolta but the film's crew were working for the company while they completed the film on the weekends, in between shooting documentaries. Edisonvolta did not bear a grudge for Olmi's obfuscation of his intentions for *Time Stood Still* and his productive relationship with them benefited him when he sought to film all of *Il posto*'s office sequences in the company's buildings. But the film contains much more personal reflections on Olmi's previous work than just using his employer's offices as locations. The director himself went through a similar hiring process to the one depicted in the film and he has shared in interviews that specific moments in the film, such as the scene of the green, intimidated employee nervously seated in front of his boss's desk, were recollections of his own experiences at Edisonvolta.[22] Olmi's stand-in, Domenico (Sandro Panseri), frequently finds himself astounded by this world, unsure of how to respond to its rules and regulations.

Modernization and the estrangement of workers from the outdoors seem to suffocate and dehumanize the workers of this unnamed company, threatening to efface their personalities and idiosyncrasies. Critics' comparisons of Domenico with Keaton were quite apt, as the silent Keaton characters often bumbled along struggling to deal with the sudden onslaught of modernization, albeit in America in the 1920s. The character-defining interplay between work and laborer that Olmi presents in the Edisonvolta films through long takes, and that returns in *The Tree of Wooden Clogs*, does not exist here. Whatever the workers do, which is never specified and appears to be mindless office work, provides no gratification. Although Olmi would continue to use long takes for non-work-related scenes in this and his later films, he utilizes other techniques to contemplate the workers' humanity and the preservation of their individualities. In *Il posto*, this is most often achieved through frequent departures from Domenico's commonplace narrative of getting a job and peripheral figures that extend the film's diegetic sphere.

Describing Domenico's story as commonplace is accurate, but this characterization conceals the film's appreciation for his personality. He is in his late teens or early twenties, on the cusp of entering the new Italian society that promises so much economically that he, like many of his compatriots, leaves behind traditional forms of labor in his village to find employment in the city as a clerk. At his interview, a young girl named Antonietta (Loredana Detto, in her sole acting role and who was later to become Olmi's wife) catches Domenico's eye and he becomes infatuated with her. They both pass a number of pre-employment tests (some related to skills, others testing their psychological makeup) but are eventually placed in different departments: he as a runner in administration, as they do not need any clerks at the time of hiring, and she as a typist in a separate building. After several attempts to find her, they cross paths one day in a corridor and they agree they will try to meet at the company's New Year's Eve dance. Domenico goes to the dance without seeing Antonietta and the film concludes with the revelation that a clerk has died and left an opening that Domenico can fill.

But the film reveals much more of Domenico than his unexciting prospects for love and his destiny for the tedious office clerk position. For instance, in a scene after they have completed some of their pre-employment tests, Domenico and Antonietta window shop for items they cannot afford and then stop at a café. During the sequence, Olmi focuses on the few delicate gestures that bring them together, overcoming the awkwardness between them. In the process of making his way through a crowd in the coffee shop, Domenico loses his spoon on the way back to the table. Antonietta tells Domenico not to worry about it and reaches across the table to stir his coffee with her spoon. Domenico's provincial naïveté leaves him helpless, prompting him to mimic Antonietta in handling his cup and plate. Becoming aware that they are running late after they finish their coffee, the couple rush back to the office building so they will not miss the rest of the pre-employment tests. They reach a busy intersection which Domenico quickly crosses but then realizes that Antonietta was too nervous to brave. Domenico rushes back and grabs Antonietta's hand and leads her across the street and they continue to run, fingers entwined, until a police officer fusses at them for dashing across a park. The camera tracking the runners serves as a formal counterpoint to the rigid enclosure of the couple's movements and actions in the office space and during the tests. Similarly, when he begins his job the next day, he refuses to wait for the elevator and the camera pans upwards as he runs up the stairs, unwilling to allow the office to constrain him fully. Wordlessly, these moments give impressions of Domenico's character, his quiet noncompliance with the rigid order of the corporation.

The film itself refuses to comply with the order of a linear, realist narrative. In *Il posto*, peripheral figures consistently shadow Domenico at the borders of his story and slightly overlap and suggest the other lives and many narratives that could also have been at the center of this film. On the day his application process begins, he meets Antonietta during one of the pre-employment tests. In a scene following a series of tests, Domenico waits for Antonietta outside of the building. After she spots him, a single take tracks them as they walk down the rest of the block. When they pass a man looking into a wine shop window, Antonietta brushes past him and then glances in his direction. Domenico then looks at the man as they both walk off the screen and the shot's tracking stops and the camera remains with the mumbling man momentarily. A similar figure appears during the scene when Domenico first arrives at the office building lobby to begin his interviews. Two men enter after him. One well-dressed man, likely a boss, enters prompting the doormen to stand up from their chairs and interrupting Domenico's enquiry about the exam's location. After the boss travels through the lobby, Domenico is told that he needs to go to the fourth floor. In the same take an old man enters, and as Domenico crosses the room the man asks one of the doormen where the welfare office is, prompting a quizzical look. After the old man repeats himself, the doorman waves his arms in exasperation and a cut is made to Domenico arriving at the personnel office.

There are other examples of these characters throughout the film: a woman furtively wrapping her meat up in the cafeteria, and a man singing on the bus. With these figures, Olmi allows the protagonist to exit and leave us with unfamiliar characters that have nothing to do with Domenico's search for a job or his love life. These moments give us pause as we recognize the challenge to the traditional conventions of classical narrative film language, such as visual narrative causality and linearity, as thoroughly detailed by David Bordwell.[23] Because Olmi provides no indications as to the peripheral figures' purpose in the film, their casual appearance leaves us with many questions and a supplication to consider their humanity.

In one of the most insightful essays on *Il posto*, Elizabeth Alsop writes that the film's "use of montage, ellipses, and surreal, even oneiric imagery suggests a desire not to be tethered to the present; to not have to portray reality simply 'as it is,' but instead to poeticize it and in the process, particularize it."[24] Although she is not referring to the peripheral figures in this quote, their mysteriousness also augments the film's oneiric qualities, calling us to review reality and unravel details as if we were recalling the particulars of a dream. Their presence has the deliberate intention of outlining the human effects of the boom, requiring viewers to identify with and imagine the lives of those who often escape their line of vision. As Millicent Marcus states, "Olmi's concept of artistic responsibility shares with [Neo-Realism] the same ethical impulse, which resides at the core of all *engagé* art."[25] Like many of the filmmakers from various New Wave movements that developed across the world in the sixties, such as Jean-Luc Godard, Miloš Forman, and Oshima Nagisa, Olmi is a modernist, self-reflexively calling attention to the form of cinematic language and conventions, challenging a passive consumption of his films. As we watch *Il posto*, we are caught off guard by the interruption its extra-narrative characters cause, specifically in the extended sequence that exits the office building and peeks into several of the worker's home lives.

This sequence appears a little over halfway into the film and introduces us to Domenico's destined office space and co-workers. Peter Bondanella suggests that in this scene "Olmi's depiction of the simple, day-to-day actions of the office staff shows that they conceal a great wealth of human interest; yet the juxtaposition of the compulsive mannerisms they exhibit at work and their more spontaneous, if often strange, behavior at home demonstrates clearly the alienating effects of the workplace."[26] The fracture in time disaffects us temporarily from the film's otherwise typical linear path. It is unclear whether these brief vignettes occur during Domenico's orientation to the workplace or if they are taking place in the past. Bert Cardullo reads the scene as mapping out "the lay of the adult land, as well as a set of possible futures—limited though they may be—for this young office worker."[27] However, the film's tendency to linger away from Domenico and provide brief sketches of others on the fringes of the narrative's world supports the impression that the sequence is less interested in foretelling Domenico's future than it is in stimulating active re-imaginings of our own world.

Like the rest of the film, the sequence has an underlying comic tone that cherishes the characters' idiosyncrasies in the face of the company's absurdities. As the scene begins, we witness the workers occupied in their daily tasks and we are given cues to the quirks and odd habits that the film will explore outside of the office. A man with glasses sits near the front of the room and scribbles notes down from a card catalogue (later we discover he is a budding novelist); an obese man throws paper balls over the novelist's shoulders as he clears out his desk; an older man cuts his cigarettes in half to fit them into his cigarette holder; another man combs his hair and carefully adjusts his sideburns; and a man in the back changes his light bulb when it fizzles out. Another worker enters the room unsubtly eyeballing a young female worker before asking the office head to check some documents. When this visiting worker discusses the novelist with another colleague as a "brownnose" and remarks on his inability to see, the film cuts abruptly to the apartment of the subject of their conversation.

The novelist lies in bed, writing with the paper close to his face, but then rises to look out his window when he hears music from the street. A cut is made to the window's view of a lively gathering taking place outside. Immediately following this shot, we are brought outside of the novelist's room and into the hallway of his floor. His landlady glances through the peephole in the door and complains about him not paying his bills and leaving the lights on. He turns out the ceiling light and covers the top of his desk lamp as he turns it on and continues writing. The novelist's viewpoint outside the window reinforces his inability to see clearly how others lead their lives. The distance between him and others suggests that he is acting himself as a writerly type of author, imagining the lives of those he sees around him. Marcus writes of this scene, "In this vivid juxtaposition of private story and public life in the office, Olmi's point seems to be that the impersonal, mechanized bureaucracy is made up of intensely human parts, each one capable of generating his or her own versions of *Il posto*, just as the novelist office member quite literally generates stories in his spare time."[28] The landlady also acts in a writerly fashion, by peering through the door, as a curious spectator, to see what her tenant is doing. For Olmi, the curious nature of these characters' acts, and our own gaze into the more intimate details of their lives, is not reducible to simple voyeurism, but expresses how the modern individual overcomes the cumbersome barriers placed between him/herself and others.

The sequence then shifts to the home of the man who was combing his hair in the office. His wife cuts his hair while he reads the newspaper, instructing her to be careful of his sideburns. The man rises up and hides when someone knocks at the door as if someone seeing him having his hair cut at home would shame him. The setting changes again to the home of the older cigarette cutter whose cryptic conversation with either his wife or servant leads us to believe that he may have a possibly criminal business on the side. We also discover in two other segments of this multifaceted sequence that the obese paper-thrower frequents a singing club and demonstrates his talents as an opera singer and that the older woman in the office has a delinquent son (she also appears briefly before this scene during Domenico's placement interview and is chastised for using the excuse of problems at home for an absence). As the woman discovers that her son has stolen from her, a cut is made back to the office with a panning shot that circles around the room displaying the baffled expressions of her co-workers as they stare at her crying. The length of this shot becomes uncomfortable for us as the workers continue to stare at her silently. When they do say something, they proceed to use the incident as a moment to hurl petty insults at one another.

Closing this schism in the narrative on this disconsolate note, an ambiguous space opens for us to fill with our own reactions to the alienated characters and unseen lives outside of our own circles. This approaches the type of phenomenological realism hoped for in Bazin's idea of "total cinema." Bazin's friend, film critic and Catholic priest, Amédée Ayfre shared ideas, which are worth considering here, on this type of cinema in his reading of the canonical Neo-Realist works. "It can only be deciphered by a consciousness which is never rigidly directed to an external end, this 'sense' can always be interpreted and colored by consciousness according to its own standards and theories, i.e., its own *Weltanschauung*, exactly like the real world itself. The result is a fundamental ambiguity."[29] Like the Neo-Realists, Olmi resists guiding the viewer toward specific resolutions regarding the remoteness of the workers from one another and the institutional segregation enforced by industrial labor. There is no soundtrack to reinforce emotion, nor *raisonneur* to guide our reception to the social problems depicted. Instead, he allows us to react to these people and their lives as if they were before us.

The heartbreaking events leading to the conclusion of Domenico's story reiterate this artistic philosophy. Since they were separated into separate divisions of the company, Domenico has made several attempts to find Antonietta. In one of these scenes, he waits outside in the rain for her to leave the building only to see her exit with a group of colleagues, including one man with whom she shares an umbrella. Later, while still working as a delivery boy, Domenico passes Antonietta in the hall. They resume their flirtatious relationship, share details about their current positions, but as they speak, they stand distinctly apart from one another, allowing Antonietta to pretend she is just about to go into her office when her manager passes by. Before she re-enters her workspace, she asks Domenico if he plans to attend the New Year's Eve party thrown by the company. She says goodbye and briefly enters her office, afraid that her manager will see her chatting, but then quickly reopens the door to wish him a Merry Christmas. After she retreats behind the door again, Domenico stares after her longingly.

Upon receiving tacit approval from his parents to attend the New Year's

2. Time Standing Still and Moving Freely 51

dance, Domenico heads into Milan, gazing out from the tram window at the city streets decorated with lights and filled with activity. He arrives at the party and is given a hat, a party favor, and, because he is not accompanied by a woman, a bottle of wine. Besides an older couple, he is the first to appear at the empty dancing hall. He sits by himself and the couple beckons him over, not too subtly displaying their wish to share his recently acquired bottle. A band at the front of the hall continues to play and the tables on the sides of the hall slowly fill up with more guests. Among the late arrivals is a girl who, from a distance, resembles Antonietta and we suspect Domenico has not yet spotted her. Following a close-up of the girl, we see that it is actually someone else. She lacks Antonietta's radiance and when she invites Domenico to dance, his face expresses disappointment and he ignores her initial advances. The girl eventually grabs him by the hand and leads him out to the dance floor. He ends up enjoying himself, laughing through a line dance, and indulging in some wine. But the party ends suddenly and cuts back to the concluding scene at the office, informing us that the novelist has died. After the party, we sense that Domenico will never be able to form a relationship with Antonietta. The film indicates that while the boom's revamped city life and white-collar work are conducive to meeting people, often the relationships that form in these environments suffer from institutional division and interference.

The closing moments also expose the disaffection that thrives within this institutionally guided culture. In a similar slowly-revolving panning shot to the one used to follow the revelation of the thieving son, the camera circles around the office as the workers stare reverentially at the unoccupied desk of the novelist, as if they are attending his funeral. A cut is made to the novelist's home in a near graphic match of the home when it was occupied. The room is now barren of life and any personal items, the mattress rolled up and the closet empty. Domenico is then invited into the office and placed at the novelist's desk after the office head and the opera singer peruse through the recently departed's items, labeling them personal or work-related. The office head's befuddlement over the discovery of a book chapter in the desk speaks to how little the novelist's co-workers were invested emotionally or socially in him or his interests. A petty argument ensues over who will sit at his desk at the front of the office and enjoy the position's better lighting. Domenico, naïve to the politics of desk seniority, willingly moves to the back when asked, leading to a game of office musical chairs as the other workers scramble to move their things forward. One of the workers begins rotating a cyclostyle and the repeating and increasingly loud din it produces runs through the last shot of Domenico seated at his desk and continues through the closing credits.

The final shot of Domenico, a close-up of his face wide-eyed and suddenly alert at what a life will mean in this office, is gut-wrenching. It echoes the calls to action in the final scenes of *Ladri di biciclette* (*Bicycle Thieves*, 1948) and *Germania anno zero* (*Germany Year Zero*, 1948), presenting us with visions of unjust and miserable societies and asking what will be done. Olmi is not a Neo-Realist, but he does share the movement's philosophy that films should present the world as ambiguously as possible, resisting propagandistic spoon-feedings of ideologically charged answers to audiences. The oneiric characteristics of Olimi's style, as demonstrated through the peripheral figures and the extended extra-narrative sequence of the film, both enables him to continue the experiential principles that guided Neo-Realism and separates him from their strict adherence to depicting the world without representing the disjunctions caused by the tendency of consciousness to conjoin imagination and memory and its freedom from being constrained by a linear conception of time.

In *I fidanzati*, the separation between Olmi's style and Neo-Realism becomes much more pronounced. Olmi had previously worked with others to edit his features, but after experimenting with the extra-narrative sequence in *Il posto* he felt comfortable enough to edit an entire film on his own.[30] *I fidanzati* is one of the most formally radical Italian narrative films of the 1960s and fully develops a temporal displacement that combines the past, the present, the future, and fantasy. However, cinema history has largely overlooked the film in favor of many of the other excellent Italian works from the period. Even at the time of release, the film gathered some awards at festivals but was overshadowed by releases made by Italian filmmakers with more established reputations. Visconti's *Il gattopardo* (*The Leopard*, 1963) beat *I fidanzati* for the Palme d'Or at Cannes, in the same year Fellini's *8½* (1963) was shown out of competition at the festival.[31]

The film's relatively cool reception then and now may be due to the mistaken perception that Olmi simply mimicked the style of Alain Resnais's two contemporary successes *Hiroshima mon amour* (Hiroshima my love, 1959) and *L'année dernière à Marienbad* (*Last Year at Marienbad*, 1961). Fernaldo di Giamatteo wrote in 1963 that there was a "disease of Marienbadism" breaking into Italy, expressing his concern that "the poison of aestheticism and moral indifference could apparently seep into Italian cinema as well."[32] In his exploration of modernist cinema, András Kovács also compares *I fidanzati* to *Last Year at Marienbad* by placing Olmi's film alongside it in a grouping of works in the *nouveau roman* trend.[33] During Charles Thomas Samuel's interview with Olmi the apparent similarity was directly addressed. When he was asked if *I fidanzati* had been influenced by Resnais, Olmi responded that his style had nothing to do with the French director's, whose style he defined as "wholly metaphysical."[34] Indeed, the only similarity between the styles of Olmi and Resnais is their propensities to freely move back and forth in time. Resnais was certainly not "morally indifferent," but the temporal transitions in his films have different motivations than Olmi's. Emma Wilson accurately describes Resnais's style as "mold[ing] the form of his films to the structures and temporality of traumatic experience," a design plainly dissimilar from Olmi's time-shifting, which anchors itself in the impressions, desires, and memories of his characters' relationships and the responsibility they feel for their social and familial obligations.[35]

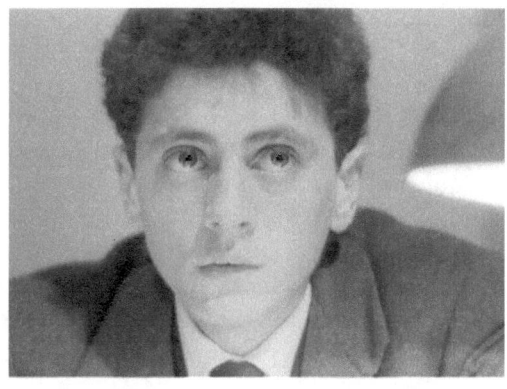

Domenico (Sandro Panseri) contemplates his fate in the office of *Il posto* (1961, Titanus).

Tullio Kezich writes of Olmi's style in *I fidanzati*, "Reality and memories, experiences and dreams mix themselves in this chronicle of the existence of Giovanni," adding that "the work appears with a superior ambiguity of total, exhaustive representation."[36] *I fidanzati* is capable of "total, exhaustive representation" because of the manner in which it invites us to revisit experiences and reconstructs lives and realities of the past, dreams, and the future. In *I fidanzati*, the time-shifting mostly occurs at the beginning and ending of the film, and sporadically at other points when a person or an object reminds Giovanni (Carlo Cabrini) of his fiancée, Liliana (Anna Canzi), or of his father. It packs the majority of its narrative into these scenes. Giovanni has been asked to transfer to a factory in Sicily for a year and a half to assist in setting up a new department. However, he leaves a troubled relationship behind that we find out may have been complicated by an affair. The relationship seemingly reignites while Giovanni is still in Sicily, but the film ends with Giovanni hurriedly speaking to Liliana on the telephone before he rushes to work during a storm, leaving their reunification up in the air. The film's shifting of time does not allow for a simple reading of the order of events in the narrative and so when this affair and the consequent reconciliation occurs, or if it happens at all, remains unclear.

Those familiar with Italian literature will recognize that this story shares several similarities with Alessandro Manzoni's nineteenth century novel, *I promessi sposi (The Betrothed)*, a cultural touchstone many Italians would certainly associate with Olmi's film.[37] This connection is worth mentioning here because of the cause of Renzo and Lucia's, the lovers, separation in the book. Don Rodrigo, a local noble, has feelings for Lucia. He uses his power and authority to prevent their wedding, setting off a series of events that keeps the couple separated from one another for years. In Olmi's film, the economic boom and the needs of a corporation, not a single powerful entity like the noble, divide Giovanni and Liliana. As in the novel (whose subtitle, *A Tale of Seventeenth Century Milan*, divulges its similar aspirations to document a cultural moment), most of the film does not focus on the relationship, as the film's title would suggest, but on the dividing forces of society fueled by the boom and Giovanni's investigation of Sicily and its rapidly changing labor landscape. Through much of *I fidanzati*, Giovanni is a participatory documentarian, listening to colleagues speak about Sicily and Sicilians, taking in local culture, and witnessing the societal aftermath of the boom.

Olmi's many uses of peripheral figures in the film imply the societal upheaval instigated by the economic miracle and draws our attention to alterations in domestic life resulting from the demands of modern labor. Italians have traditionally placed great importance on their family identity and been sensitive to the type of disruptions to family life seen in *I fidanzati*. Rudolph M. Bell notes the role the family has traditionally played in virtually every aspect of Italian life. "The individual without family is anomic; groups larger than *la famiglia* are secondary. In politics, in work, in the economy, in religion, in love, indeed in all of life, perceptions exist and decisions are made primarily in terms of family."[38] We witness the turmoil caused in the lives of individuals inside and outside of Giovanni's life as the boom threatens the center of their values by removing them from their loved ones.

During the film's dancehall opening, Olmi cuts between the dance and Giovanni at work and flashes of his relationships with his fiancée and his father. At the dance, Giovanni and Liliana treat each other distantly, as if their relationship has soured because of Giovanni's acceptance of the job offer in the South or possibly because of the affair that we discover later.[39] In one of the asides from the hall, Giovanni's superiors ask him whether he is married. After answering no, he is told "good. Fewer complications. You know how it is with transfers." A cut is then made to Giovanni as he exits a room where his father sits. He leaves and says something to his father, though no dialogue is audible. A sound bridge guides us into the next scene where Giovanni discusses his father with an unidentified official. Contextual evidence, provided through the order of shots in this sequence, suggests the man is a manager at a rest home that Giovanni's father may live in or where Giovanni is thinking of placing him. As the two men speak about the melancholia of the home's residents, a montage of shots of lonely and despondent old men follows.

Giovanni's father appears again halfway through the film, while his son is at a Carnival festival.[40] The documentary-like observation of this event adopts Giovanni's viewpoint through point-of-view shots as atemporal and spatial excursions break up the scene of the party. Among a huge crowd in a piazza, partygoers wear masks and costumes, and people hurl confetti at one another while others dance. When we see an old, drunk man dancing around, the film transitions to Giovanni's father who rises out of bed as a caretaker chastises him for drinking too much. Giovanni also appears momentarily in this digression, handing some documents over to the caretaker, and then vanishes as his father continues to be fussed over before the film returns to the festival. Giovanni's thoughts on leaving his father behind are not shared with us, but the flashes of his father while he is at the party haunts the scene and soberly counterbalances the jovial atmosphere. The fragmented editing language Olmi employs to visualize the protagonists' perspectives in *I fidanzati*, and in the majority of the rest of his narrative films (and tellingly does not use in films such as *The Scavengers* and *The Tree of Wooden Clogs*), is one of the methods he uses to characterize the conflicting desires of the modern personality.

Other examples of the boom's impact on families edge Giovanni's narrative. On his first night in Sicily at the company hostel, Giovanni encounters an exhausted waiter, who rebukes him for coming into the dining hall so late before asking whether he prefers soup or pasta. When the waiter brings out the food, he offers an explanation for his irritable behavior by detailing the stress of preparing 100 to 150 meals per day. His family is separated because his wife is staying near his hospitalized son and he has to manage his home alone. After dinner, Giovanni walks into a lounge and sits in the back of a dark room, lit only by a television set. A group of silent men fill the seats, their faces void of any pleasure. Lively jazz music plays on the TV's speakers, but it does nothing to lighten the mood. The waiter's eagerness to discuss his family life and the detached individuals at the hostel denotes the extent to which the boom has isolated both locals and migrants from their families and loved ones.

Even at the plant, the dividing line between the professional world and the family is pronounced in the replacement of agrarian, family-based working environments, with the customs of the modern corporation. As Giovanni exits an office on his first day of work, an extended family, including several children and elderly adults, of a worker wait in the hall. The secretary reminds the employee that they cannot bring their entire family to work. The moment is humorous but also serves as one of the film's many examples of the contention between Sicilian society and the expectations of globalized industrialization. Olmi's Edisonvolta documentary, *Il grande paese d'acciaio*, observed many of the same tensions. Both films use of Sicily as a primary location for their observations on the boom is particularly fitting as the island was one of the last outposts of Italy to resist assimilation into an Italian national identity and the boom's corporate culture. Southern Italy, specifically Sicily, has consistently struggled economically while the North has become an economic center of Europe. Some have argued that the cause of Sicily's inability to progress is its specific subculture, a perspective reiterated in the film by the northern Italians at the worksite.[41]

After Giovanni's plane touches down in Sicily, a few of his new colleagues greet him at the airport and take him to the company's hostel. On the drive there, Giovanni gazes at the ruins and peasant houses of the Sicilian countryside. An accident nearly occurs when a horse-drawn carriage pulls into the road. The driver of Giovanni's car then proceeds to give a thinly veiled jab at Sicilians in his exclamations, "He's in the middle of rush hour traffic and he acts like he's in the country. He rushes out like a bullet. Some people are so rude. That animal belongs in the wild, not in the middle of traffic." During another car journey, on the way to the Carnival festival, one of Giovanni's co-workers opines that Sicilians would be better off driving bumper cars than being permitted to drive automobiles. Many of these moments characterize the Sicilians as unable to keep up with the pace of the modern world, of being stuck in the ways of the past. Two conversations at the plant, in which Giovanni just listens, repeat similar characterizations of the islanders. "They have a different work ethic and it goes back generations." "They're just a little crazy. The sun's real hot and they never have a chance to blow off steam." But unlike his colleagues, Giovanni is fascinated by the Sicilians. Their culture, and the environment that has created them, offers a reprieve from his demanding job.

After one of these conversations, Giovanni ventures by himself into the countryside. Unlike a tourist, he does not visit any of the ancient Greek ruins or Mount Etna. Instead he treks around to view Sicilians at work, and in their free time. He approaches a field, where laborers are digging up salt from seawater basins and piling them into mounds. None of the corporate atmosphere of his plant can be found here. He watches a pair of the workers attach sheets to a windmill and rotate it. The only sounds are of the workers digging, the windmill being prepared and Giovanni greeting those he encounters. As we watch the workers, their lives and bodies become inseparable from their work: their leathered skin and broken smiles complement the cheerful attitudes they have while they accomplish their tasks. The workers do not necessarily appear backwards, but they are not wearing safety equipment and do not make use of any of the advanced technology that we see used at Giovanni's plant. The texture of their tools (the wood of the shovels and the windmills; the straw hats they use to shade themselves) implies the simplicity of their methods, and their ability to comfortably meld their occupations with their lives.

The Arcadian nature of the locals' life is further attested to when Giovanni stops at a local church. In the church's courtyard, a car with a megaphone attached to its roof drives slowly around the building announcing that a wallet containing 5000 lire and some important documents were lost. "Whoever finds it is welcome to keep the 5000 lire." Children inside of the church sing and Giovanni, seated near the back, watches as a dog enters the church. The children finish singing and a priest reminds them not to run, talk, laugh, or spit when they come into the building. The dog loudly barks, interrupting the priest's castigation to the clamorous delight of the children. The cleric's attempts to keep the children seated in the pews fails as they join the dog in circling the church. Beyond greeting them, Giovanni does not interact with the individuals in any of these scenes, but he obviously admires them. His, and the film's, appreciation for their way of life reveals that Olmi shared Pasolini's belief that Italy was becoming "homologized." Pasolini felt that Italy's lower classes "had lapped up the consumerist myths of neo-capitalism and lost any kind of cultural autonomy they might have possessed in the process."[42] He laments, "The peasants' world, after a nearly 14,000 year life span, has practically ended with one blow."[43] The Sicilians in the film have resisted integration into this world, an idea reiterated in the Carnival scene, which, accompanied by the scenes of everyday Sicilians enjoying their lives, arouses Giovanni's memories of his own home in the North.

By the end of the film, Liliana has transformed into a peripheral figure for Giovanni, someone whose absence we may even have forgotten. Liliana and Giovanni's father correspond with a lifestyle that Giovanni associates with the Sicilians. His loved ones' lengthy disappearance from his life and the film symbolically reflects the disappearance of the traditional lifestyle the Sicilians enjoy. Antonioni's *L'avventura* (The adventure, 1960) features a similar symbolic relationship between the disappeared and the changes in Italian society. Peter Brunette notes that Antonioni's film "functioned … as social criticism, however disguised. Some of it pertains specifically to the Italian context and some of it is intended as part of a more global criticism about contemporary life in general."[44] Like Olmi's peripheral figures, Antonioni also shattered conventional narrative devices through the disappearance of a lead character in the first quarter of the film. A group of friends go on a sailing trip together and one of them, Anna (Lea Massari), disappears. At first her companions search for her, but about halfway through the film her absence no longer concerns the other characters and they cease looking for her. "This double disappearance creates a gaping hole in the film, an invisibility at its center, which suggests an elsewhere, a nonplace."[45] This elsewhere created by the loss of these figures, in both *I fidanzati* and *L'avventura*, is a space for us to piece together what causes these vacancies.

In Olmi's film, Liliana is seemingly redeemed in the sequence near its conclusion that begins with his reception of a letter. The film does not share its contents with us, but after examining it Giovanni lies down on his bed, cueing a cut to a lakeside scene in an unspecified location and time. We see Giovanni and a woman from the dancehall sequences amongst a group of friends. The friends leave the pair alone to philander as sensuous jazz music accompanies the dialogue-free scene. The scene then shifts to Giovanni speaking with Liliana about the suggested affair before she asks if he still wants to marry her. Following their conversation, the film returns to Giovanni in Sicily. The chronology of this event, or the subsequent scenes with Liliana, is unclear. The scene's structure throws into question whether the letter has brought to mind painful memories and anxieties or if he is fantasizing about a situation that would allow him to pick up the pieces of the relationship he left behind.

As Giovanni sits on his bed, images of he and Liliana together interrupt shots of him staring pensively in his empty room. In the form of letters, a voiceover conversation between the couple then commences. Throughout this lengthy sequence, Giovanni is repeatedly placed on the left side of the screen, looking right while Liliana is placed on the opposite side, looking towards the left, suggesting both the distance between the lovers and their longing for one another. Olmi fragments shots of their amorous glances into blank spaces with scenes of them together, or things or people they speak of, in various settings. In her first response to him, she dictates her letter as if she speaks to him across the room. She begins cautiously, explaining her hesitancy to reply to him without allowing us to place with any certainty when this communication transpires in relation to the affair or how long they have been apart from one another. She updates him on his father, who still lives in his apartment and not in a rest home. They continue responding to one another's letters in this manner, increasingly reminiscent of their first encounters, and their time together at the dance hall, *Speranza* (hope). The repeated musical motif played in the dance hall sequences, which recommenced earlier as they discussed the affair, picks up a bouncy melody as shots of the couple happily rejoined run between their conversation and then turns to a somber tone when a reference is made to the couple's difficulties. A brief interlude showing Giovanni swimming joyfully in the ocean temporarily pauses the conversation but then their letters resume with alternating shots of the couple framed individually, again on opposite sides of the screen, as if they walk toward each other. When Liliana determines that their time apart has brought them closer together than they were before, the music reaches a crescendo, and the sequence climaxes with a shot of them kissing.

Immediately as this charming scene concludes, the film brusquely

2. Time Standing Still and Moving Freely 59

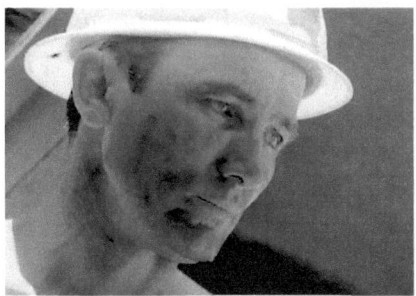 

Throughout the scene in *I fidanzati* when Giovanni (Carlo Cabrini) and Liliana (Anna Canzi) narrate their letters to one another, Olmi places Giovanni, looking toward the right, on the left side of the screen and Liliana, looking toward the left, on the right (1963, Titanus).

adjusts its tone. The music stops and wind howls over the soundtrack as the film returns to Giovanni, alone, in Sicily trying to reach Liliana on the phone. All of the optimism emanating from the lovers' reconciliation has suddenly disappeared. Giovanni's job clouds whatever vision he may have of one day being able to fulfill the scenes of the rekindling of his romance with Liliana that we have just witnessed. The storm tearing through the countryside initially prevents him from hearing Liliana.[46] We do not hear her voice, but Giovanni's responses to her indicate that she was not expecting his call and that they have not regularly communicated. He tries to justify contacting her because calls are half-rate on Sunday. Before cutting the conversation short when the operator reminds him of his limited time, he expresses his wish to miss work, a want that correlates with one of Giovanni's co-worker's derogatory comments earlier in the film when a co-worker expresses exasperation with the Sicilian work ethic and a particular custom of the locals. "Just think: at first when it rained, they wouldn't come to work. Everything stops here when it rains. They don't have an industrial mentality and there's nothing you can do." Giovanni's inclination to stay home during the storm specifically aligns him with the Sicilians' resistance to industrial mentality.

As suggested above, Olmi's editing language is then not inspired by French New Wave filmmakers such as Godard and Resnais. Rather, he reformats the Neo-Realists' political commitment in conveying social problems ambiguously, combined with an emphasis on the virtues of traditional working lives. Bazin foresaw an evolution from Neo-Realism with films that inherited aspects of Neo-Realism combined with other styles. "Neo-Realism does not necessarily exist in a pure state and one can conceive of it being combined with other aesthetic tendencies. Biologists distinguish in genetics, characteristics derived from different parents, so called dominant factors. It is the same with Neo-Realism."[47]

Olmi gained a sense of how to present the reality of his workers through the works of Flaherty and the productions of Grierson more than from De Sica or Rossellini. But Neo-Realism introduced a kind of experiential cinema that left spaces for audiences to fill that Olmi incorporated into his films. Bazin writes that in Neo-Realist cinema, "The assemblage of the film must never add anything to the existing reality. If it is part of the meaning of the film…, it is because the empty gaps, the white spaces, the parts of the event, that we are not given, are themselves of a concrete nature: stones which are missing from the building. It is the same in life: we do not know everything that happens to others. Ellipsis … in Rossellini's films … is a lacuna in reality, or rather in the knowledge we have of it, which is by its nature limited."[48] As demonstrated above, Olmi's experiential film language in *I fidanzati* leaves gaps for us to fill, expecting us to take responsibility for our reactions to the boom's permutation of everyday reality. The Sicilians in *I fidanzati* embody a response to these problems that was provided earlier in *Time Stood Still*, namely that the rampantly spreading white collar world could incorporate the values and provide the sense of immaterial gratification that was previously gained from pre-industrialized work in nature. Unfortunately, in Olmi's post-boom films of the late 1960s and the 1970s, covered in the next chapter, the way of life represented by the Sicilians and Natale has all but disappeared and few seem capable of finding joy in the office-bound life their work constructs for them.

3

Disillusionment with Success During *gli anni di piombo* in Olmi's Post-Boom Trilogy

For many Italians, the defining era of the twentieth century in Italy was not the boom or the fascist period, but the events of the late 1960s and 1970s often known as *gli anni di piombo* (translated often as the years of lead, or the leaden years). Many of these events corresponded with Italy's new globalized culture and a generation of discontented youth. Italians' ties to Catholicism were loosened and secularization in Italy led to people searching for new social communities, a demand for increased social services, and further education rights.[1] The period began with the student and worker-led movements that shut down all of the universities in Italy and continued through the terrorist activities of groups on the left and the right, culminating in the kidnapping and execution of the politician Aldo Moro by the Red Brigades, and dying down by the early 1980s. Historian Richard Drake writes, "No other industrialized country in the contemporary world had experienced anything at all like Italy's fifteen-year-long affliction with terrorism. More than twelve hundred people died or suffered grievous injury from this violence, which from 1969 to 1984 included thousands of terrorist attacks."[2] It was a period of extreme turmoil that deeply informs Italian culture to this day.

Yet, during this period, unlike the Neo-Realist depictions of social problems during the Italian reconstruction after World War II, most of Italian art cinema did not directly reflect the troubling circumstances occurring daily across the country but left head-on engagement with these events to Italian comedies and *poliziesco* films (crime films).[3] However, prominent Italian art filmmakers were still addressing these issues in their own fashion. Pasolini and Bertolucci, both self-proclaiming Marxists, continued to make films that confronted middle class morality. Rossellini was on a quest to enlighten the masses away from corporate culture and "give a general sense of direction" through his many history films made for television.[4] Antonioni's works in the late 1960s and 1970s consider global phenomena (American counterculture in *Zabriskie Point* [1970]; a rare extended look at Communist China before it reopened its doors in *Chung Kuo-Cina* [Chung Kuo-China, 1973]; and the societal upheaval caused by colonialism in *The Passenger* [1975]) that were interwoven with Italian unrest of the period. Both Olmi's history films, which are covered in the next chapter, and his contemporary-set films of these years were similarly based in the milieu of post-boom Italy. In the three films considered in this chapter, Olmi continues to present microcosms of everyday people, most of whom, have attained financial wealth that would have been well beyond the reach of previous generations. He reveals the cracks in these worlds through the fragile loneliness of modern life and the discontent of a society, now driven by consumption, often aching to re-commune with nature.

The promised stability provided by fiscal prosperity proves illusory in *One Fine Day*. Committed to fashioning stories woven out of reality, Olmi realized that the business culture of the late 1960s was alien to him as he had not worked in an office for more than a decade. His previous features, with the exception of his film on Pope John XXIII, were populated by characters (low-level office workers and manual laborers) and in environments with which he was intimately familiar. He prepared for *One Fine Day* by spending a month in a publicity agency to acquaint himself with the world of transnational business, executives, and the advertising field.[5] Many of the actors in the film were employees of the agency and Olmi based his protagonist's personality on the lead actor's own disposition.[6] Olmi allowed the actors own lives to intersect further with their characters by letting them guide the dialogue, purposefully replicating the strategy of *commedia dell'arte* in an additional effort to ground the film in the realities of the advertising industry.[7]

In many ways *One Fine Day* is, in the words of Basil Wright, "the world of *Il posto* seen from the other end," or the unrewarding life that Domenico may have envisioned for himself in his new position.[8] Bruno (Brunetto del Vita) works at a Milan advertising agency and becomes temporarily promoted when a colleague, Davoli (Vitaliano Damioli), has a heart attack. Although married, he has multiple affairs, including one with a young interviewer (Lidia Fuortes), whose name is not given, hired by his firm to conduct research. Driving in heavy winter conditions with an account executive (Giovanna Ceresa) after a meeting, he suddenly notices some liquid on a rear window. When he pulls over to see what has happened to his car, he discovers that he has hit a worker, Stucchi, who was pushing a cart on the roadside.[9] This accident has only amplified a mental and emotional crisis for Bruno that he has been experiencing at least since Davoli's heart

3. Disillusionment with Success

attack, bringing him to a moral inventory regarding his relationships with his family, friends, and business associates. Already trying to deny the seriousness of the situation, he discovers that Stucchi has died. Bruno's lawyer (Walter Sardi) arrives and Bruno, the account executive, and Stucchi's co-worker all provide testimony regarding the accident. In their questioning, the Carabinieris' approach to this particular incident is to frame Stucchi as a man who died because of drunkenness and because of the poor road conditions.[10] A trial of the accident commences and concludes without finding fault with Bruno.

Retrospectively, Olmi has looked back on the film as both an omen of the troubles in Italy of *gli anni di piombo* and as symptomatic of the irresponsibility of the international ruling class that led to the global financial crises of 2008 and 2009.[11] The death of Stucchi breaches the narrative, opening a window outside of the narrowly focused business world and into the lives of those brushed aside by the boom and the young people who, by the late 1960s, were filled with angst toward filling the unsatisfying, dead-end jobs of their parents. Olmi widens this breach further through several characters who yearn for a sense of purpose in their lives or who suffer from seclusion.

In a side story running parallel to Bruno's, in two scenes at the beginning and toward the conclusion of the film, we see the interviewer, Bruno's paramour, walking around with and visiting the art studio of a colleague (Raffaele Modugno) from the agency as they discuss their lives and work. As the first scene begins, we see them preparing to leave the agency together for an informal date. Walking out of the building, when asked what she is working on, she replies "Martian food," and then playfully asks him if he is a Martian, setting up the characterization of the young man as "alienated." During their evening together, the interviewer dissects the man as if he was a subject for one of her professional research assignments, seemingly unable to treat him in a way that acknowledges the attraction she genuinely feels for him. Her colleague also grapples with difficulties in connecting with others, preferring to eat alone and rush away from the office as soon as he can, despite the interest in others manifest in his paintings.

The two friends buy some food and wine before heading up to the attic art studio that the man shares with several friends. When he turns the light on to reveal his artwork scattered across the rooms of the studio, the budding novelist of *Il posto* springs to mind. Like the unfortunate writer from the earlier film, this artist also seeks to imagine the lives of others through creative means, crafting an outlet for his withdrawn interest in others. The interviewer is awestruck when the room lights up, unprepared for her co-worker to share this side of himself. The artist is framed in the space through multiple doorways, giving the impression that he has unseen layers that the interviewer has not imagined, mostly because he wants to remain invisible.

She asks which painting was most recently completed and he points to one hanging on the wall near his bed. It is an austere, unembellished representation of two houses: one, a larger building placed in the foreground and a smaller one off to the other's side, set further in the back. He tells her that the name of the painting is "La solitudine di tre persone" (The loneliness of three people), and states that two people live in the larger house and one person lives in the back. She enquires which house he lives in and he responds that he resides in the smaller one, but that he thinks the other two people who live together are probably lonelier than he is. His own rationale for distancing himself from others leads him to conclude that the rest of society aches for isolation, evoking the aphorism of Sartre's Joseph Garcin in *No Exit* that "hell is other people."[12] But they avoid breaking the surface of the artist's preoccupation with his own loneliness or that of others' in their floundering conversation.

After a few drinks, the two sit opposite one another, he laying on his bed and she in a chair facing him. Instead of testing the potential for romance with the strikingly beautiful interviewer, he secludes himself in his thoughts. Unable to perceive his feelings, she first asks him why he no longer speaks and then pointedly asks if he wants her. His languid reply does not exhibit any amorous intentions at all but does deny his self-professed solipsism. The camera pans around the attic, seemingly hunting for clues to the man's character as he voices his wish to not think at all, his hopes to be united with everything around him, and his disappointment when he reawakens to his alienated existence. Olmi's choice to have the actors improvise their conversations and the camera's framing of the young man exposes the many feelings and hopes of young people that remain bottled up in professional lives that consume them.

The artist's opposing social and anti-social desires initially loom over his final meeting with the interviewer later in the film. Her need for a physical relationship were unfulfilled by the artist and so she capitulates to the advances of the much older Bruno. Her attempts to explain where she has been in the month since they last saw one another perplex the artist, who still disregards her feelings for him. Only when they dance at a club, putting aside their attempts to verbalize their estranged condition, do they overcome the obstacles erected by post-boom social mores, a suggestion that the alternative youth culture of the 1960s offered solutions to a generation seeking more than what mainstream society currently offered them. There is a poignant irony in the couple's difficulties to connect with one another, considering the advertising agency's primary objective is to understand people's needs and wants in order to know what to sell them. At their

3. Disillusionment with Success

company, committees meet to discuss how to emphasize male virility in ads to sell deodorant and develop a separate product to help customers digest their food. Olmi shows the interviewer speaking with various people, none of whom leaves more than a passing impression, accentuating that to the agency these individuals are nothing more than a collective grouping of statistics that will dictate how they will market their products.

This same ethos governs relations at the agency. During the film's introduction to the workplace through brief scenes of meetings and advertising artists debating how to give prominence to an armpit in a campaign, one of the firm's administrators, Davoli, appears noticeably uncomfortable at a presentation. No one says anything or follows him as he steps outside and the meeting continues. We discover later that he has suffered a heart attack. Crosscuts between a shot of the blinding light of the projector in the conference room and the administrator attempting to recover prefigure Davoli later telling Bruno that he does not know what to do with his life outside of work. Their jobs ravenously devour their psyches until they have no other reason for existing outside of the office. Olmi's time-shifting in *One Fine Day* often stresses the advertisers' inability to direct their thoughts inward or to permit their personalities to inscribe themselves in their work.

Only following the accident does Bruno turn introspective, questioning the morality of his actions at and outside of work. Before he begins sleeping with the interviewer, we see him meet a nameless woman at a hotel. Undressing, they do not exchange passionate declarations or conversations about one another's lives. Bruno lies on the bed and gazes at the ceiling while his companion stares at him and takes the last few puffs on her cigarette before they have sex. But even as they begin to kiss, Bruno turns his head away, his mind elsewhere. His sexual interplay with the interviewer has the same frigid air to it, devoid of any hint of love or emotional exchange. In a flashback scene Bruno recalls after the accident, the young woman turns off the light before undressing wordlessly and with an expressionless mien. In earlier scenes, Bruno has repeatedly tried to disguise his relationship with her as professional, even when he takes her out to eat to a candlelit dinner accompanied by violin players. In their interactions, she has consistently called into question his intentions, and finally in the hotel room, while staring out the window, she tells him he can have her but that she has grown tired of his constant feigning.

The accident prompts Bruno to lose composure, depriving him of his psychological drive to sell himself to others. Following the presentation of a new product, Bruno drives toward the airport with his account executive. Out of nowhere we hear a startling noise, as if something has either hit the car or a part has broken. Bruno looks over at the rear-right side window and sees that an oily substance has covered it. After guessing at what may have happened, he decides to pull off to the side of the road and inspect the vehicle. He learns that the sound occurred when the car hit a worker, Stucchi, and the substance on the window is likely his blood. With Stucchi's friend, Bruno pulls the man out of the snow and onto the road prior to running back to tell his companion to drive the car back so they can transport the injured worker to the hospital. Only moments before, Bruno was talking himself up as Davoli's replacement and congratulating himself on how he will impress the head-office in Frankfurt. The sudden introduction of out-of-focus shots from a handheld camera augment Bruno's destabilization once the gravity of Stucchi's injuries dawns on him.

Once at the hospital, a group of nurses and nuns bring Stucchi inside for further examination. We see no wounds suggesting that his injuries are severe as he lies in a hospital bed, mumbling about his children. Bruno assures himself that the man is not hurt and returns back to the local office. Once at the office, he places a call to his company to let them know he will not make the trip to Frankfurt, and when he hangs up the phone, the film makes a momentary, opaque transition to the site of Stucchi's accident with a panning shot, from a moving car, of a man sorting through roadside debris near a tipped over cart. This may be either a reimagining or reconstruction of the events that led up to the collision with the peasant worker or a flashback to something he perceived after the accident but that did not immediately register.

Objects and quiet moments of reflection trigger other shots relating to the incident throughout the night. As Bruno inspects the car outside of the office in foggy-evening air that suffuses the scene with eeriness, he touches a small nick on the arch above a wheel, and a shot of the accident site flashes through the scene, panning over the accident's aftermath and then pausing on Stucchi's hat in a roadside ditch. Moments later, Bruno returns to the office and watches from above when the carabinieri arrive to commandeer the vehicle for the ensuing case, and a rapid montage of flashbacks, imagined events, and shots of unfamiliar individuals punctuate the sequence. The last of these unfamiliar figures gazes into the camera distraughtly. She is a middle-aged woman whom we later ascertain is Bruno's wife (Maria Crosignani). Left alone in the building, Bruno's thoughts return to her through a handheld point-of-view shot that walks through the doorway of a living room, taking the area in, as if looking for someone, until the camera rests on his wife, in a doorway on the opposite side of the room. A close-up of her, now smiling, follows, and a younger female voice off-screen asks, "Is it Dad?" Bruno's wife responds affirmatively and another cut returns us to the office, Bruno looking forward as if his wife acknowledges him in the present. One further cut back to Bruno's wife in close-up in the home is made as she looks down. In the next shot

3. Disillusionment with Success 67

Bruno also lowers his gaze at the office, sighs and then walks to a chair to sit down.

The memory of his wife impels Bruno's thoughts to the bedroom scene described above with the interviewer and then shifts to a scene of a conversation with Davoli about his life flashing before his eyes during his heart attack. Davoli shares, "You see moments of a forgotten life, that were not remembered. Faces of people you've forgotten. You have a sense of regret for things that have become obscured." Bruno is awoken out of his contemplation by his daughter's arrival, sent by her mother to bring some things for Bruno's overnight stay in the building. Perplexed that his family already knows of the day's events, he calls around to ease his fears and prevent himself from panicking over the accident. Pretending to be one of his lawyers, he phones the hospital and discovers that Stucchi has died, inducing another wave of rupturing images from the accident, his affairs, and his dogs at his grandfather's home in Tuscany. In this scene, the film allows us to effectively time travel with Bruno as he journeys from one location to the next, conversations being revisited and seemingly occurring in the temporally central present with him. His thoughts rush through the past as guilt overwhelms him, bringing him to a reckoning of his role and position in society.

Olmi has referred to advertising as a "kind of crime."[13] In the film, the advertising agency emblematizes how a consumerist culture distorts our perceptions of reality. The accident elicits in Bruno a renewed vision of the social realities surrounding him, a forced reassessment, that he cannot shake, of the moral consequences of his actions at work and with his family. As the film nears its conclusion, the advertising campaign consuming Bruno's time during the film has suffered setbacks in its conception and design. The Frankfurt corporate office is not pleased and speculates that anxiety over the impending trial has impeded Bruno's work. But even after the trial ends in Bruno's favor he has not regained the carefree mindset that directed him before the accident. Following the trial, Bruno, his wife, and daughter quietly celebrate the court's verdict at the family's countryside home in Tuscany. Earlier in the film, Bruno revealed in a discussion with his boss from Frankfurt that he bought his grandfather's home after he had established himself in his career because the land was not worth much after all the farmers left the area to move to the city. Seeking to recalibrate himself, Bruno periodically uses the home to return to his roots and to nature. A car arrives to pick up his daughter and Bruno and his wife are left alone. They sit in a darkened room in front of the television, and after his wife mentions that she would like to invite a family over, Bruno agrees and states, "Now everything should go back to normal, like before." Bruno's wife falls asleep against his shoulder as a voiceover on the television narrates a documentary (the film on TV is one of Olmi's Edisonvolta films, *Un metro lungo cinque*). When he looks down at his wife, terror clouds his face prior to a quick shot of Stucchi in pain intruding upon the scene, hampering Bruno's plans to reclaim his former life. Bruno closes his eyes and lays his head back in resignation, as if reminded by the workers in the documentary that his conscience will not permit him to ignore the lives he has affected.

A year prior to *One Fine Day*, Olmi had completed *Ritorno al paese* (Returning to the village, 1967), a short film for the RAI network, narrated by and featuring Mario Rigoni Stern, a novelist who wrote the screenplay for *The Scavengers*, journeying home from the city to his home in the countryside. *Ritorno al paese* encapsulates Olmi's consistent suggestion that nature cleanses the clutter created in the mind through life in the city. Like Bruno, Stern's dogs scampering through open fields provides him with a sense of ease and freedom that the crammed city constrains. A decade after the boom's effects reverberated throughout Italy, the yearning to return to the countryside in both of these films partly diagnoses the period's social problems and spiritual uneasiness to a general dissociation from nature. Bruno and his compatriots are lacking the unification with the natural world and smaller communities that Olmi's films suggest can give life purpose and spur ideas to solve problems.

But Olmi's films do not propose completely withdrawing from cities as the cure to society's problems. Even in the Tuscan countryside, Bruno cannot evade his new awareness of the realities beyond his world. Olmi abstains from providing quick and easy answers through Bruno to the unease already brewing in late 1960s Italy. Writing during the early 1970s, Pierre Leprohon addressed the apparent inertness of Olmi's protagonists. "Not surprisingly, the passivity of Olmi's heroes has infuriated a number of critics committed to the cinema of protest. Yet it remains to be seen whether this resignation, this silent accusation, is not more convincing than the obscure symbols or ranting expostulations beloved by the specialists of alienation."[14] Leprohon correctly characterizes some of the charges critics would cite against Olmi for many years. However, Olmi's films do more than accuse and resign responsibility. As stated in the earlier discussion of *Time Stood Still*, Olmi often uses beautiful scenes of the natural world to alter our perceptions of the world. In *One Fine Day*, *Ritorno al paese* and in much of the rest of his work, this kind of visual counterpoint meets Anat Pick's reading of Bazin's concept of "total cinema." "Total cinema delivers us from one form of subjective investment to another that reflects on our participation in the environing world. The extinction of subjectivity is not therefore a withdrawal but a mode of involvement."[15] Total cinema aims to present the world, in this case the natural world, objectively, as a space that we can use to reflect upon reality. But in juxtaposing the environment with this story, Olmi offers the natural world as a stimulant to thinking of how to address the problems created by post–World War II industrialization.

Not all of Olmi's works end so openly nor do they all avoid featuring protagonists who take action. In *In the Summertime*, Olmi follows a compassionate and tenderhearted outsider who is punished by society for acting on his convictions. As with many of Olmi's short and feature films from the 1970s, this work was made for television, predominately to be shown on the RAI network on black and white screens, although it was shot in color. Early development of *In the Summertime* featured a narrative involving a professor who fell in love with one of his students. However, the only remaining element of this idea in the film is that the lead character (Renato Paracchi) is known only by the nickname, the professor.[16] Fortunato Pasqualino, an Italian philosopher and writer, assisted Olmi in evolving the narrative to include a recent news story of a trial involving a man who sold invalid titles of nobility.[17]

Critical reactions to the professor's odd mannerisms and behavior, and the overall tone, vary as much as they did with Domenico in *Il posto*. Italian film scholars, such as Luca Finatti, following comments made by Olmi, position the professor as a Christic character, marking the tragic elements of the film and underscoring the redemption of the female lead (only known by the title the professor bestows upon her, the princess) through the professor's declaration of her royal characteristics.[18] The few English language critics that have written on the film often note the professor's similarities with Charlie Chaplin's Tramp. Ignoring the comic touches in *Il posto*, David Thompson remarks that *In the Summertime* is "the first, promising sign of comedy in Olmi with a note of Chaplinesque social criticism and a defense of eccentrics that veers towards whimsicality."[19] Basil Wright correctly identifies the specific influence of Chaplin's *City Lights* (1931) on the film.[20] However, the professor's similarity to the Tramp character himself ends with the character's awkwardness and benevolence. It would be a mistake to equate the depiction of the professor's eccentricities with comedy. Instead of eliciting laughter through slapstick, his irregular behavior irritates initially, and his physical unattractiveness repels our natural inclinations to identify with him. But over the course of the film, his sincerity and pure intent surmount resistance to his foibles.

The professor's artlessness and the satisfaction he receives from his mission/profession modifies Olmi's use of atemporal cutting in the film. These moments are limited, but when they do occur they are not provoked by guilt, absent family members or romantic longing, as in many of Olmi's other time-shifting works, but by the professor's genuine concern for other people and his imagined impressions of strangers who he deems possess the qualities of nobility. The professor first encounters the woman (Rosanna Callegari) he will later christen princess on the street. Distraught from a quarrel with an unidentified man, she runs right into the professor's arms and pushes him away when he offers to assist her. Moments later, waiting in a lobby to speak with his employer, a two-second shot of the woman flailing her arms at the professor crosses through his thoughts. Unlike Bruno in *One Fine Day*, the professor is deeply invested in other lives at the commencement of the film.

When he returns home, a letter requesting a nobility title sparks his imagination. With a quill pen, the professor congratulates his customer in a letter, which he dictates aloud to himself and then continues to recite while in the shower. Olmi intersperses shots of the newly denominated noble taking a photo with his family during the professor's soliloquy. The man's relatives do not wear especially fine clothing, nor are they seated in a luxurious estate room, as in a Renaissance or Enlightenment era nobility painting. Wealth does not distinguish them nor give the man an inherent title to nobility. Rather, the professor reminds him that to make himself worthy of the title conferred the noble must commit to actions and behavior worthy of his dignified status. Cutting between the professor's apartment and the photo studio, Olmi charts the professor's innate ability to look beyond monetary wealth, the primary qualification of success in the post-boom world, in his estimation of an individual's character.

Exiting the line at the post office after he has sent the nobility certificate requested in the letter, the professor bumps into an elderly man that grips his attention. Their only exchange is limited to the professor's apologies and the man's assurance that he has taken no offense, but the professor is transfixed. The professor then follows the man until he reaches his apartment, though he loses him once he arrives at his floor. Desperate to acquire the man's name, Querciai, he rings a doorbell and waits for his new acquaintance to answer the door. The professor then runs to the archives of Sforza Castle to locate Querciai's family coat of arms and copies it in his pocket sketchbook. Once at home he writes another letter, this time addressed to Mister Querciai, again dictating the correspondence to himself as the film flashes back to his brief experiences with his esteemed subject at the post office and the train station. The professor's abnormal actions in these scenes call attention to his invasion of others' privacy and his lack of respect for social norms. But it is precisely these behaviors that allow him to challenge ideas of relationships between people that Olmi found relevant in an epoch of such political tension as *gli anni di piombo*.

In the early 1970s, Olmi stated that he made a film with a character like the professor because of the alternative perspective he offers. "I believe crazy people will save mankind. I am not talking about pathological cases, of course, but those who see more profoundly than the sane—like that man in Dreyer's *Ordet* (1955) who lives on a level of wisdom above the earth."[21] Olmi's likening of the professor to Johannes (Preben Lerdorff Rye), who believes himself to be Jesus Christ, and the hope that such individuals can "save mankind," unveils his rationale for molding the professor as a Christic figure. Olmi offers Christ, through the professor, as an antidote to the political tensions and social ills of *gli anni di piombo*. In doing so, he is using Christ's teachings about love to challenge a society that has lost its ability to cultivate trust and respect among its citizens. His comments on Christ reveal that Olmi sees Christ as a peaceful rebel, one who would even challenge social conventions and rules to demonstrate his love. "The advice of Christ is not so much in obeying the rules, as is perceived, but it is loving your neighbor as yourself.... In a certain sense, it is actually disobedience that brings us to Christ the man, one like us, that we could meet on any day of our existence, or in whatever time or place."[22] The professor is also a rebel of sorts, defying societal conventions because of his admiration and love for others. As the film progresses, the altruistic impetus for the professor's strange habits becomes more apparent, challenging our initial preconceptions of him and his conduct.

However, in comparison with other films with Christ figures, even Olmi's *One Hundred Nails, In the Summertime* only very subtly alludes to Christ. The professor never delivers his own Sermon on the Mount, nor does he seek to convince a large group of people of his philosophy. Sparse visual references through a few close-up shots of bread shared by the professor and the princess and a tense garden scene scarcely denote events such as the Last Supper and the Garden of Gethsemane. Olmi is less concerned with audiences recognizing Christ in the film than in presenting Christ-like love through the professor as a return to more communal relationships that elevate one another and enable individuals to take pride in their contributions to society.

Although officially employed by a publisher to draw maps for a history book, the professor's passion lies in increasing others' self-esteem and recognizing the true character of individuals. At his day job, he continually draws his bosses' ire because he will not compromise his beliefs or his justifications about what certain colors represent. He resists their advertising-minded rationale for their selection of colors with arguments of how those they have selected misrepresent the spirit of the subjects. The professor's dedication to his work and refusal to participate in activities he does not fully support disputes the mentality ushered in through the boom, which suggested that individuals should be willing to sacrifice their personalities and their lives in their communities for any job in the city that offered security and moderate wealth.

Fontanesi (Gabriele Fontanesi) serves as a foil to the professor's genuineness and kindness, also filling the role of the millionaire from *City Lights*. The two were classmates who become reacquainted with one another in a café at the beginning of the film. Waiting to place a call, the professor stares at Fontanesi flirting with someone on the café's phone. Fontanesi has his red hair slicked back and always wears sunglasses. He constantly laughs at everything in accordance with his general insincerity. Even after the professor provides additional reminders of their time together, Fontanesi's reactions disprove his claims to know his former classmate. The professor joins Fontanesi as he shops for a car, and in their conversation the more affluent man states his belief in the importance of wealth while dismissing the professor's satisfaction that he receives from his heralding work. When the professor rehashes his recent disagreement with his official employer, Fontanesi associates the mention of colors with his new color TV and he invites the professor over to his home the next Sunday.

The absurd garish décor and layout of Fontanesi's house dumbfounds the professor when he arrives. The glass front doors bang open repeatedly as a recorded message, announcing that the host will arrive in a few minutes, blares through the lobby. Abstract sculptures and multi-colored, glass panel walls clash aesthetic styles and tones, reinforcing impressions of Fontanesi's depthless character. The professor notices movement in the home's backyard and catches glimpses of a neglected toddler, presumably Fontanesi's son, playing outside unattended by anyone. Screeching tires at the front entrance announce Fontanesi, who bolts upstairs with a young couple, Mario and Stella, only slowing his gait momentarily to give a vacant greeting to the professor.

The rest of the house, with its cold metallic walls and bareness, has the same pretentious design. No picture frames of families adorn the walls, nor do books line the shelves. Nothing in the house reflects anything the owner values or cherishes. Charles Maland's description of the world of *City Light*'s millionaire character also applies to the vapid reality of Fontanesi. "The millionaire's world…, although one of economic prosperity, …is also a schizophrenic world, shifting between celebration and coldness, welcoming inclusion and harsh exclusion, alcoholic camaraderie and suicidal sobriety."[23] Fontanesi does not fluctuate as rapidly between these poles as the millionaire, but his empty personality simultaneously suggests these opposing characteristics in his relationships. No one mentions the child in the back of the house and no one asks about the whereabouts of Mrs. Fontanesi. In contrast to the professor, Fontanesi is only interested in people for the immediate gratification of his ego. The disappointment the professor feels in the expectations he had of his former friend, combined with the orgiastic passing of Stella from

Mario to Fontanesi, overwhelms the professor, who awkwardly dashes out of the house to jeers.

The incident augments the professor's status as an outcast in his society. His division from others is also reiterated through the film by his constant phone calls that are never answered. No one wants to interact with him. His vision of measuring the worth of individuals based on their comportment does not comply with the zeitgeist. Not until he forms a friendship with the woman from the beginning of the film does the professor find someone who encourages his benign worldview. Since their initial contact, the professor has espied her in the street and shared an elevator with her, but only when she rings his doorbell as a salesperson do they have a real conversation. Due to the professor's humble deportment, she does not remember their previous meetings until they start talking. She recites a soulless sales-pitch, hawking household items. The professor discloses that he has no use for her wares but offers to buy them anyway. He only has a large-denomination bill and insists on accompanying her to obtain change so he can buy her goods. Under pressure to eat something by a restaurant owner that they ask to give them change, the two share a meal, enabling them to review why she was so angry the day they first met. She confides in the professor that she was running away from a lover's squabble, but the man was just one of many and she falls in love with new men constantly, placing her, in a Christic reading of the film, in the role of the penitent Mary Magdalene. When she observes that he appears to have few friends, he invites her to meet Count Carlo.

In a cab on the way to the Count's home, the professor unfurls his criteria for defining nobility, omitting the state's or ancestry's role in determining the elevated status of the titles he awards. He insists that nobility reveals itself in a person, linking this idea to Count Carlo's belief that every object reveals the soul of its creator. These attitudes give voice to Olmi's repeated emphasis on the value of work that permits workers to align their professions with their lives and beliefs. Count Carlo's home and his lifestyle, both of which diametrically oppose the world of Fontanesi, correspond with these principles. The arrangement of the art in Count Carlo's home reflects the sensibility of someone who surrounds himself with objects that have personal significance to him. The Count switches on an automated musical cabinet that rotates a ring of bows across the strings of several violins to play a lively melody. He describes his musical instruments with enthusiasm, detailing their history and why they appeal to him. At one point as they listen to the cabinet, the Count places his hand on one of its shutters, and proclaims, "This machine was not made by other machines, but by a human being. If you place your hand here, it feels like its breathing, as if it was alive." The princess looks at the Greco-Roman statues around the room and the paintings that hang on the walls. With the deadness of Fontanesi's home in mind, this sequence not only resonates with some of the ideas behind Walter Benjamin's theses about art in the age of mechanical reproduction, but also decries the notion of art for art's sake.[24] The Count takes pride in objects, still or automated, that have both their own aura, or uniqueness, in the Benjaminian sense, and that also inspire him.[25] He has an appreciation for the authenticity of an object given by its creator, just as the professor venerates the aura of people and their praiseworthy traits, no matter how common they may be.

The professor elaborates on his friend's sensibilities while he and the princess listen to the Count operating a player piano. She notices that it produces music automatically, but the professor describes to her how the Count gives expression to the music through a device that allows him to emphasize specific notes on the piano. To the professor, personal expression is of paramount importance in providing a sense of authenticity. He states, "For example, how many ways are there to say I love you? The words are always the same, but it's the expression that communicates how much one truly loves." The professor's life testifies of this principle through his relationships and the significance for him that small gestures or acts of kindness have in ennobling a person.

The professor does not have any romantic aims with the princess. Finally, having found someone willing to listen to him, he lives up to his own title, hoping to impart knowledge. At the princess's doorstep after their visit to the Count, she asks him about his own nobility and he responds that he actually has a higher unspecified title than count. He then places his hand on her face and accords her the title of princess. When she states her disbelief in princesses in the contemporary world, in hushed tones as if performing a sacred ritual, he contends that there have always been princes, princesses, and nobles, and that more and more will arise until all people discover their nobility.

However, institutions will not have a hand in this grand exaltation as their hegemonic aims hamper personal growth and self-esteem and sever constructive relationships with others and with nature. During a day out in a garden, the professor guides the princess away from a tour group because the scientific titles bother him and distract him from experiencing the beauty of the surroundings. When they come across a flower naming ceremony, the professor exercises his own authority to name a rose after the princess, but officials angrily grab the flower away from them. Infuriated when one of them calls the princess a bitch, the professor kicks the offending man in his shin. Not only does this scene reprise Olmi's consistent indictment of the institutionalization of nature but the director again uses images of the environment to offer a contrasting view of reality to that

3. Disillusionment with Success

The professor (Renato Paracchi) waves to the princess from his jail cell at the end of *In the Summertime*. The scene recalls the conclusion of Chaplin's *City Lights* (1971, RAI-Radiotelevisione Italiana).

offered by the boundaries of city life. *In the Summertime* presents the denial of an individual's own discovery of self-worth as an additional consequence of society's seizure of the natural world.

Society has to expel the professor because he threatens its stability with his belief in the authority of the individual to define the value of people and things. After his altercation in the garden, he becomes separated from the princess and returns home with an injured foot. Aware that law enforcement may be searching for him, he asks the doorman of his building to deny that he is at home. The doorman agrees and continually visits the professor throughout the night, bringing him coffee and home remedies to heal his foot. The professor thanks him with a coat of arms and a title of nobility. The next morning the police take the professor away, seemingly for accusations of fraud rather than for the incident in the garden, and the doorman, a Judas figure, hides as the authorities escort the professor out of the building. They fingerprint the professor, take mug shots, and room him with two prisoners who derisively offer to buy nobility titles. Tellingly, at the trial, it is not the professor's nobles who accuse him of deception. It is their relatives and his former bosses at the publishing company. The court calls the princess to the witness stand and she denies the prosecution's charges against the professor, stating her belief in the authenticity of the professor's titles.

The film's denouement begins immediately following the princess's testimony. From his cell, the professor spots her walking on the street and calls out to her. As they stare at one another from a distance, the rumbles of a plane roar overhead. We hear this noise during multiple scenes in the film, stressing the professor's traditional perspectives in contrast with the new technologically driven world. The princess may have come to pick him up after he has served his sentence, or perhaps she just happens to walk by the prison. This ambiguity requests us to consider why society rejects the professor. This is also the only section of the film that visually adapts a sequence from *City Lights*. The Tramp was not in a jail cell, but whether the woman (Virginia Cherrill) whose sight has been restored, thanks to him, and sees him for the first time, accepts him, remains an unanswered question in the film's closing shot. William Rothman writes that by ending the film this way, Chaplin requests a thoughtful reaction from his audience. "By calling upon us to imagine that the screen is not a barrier, Chaplin calls upon us to reflect on the limits of the medium of film and to ask ourselves whether or not we wish for these limits to be transcended. Do we wish for the Tramp to be real, if that means we must give our love to a human being of flesh and blood? This is a philosophical question about the human capacity for love and for avoiding love."[26] As in Chaplin's film, Olmi does not show us the princess's reaction to the professor's call, ending the film with a freeze frame of the professor staring out of the cell. Denying us a view of the princess's action here denies us knowledge of the professor's fate and calls upon us to ask ourselves whether we would accept him into our world.

Unfortunately, *In the Summertime* confirmed in many critics' minds, during *gli anni di piombo*'s heated political tensions, which even surfaced in major cultural events such as the Venice Film Festival, that Olmi was out of step with contemporary European art cinema. For this particular film, Olmi asked his distributors, RAI, not to enter the film at Venice because he was aware of the pummeling he might receive from critics. Ignoring Olmi's request, the television company wanted more exposure for the film and decided to take it to the festival without the director. It was assailed by all but a few.[27] Since the mid-1960s he had been receiving negative reviews about his films' reticence to directly engage with political events at hand. The films were also not performing well in their very limited theatrical distributions. He supported himself through working on additional programs for RAI, including for the popular *Carosello* (*Carousel*, 1957–1977) program, that skirted around the regulations of public television by advertising with sketches or short stories lasting exactly one minute and forty-five seconds, with the last thirty seconds dedicated to product publicity.[28] Other Italian cinema icons such as Sergio Leone, Gillo Pontecorvo, and Totò also contributed segments to this long running series.[29] While working on one of these programs, Olmi encountered a family that triggered an idea. He saw in the family many of the problems that were plaguing Italians during *gli anni di piombo*. He decided that his next film, *The Circumstance*, would feature characters specifically mirroring the lives of these people.[30] In retrospect, Olmi revealed that he felt he betrayed the family because he was not forthcoming about the unfavorable manner in which he would depict them. However, when the family saw the film they recognized themselves and instead of becoming angry they began a close friendship with the director.[31]

Their disappointment with the film's portrayal of them would have been completely understandable. The members of the Riberti family in the film are distant from one another and the majority of them, besides Beppe (Massimo Tabak), the eldest son in his mid-twenties, and his wife, Anna (Barbara Pezzuto), are miserable. The family, like their offscreen counterparts, is descended from farmers but the wealth they gained during the boom planted them in the middle class and they now pay ranchers to maintain the dairy farm where half of the family lives. The mother, Laura (Ada Savelli), a notary public, and Silvia (Raffaella Bianchi), a teenage daughter, currently stay at the family's summer home. Tommaso (Mario Sireci) is in his early twenties and is the second eldest child. Unemployed and not interested in school, he lives at the family farm where he spends all his time designing robots. Beppe and Anna also live on the farm but separate from the main home in a cottage they have built by themselves. The father, Mister Riberti (Gaetano Porro), an engineer, lives in his own apartment but for the majority of the film he attends a company retreat.

The Circumstance has the most complex editing structure of any of Olmi's films, reinstituting the continual mixture of past, present, and future that he had only used sparingly since *One Fine Day*. Chris Fujiwara notes that "the film has extraordinary fluidity: as Olmi's short flashbacks overlap, it becomes difficult to tell whose subjectivity, if anyone's, is organizing the narrative."[32] Olmi divides time equally between several characters, transitioning between the different stories as they intersect and diverge into different directions. As with many of Olmi's other time-shifting films, the motivations for the breaks in the narrative mostly stem from quiet moments that bring characters to meditate on their desires and social and family responsibilities.

Laura's children do not respond to her parenting favorably. She transfers her mothering to a young man that she escorts to a hospital after his motorcycle catches fire during an accident, leaving him unconscious and with a scorched face. At the hospital, the doctors scrape off the burned skin from the man's face, causing her to cringe and retreat outside, precipitating images of the accident and its aftermath to encroach upon the scene. Laura never discusses the incident with her family. She feels at ease with a large group of friends residing near the family's beach house but discussing the experience with them only aggravates her anxiety over the boy. The accident continually replays in her mind and drives her to visit him. The day after the accident, the hospital has still not located the young man's parents. Laura takes it upon herself to pay for a better room for him and also asks him if she can repair his medallion that she found in the back of her car.

The young man fulfills her mothering instincts because his invalidity obligates him to passively accept her care. She wants to tend to her family, but often comes across as desiring to control her children's lives. In response, they push her away. She derides Tommaso's inventions and accuses him of wasting his time when he could prepare himself to enter school. After their child is born (an event she misses because she spent the night in the hospital with the injured young man), she pleads with Beppe and Anna to stop "playing" in the cabin they built and move in the main house, a demand they respectfully decline.

Her inability to reach Silvia appears to affect her the most as evidenced by an intricately patterned sequence. As Fujiwara indicates, there are scenes where a character's subjectivity will feature another character and then the film seeps into the subjectivity of the second character. After Laura returns one day from the hospital, the film follows Silvia's wandering mind, seemingly incited by her mother's announcement of her arrival and a zoom-in on a watch we later discover is a gift of affection from a lover near the family farm.[33] Olmi blends together shots of Silvia in several locations (1. bikini-clad and lying on her bed; 2. with her suitor at the farm; 3. and moments at a neighbor's house with Fabrizio, her admirer at the beach house) with an interval featuring her mother. Fragments of an overheard phone call regarding the farm's management trigger a cut from Silvia in her bed to Laura, now in her house-robe, at an unspecified time. As Laura speaks, images related to her conversation (the farm and its cows) swiftly flash through the sequence before returning to her at the summer home. Laura hangs up the phone, and we see her in the foreground, blurred, looking at her reflection in the mirror. Laura looks away from the mirror and the film cuts to a medium shot of her sitting down. When the phone rings, she picks it up, but then the film repeats the shot of her looking in the mirror. We are then brought back to the medium shot setup of her seated as she hangs up the phone. This is followed by a point-of-view shot staring into Silvia's empty room before flowing back into the young girl's reverie of her lovers. This interlude denotes Laura's identification with her daughter and her frustrated attempts to assist her as she blossoms into a sexually curious young woman. The undefined figure in the foreground of the shots with the mirror at first do not immediately register as Laura looking at herself

3. Disillusionment with Success

through a reflection. Initially it even seems as if the blurry figure may be Silvia looking at her mother because this temporal aside began following the daughter's train of thought. Through the oneiric merging of their introspective meditations, the mutual dissatisfaction the scene emanates magnifies the mother and daughter's dysfunctional relationship and epitomizes the generational conflict at the heart of the film.

Other young people have problems connecting with Laura as well. She does not reprimand a young woman she catches eating on the job in her office but tells one of the other employees to remind the offender of work regulations. More pointedly, she treats one of Tommaso's friends with suspicion, forcing him and his girlfriend, Mimma, to leave one morning from the farm when they enquire if her son has woken up yet. This last event immediately precedes her final visit to the hospital. This sequence begins with Laura ascending the stairs to the hospital, but before she reaches the top, the film cuts away to her journey there mixed with images of her anticipation to see the boy smiling at her as she enters his room and gives him his repaired medallion, a reminder of a day when he and his girlfriend were especially happy. A cut is made back to Laura finally completing her climb and then to a similar shot of her entering the room, but it is empty, with the mattress rolled up and the sheets stripped off the bed. The boy's father finally checked his son out of the hospital. Disappointed, Laura does not accept a nun's offer to retrieve the boy's contact details but returns once more to the site of the accident, unable to shake the emotions the boy stirred in her. Later, she looks fondly at the medallion before placing it in a drawer. Laura longs to connect to her children and other young people, but on a basic level she does not understand them, a failure symptomatic of the larger problems in Italy that led to the student protests and violence during *gli anni di piombo*. The opportunity for her to dote upon a young person who cannot resist her, temporarily allowed her to fantasize that she could bond with a younger generation.

Mr. Riberti's job does not even permit him to desire for meaningful relationships with his children. Work occupies so much of his time that he lives on his own to be closer to his job. The harbingers of the global mid–1970s recession already place pressure on businesses to scale back and layoffs threaten everyone at Mr. Riberti's company. All of his colleagues are anxious, forced to attend a work retreat where they play a game that aims to predict their worth to the company. Older employees complain they feel left behind and cannot understand a field they have worked in all of their lives. Rumors float of staff arriving at work only to find their offices cleared, leading to some workers quitting rather than agonizing over if they will be next. When Beppe's child is born, the stress of losing his job delays Mr. Riberti's decision to take time off to welcome his new grandson. He asks Laura to phone her friend, his boss's wife, with the excuse of announcing the birth to remind his supervisor of their social ties so he can safeguard his job.

Beppe and Anna want no part of such a world. They are hippies, representative of the counter-culture movement in the cabin they have built on their parents' farm. The scene of their child's birth functions as the film's moral center. A heavy storm prohibits them from driving to the hospital, forcing them to have a homebirth. The urgency of the moment invigorates Tommaso, his friend, and Mimma. When they learn Anna has begun giving birth, Mimma fetches Rina, one of the farmers' wives, to act as midwife while Tommaso calls the doctor. Following the birth, shots of the rain's mist circling the cows in the night air and the ambience of the farm prefigure the beauty of the simple life of the laborers in *The Tree of Wooden Clogs*. Tommaso escorts Doctor Brusati back to his car when he has completed examining the newborn. Addressing the night's confusion and panic, the doctor states, "Bringing a child into the world is a normal, natural act. We forget that nature is perfect, a sign that we are losing confidence in life."

The birth scene's pining for a more uncomplicated existence corresponds with other representations of Italian society's transformations in the film. The home blends the farm's rustic background and Christian art with a ubiquitous contemporary middle-class taste. Murals of farm life ornament the walls, along with a large cross in one of the bedrooms. In one scene in this room, Tommaso's friend asks his girlfriend if she would like to have sex there and she replies that she would feel like she was in church. Other rooms, such as the main dining room, share similar features, remains of religious-themed murals left uncovered in rooms otherwise fitted with wallpaper. The house actualizes the diminished role of religion and nature in the family, using Christian icons and agricultural imagery as art and decoration but not for spiritual inspiration.

Silvia's story exemplifies the changing sense of morality that swept through Italy in the 1960s and 1970s. Donald Sassoon writes that Italian youth of the time "were faced … with a new sexual ethic coming from the country that their own political establishment was presenting as the model of the good society, the USA, while Italy appeared to remain under the influence of the clergy."[34] But the clergy is completely absent from Silvia's life and her parents grew up with post-war standards amid increased secularism and developed a hands-off approach to the sex lives of their children, leaving her with no one to offer her guidance on how to navigate her awakened libido. She appears to be around fifteen or sixteen and spends most of her time with her friends and avoiding her family. She responds to her mother's pleas for her to come home early with apathy and when Laura tells her daughter to prepare to visit Beppe's new baby, Silvia asks why she should care.

If we were not privy to her thoughts and her relationship with her blind friend, Francesco (Giorgio Roncaglia), we would assume that Silvia is the stereotypical self-centered teenager. But most of her detachment originates from divided feelings as she deals with her feelings for the two boys that vie for her attention. She does not know how to handle the advances of one of her boyfriends, Fabrizio, who wants to have sex. Silvia, Fabrizio, and other teenagers spend much of their summer at the home of the Frandoni family, neighboring the Riberti's summer home. In their first scene together, a repeated wordless flashback suggests that Fabrizio made a move on her in a secluded area near the neighbors' pool, which she rejected and now holds against him. Her confusion about her feelings for Fabrizio and the boy she visits outside of her parent's cabin, and how she copes with her maturing sex drive, leaves her unable to commit to either of them. In one of the group's outings to watch the sunrise, Fabrizio quietly tells Silvia, "I bet you still haven't been with anyone … girls are always afraid of their first time." She does not respond to his kisses and exhibits no emotion in his presence. At the farm, her other lover, to whom she also remains unresponsive, calls her and waits outside for her, pleading for her to explain why her feelings have changed.

Francesco gives a reprieve to Silvia in the midst of her angsty love life. She admires him and his passion for music. Finatti describes this boy as "the only positive character" in the film but concludes that "his presence in the story is unfulfilled, without any dramatic weight, a poorly realized sketch."[35] But Olmi deliberately under-develops the boy because he is another of the director's peripheral figures, a barely present character that briefly appears in Silvia's scenes, drawing her, and the audience's, interest. Francesco is the Frandoni's son and the film occasionally finds him sitting alone, reading or listening to classical music. In an early scene, he enlists Silvia to help him find a record and she then sits and listen to Hayden's "Notturno in F Major" with him. Francesco's exploration and pursuit of his interests attracts her, not necessarily in a sexual manner, but as an alternative to her directionless path. At the end of the film, she follows his chauffeur's car on her scooter. She stops and watches him enter a choir hall with his arms full of his books. After he enters, she continues to sit outside, staring at the building pensively as if she wishes she also had the courage to escape the role of a jejune teenager and set out to find herself.

Tommaso is also adrift, uncommitted to anything and unsure of where to steer himself. He has erected a lab for himself in the farm's cellar where he builds robots with his friends. At dinner with his father's colleague, Tommaso listens on as Mr. Riberti describes his son's activities as a waste of a lot of time, building things that have no practical use. The co-worker sympathizes with Tommaso, rebutting the boy's father by questioning what it means to work and suggesting that often when people "play" they commit themselves the most. Tommaso is certainly committed to his experiments, but his own purposelessness also troubles him. He tells Mimma and her boyfriend that his robots will help people think, but their question on what the robots will help people think about leaves him speechless. The appearance of the robots indicates their uncertain purpose. They consist of a jumbled collection of wires and small interconnected pieces in glass containers. He has no plans to give them any form, telling his friends that they will not mimic human movements in any way. His lethargic persona inclines his family and friends to think he does not care about anything and has no plans for his future. But the film's final scene suggests that his independent thinking will find a foundation to build a future on.

Olmi prepares us for the conclusion's very direct symbolism by linking Tommaso with the farm's cows throughout the film with shots of the young man thoughtfully examining them and through a graphic slaughtering scene, where farmers shoot cows in the head with a nail-gun. In the last scene, Tommaso observes the herdsmen loading the cows into a truck and then follows it out onto a two-lane highway. When the opposite lane is clear, Tommaso overtakes the truck and the films ends with a freeze-frame, shot from the young man's point of view, of the car driving forward on an empty, misty road, suggesting that young people able to mark their own paths will find a way out of the troubles that plagued young Italians during this era.[36] Indeed, the other two Riberti children have analogous options at their disposal in the form of Francesco's example for Silvia and in Beppe's choice to reject consumerism and return to a self-sustaining mode of living with his wife. Olmi proposes that the choices these young people make will shape the future of Italy. Like the other films discussed in this chapter, nature continues to offer itself as a source of redemption, providing a refuge for those seeking to escape the meaninglessness of post-boom society and culture. However, none of these works directly prescribe how society could redeem itself through the natural world. Even Beppe's emulation of the farming lifestyle is problematic in that, as Finatti indicates, he still, somewhat hypocritically, has built his home on his parents' property and takes marching orders from his mother.[37]

The Circumstance is the last of Olmi's fictional narratives, besides later short films and his contribution to *Tickets* (2005), that is firmly situated in the contemporary world. But in the history films explored in the next chapter he frames the past in an open manner that continues to invite us to give new shape to the present, including redefining how we regard our rights to the environment.

4

Revisiting the Past to Contemplate Our Freedom in the Present

Olmi's History Films

Representing history in film naturally has inherent ideological implications. As Leger Grindon notes, "The mere selection of a historical episode carries latent associations or even explicit political allegiances."[1] During the first half of the twentieth century, Italian cinematic depictions of the past exploited Italy's vaunted role as one of the birthplaces of Western civilization to form perspectives of the present and justify the actions of nationalistic governments. This appropriation of Italy's past was approved of by Benito Mussolini, who was keen to play on Italy's storied history to convince Italians of the legitimacy of his imperialistic ambitions. He organized the erection of monuments and statues, such as the *palazzo della civiltà Italiana* (palazzo of Italian civilization), in the EUR district of Rome, emblematizing his efforts to create the fiction of a continuous Italian state dating back to the age of the Caesars.[2] Aware of history's role in propagating the Fascist regime and earlier nationalist agendas, post–World War II Italian arthouse filmmakers adopted a much more cautious approach to representing history. Marcia Landy writes that the historical films of Rossellini, Visconti, and Fellini "visually address the past by deconstructing spectacle often through memory, rendering it comic, grotesque, or surreal to permit reflection on thinking historically. They offer pedagogical, essayistic, or allegorical forms in an appeal to the spectator to rethink the shapes and meanings of history."[3]

Although they share a similar goal of provoking a rethinking of the past, Olmi's history films (*The Scavengers*, *The Tree of Wooden Clogs*, *The Profession of Arms*, and *Greenery Will Bloom Again*) have little in common stylistically or narratively with those made by the filmmakers Landy references. Unlike Fellini's or Bertolucci's works set in the past, Olmi's history films are not psychologically charged investigations of memories of historical moments or the roots of authoritarianism, nor is their focus on iconic figures, as in Rossellini, (with the arguable exception of *The Profession of Arms*' Giovanni de' Medici) or the aristocracy, as in many of the historical works of Visconti. Predominantly, Olmi's history films, like his boom and post-boom films, center on everyday lives in the shadows of events generally regarded as defining their eras. *The Profession of Arms* is uncharacteristic among these films in its focus on a character with considerable power, but the film immediately withdraws that power by beginning with the death of the protagonist, deflating his importance throughout the film. The central theme of Olmi's history films, even *The Profession of Arms*, is the inability of the characters to live autonomously, free from the powers that be. They have been denied their natural rights to sustain themselves with the resources of nature as they see fit, or to love and live with who they want, because they are still subjects of their societies.

Olmi's respect and admiration for the rustic, farming world of Italy prior to the boom did not blind him from understanding its dangers, nor how it was also marred by injustice in its system. Recognizing this, Olmi has crafted his historical films to stimulate thinking about history rather than drawing definite conclusions about the films' subjects. These types of history films, as indicated by Robert Rosenstone, "rather than opening a window directly onto the past,… open a window onto a different way of thinking about the past. The aim is not to tell everything, but to point to past events, or to converse about history, or to show why history should be meaningful to people in the present."[4] Through the open-ended depictions of the exploitation of his characters, these films open our own political systems, and therefore power, to interpretation, by inviting us to identify how contemporary civilizations have maintained similar limitations on our, and others', freedoms, including impinging on our claims to the bounties of the natural world.

In *The Scavengers*, Olmi contemplates the meanings and paradoxes of freedom, and its relationship to civilization and nature, through a pair of men scouring the mountains for relics from World War I. The film and its themes derived from the landscape and the local residents of Olmi's adopted home. While working with Mario Rigoni Stern on an adaptation of the author's World War II memoir, *Il sergente nella neve* (*The Sergeant in the Snow*, 1953), that was never finally realized, Olmi fell in love with Stern's hometown, Asiago, in northeastern Italy. He decided that it would be where he and his wife would raise their young family and he resided there until his death in 2018.[5] Stern and Olmi, became neighbors, developing a close friendship that led them to collaborate on a short film for the RAI network, *Ritorno al paese* (briefly discussed in Chapter 3). Tullio Kezich, who had worked with Olmi on previous films, had been working with Stern on a project based on stories about Asiago (from Stern and other mountaineers) that they hoped to form into a television miniseries.[6] Olmi joined the project later on and assisted with the final script and it transformed into a film, still for television.[7] While interviewing local residents and scouting locations, an older man at an inn serenaded them with an anti-war song. Toni Lunardi was celebrating his eightieth birthday and sat with the filmmakers, talking with them for several hours about his experiences in life as a soldier, a shepherd, and even as a scavenger for artifacts from the war.[8] The filmmakers, spellbound by the man, his stories, and his *joie de vivre*, agreed to hinge the film on Lunardi and his singular personality.[9]

In the relationship between Lunardi's character, Du, and Gianni (Andreino Carli), *The Scavengers* probes the restrictions society places on individuals to allow them to take part in civilization. Gianni, a World War II veteran, has walked back home to Asiago from the Russian front to find an empty job market.[10] This scenario resembles the situation that many of the Neo-Realist protagonists, such as Antonio from *The Bicycle Thieves*, find themselves in before they enter into hopeless predicaments that lead to their downfall. However, as Roy Armes writes, Olmi "chooses a gentler path" for Gianni.[11] Olmi is much less interested in presenting the desperation of the post-war period than in reflecting on the choices Italy collectively made prior to the boom. Gianni's brother, Francesco, has decided to immigrate to Australia to find work, an option that Gianni would likely choose as well if he was not committed to his fiancée, Elsa.

After a discouraging visit to the local employment office, where he is shown a lengthy list of the other men waiting for work, he joins forces with other jobless, recently returned veterans to form their own lumber company. At the outset, they run afoul of the law. The film transitions directly from the employment office to an angry police officer reprimanding the young men for cutting up a fallen tree stump. The cut underscores the absurdity of the situation: the government requires hefty fees for the veterans to work the land to support themselves, but it has no means to give them jobs to earn money for the fees. The officer charges that they are ruining the seedlings to justify his anger, but he has no response to their exasperated questions of how they are supposed to find work. The ex-soldiers commandeer a lumber mill, though they are anxious over the mayor's threats to send policemen to prevent them from chopping down trees in the forest. The police continue to harass them, threatening to throw them in jail if they take the timber back to the mill, despite the men's pledge to pay the city their dues after they sell it. Desperate, some of the men even brandish their guns from the war to ward off the officials. However, the city finally puts a stop to the group's efforts by indebting the men with an exorbitant sum for the trees they have felled.

Dejected, Gianni visits Elsa and tells her that they will have to separate for several years again because he has no recourse but to immigrate to Australia with his brother. But on the way home he hears Du, drunk and sitting outside, singing out of tune a socialist protest song about a politician, Giacomo Matteotti, who was murdered because of his vocal anti-fascism.[12] Lunardi animates Du with his own whimsical temperament and habits that attracted the filmmakers. In between sentences he makes buzzing and whirring noises and uses his raspy voice to shout and swear exaggeratedly when he speaks. Morando Morandini correctly observes that the film at first appears to be about Gianni, "…but when old Du enters the scene … the story becomes his."[13] Although the narrative is still ostensibly Gianni's, in that his decisions drive the story forward, the film pivots toward Du partly because of his vibrancy but also because of his personification of the freedom that Gianni desires. Gianni knows of Du from the old man's legendary reputation and expresses surprise that he is still alive. When the younger man laments that he has no freedom to live in his own country, Du scoffs at him and offers to take him under his wing to find "treasure." Gianni expresses disbelief until Du waves a wad of cash in his face.

The generational discord in Gianni and Du's relationship reconsiders several of the same problems that exist between Natale and Roberto in *Time Stood Still*. Both of the older figures in these films represent the broken tradition of living and working in harmony with nature that collapsed during Italy's reconstruction period. Du's Thoreauvian relationship with the outdoors renders him almost completely self-reliant, only dependent on others for trade. He succeeds in his occupation because he possesses a seemingly supernatural sense of which caves to examine, and where to dig for metal because of his acute ability to read his environment. But there is something incongruous in Du's claims to freedom beyond the dangers his occupation naturally poses. He does not need to risk his life blowing up holes in the ground to look for unexploded bombs and shells lined with gun powder. He has no family to support, (he often mocks Gianni and his plans to marry), he could live off of game in the mountains, and he does not spend the money he earns. Though the film never makes this explicit through dialogue or through the use of overloaded imagery in war flashbacks (there is no time-shifting at all), Du seems driven to scavenge under the surface of what nature has buried for psychological purposes, to address the trauma he experienced in war. A World War I veteran, Du often recounts episodes from the key battles that were fought in the area while he and Gianni work. He does not discuss his rank, personal memories of the war, or other soldiers. In his recollections of the war, he recounts events as if he was a distant, neutral observer. Outwardly, he shows no signs that these memories distress him but his determination to unearth the bombs speaks to urges that his exuberant personality refrains from displaying.

When Gianni travels up the mountain to test out the old man's offer, the sight of Du's cabin also reveals his preoccupation with the war. On the outside wall of his home lay piles of war helmets, mines, and large bombs. Gianni does not find Du at home, and so he probes the area, spotting the old man detonating an explosive that will blow a hole in the side of the mountain. Du tells his new colleague that he just killed 152 Germans and 149 French soldiers. Gianni is curious as to how Du's flashback mixes in allies with opponents from the war, leading the older man to recap how bombs indiscriminately killed everyone in trenches and pits. However, he abstains from answering Gianni's questions about his wartime experiences. Du's selection of a memory that happened to kill allied and central power soldiers is not random, but a result of his resolved impartiality. As Gianni indicates, his name, "Du," translates to "you" in German. Du often shouts German and Latin phrases at will and in one scene mimics a German officer, wearing a soldier's helmet and barking marching orders. He deliberately models himself as a Whitmanesque embracer of everyone, proclaiming himself as a citizen of the world. He tells Gianni he wants to banish all nationalities because he refuses to comply with social contracts that would require him to belong to anyone else.

But Du's celebrations of his limited social ties, self-sufficiency and independence are somewhat paradoxical. His philosophy has traces of anarchism, but his actions express a need for the enduring order of civilization. His recruitment of Gianni exposes his wish for offspring that will adopt his way of life. He relishes the young man's company and deeply resents Gianni's occasional absence and his eventual departure from him. The film recognizes these paradoxes and explores them as Gianni weighs his options for his future. After securing the terms of a partnership with Du (they will split all of their earnings 50/50), with a new-found hope Gianni tells Elsa of the opportunity. She immediately opposes scavenging, labeling it work for desperate people. She continues her argument by pitting the structure of a family and home against the life Gianni has begun in the mountains with Du, warning that she does not want a scavenger as a husband. She informs him of companies that will construct houses in Asiago and will need workers. But he does not want to have to wait years to rise through the low-rewarding systems that these companies will offer. He decides to take his chances with Du and break off his relationship with his fiancée. In making this choice, Gianni believes that he can shape his own future, not yet fully comprehending the anti-progressive qualities of life as a scavenger.

Du's wish to eschew society includes rejecting its technological developments. He lights his home with lanterns and candles, dismembers the weapons and bombs they find by hand and has a strong aversion to using any type of modern equipment. Over the course of the film, he teaches Gianni to lift a bomb out of the ground with a belt, how to take apart explosives by hitting them against rocks, and to use a greased feather to loosen a warhead. When he has convinced Gianni of the financial gain they can earn together, Gianni fully commits himself to their partnership by buying a mine detector with all of his earnings from the war. Du angrily mocks him and is offended by the idea that a machine can outperform him. The failure of Gianni to initially find anything besides scrap metal encourages the old man, but Gianni tells him of his determination to continue working with the machine so that Du will eventually accept "modernity." When Gianni locates a copious cache of weaponry with the mine detector, Du warms to the idea of using it. However, he is only excited by the temporary pleasure it gives him of finding something. He and his scavenging profession are entrenched in the past. The old man has no intention to turn his partnership with Gianni into a modern, enterprising company.

In a chilling scene as they transport a bomb home to dismantle it, Du's scarred impression of the world emerges from his description of a gorge they pass. Intermingled with his own machine gun sound effects, he narrates a battle between Italian and Austrian troops in which 3,000 soldiers died. He describes how the soldiers' bodies tumbled down the mountainside when they were gunned down. He then points to the grass below and states, "You see all that grass down there, how green it is? You know why it's so green? It's grown on human flesh…. War goes around and around the world and never stops." The two men walk past the camera, which briefly follows them before panning around the valley as distressing music steadily becomes louder on the soundtrack. The troubling scene confirms the old man's incapacity to look forward. For Du, nature does not instigate ideas for the future; it only reawakens his memories of war and impels him to eradicate all traces of its battles from the valley.

Gianni does not permit Du's obsessions to sway him from scavenging. However, two events do lead him to come to terms with his colleague's disconcerting, macabre fixation with war. Rumors spread around the town that the Turk, the buyer of all of the local scavengers' findings, has been swindling the scavengers and that some new buyers will arrive from Treviso shortly. In an eager attempt to obtain more goods to sell to the new buyers, a group of scavengers hastily tearing down weaponry strikes a grenade that explodes in a shack, killing several men and upsetting the entire scavenging community. The film does not show the explosion itself, but in the only sequence that excludes Gianni it follows the Turk and a group of men as they assay the aftermath of the explosion and locate survivors. The shack resembles a war zone, with bloodied, dismembered bodies strewn across the floor. Back at Du's cabin, Gianni expresses how much the event troubles him by stating that their job is almost worse than going to war. However, the fulfilled threat of danger that claims the lives of the young men in the shack is not yet enough to deter him from scavenging. He continues working with Du until he comes face to face with death when they come across a find they believe to be the holy grail for scavengers.

When Gianni began working with Du, the old man recounted his meeting with an Austrian admiral following the war who was inspecting the valley for a battleship that the Austrian army had supposedly buried in the mountains. Gianni's mine detector picks up a strong signal that leads the men to conclude they have found the battleship in a concealed, deep cavern. Du can barely contain his excitement as they blow an opening in the mountainside large enough for them to descend through. They probe the many tunnels in the cave, scurrying from end to end looking for the battleship. Though hints of the sought treasure have eluded them so far, discovered cartridges of ammunition and weapons encourage them to descend to a lower level of the cave. Below, when they reach the back of the pit, instead of more loot they find a room full of dead bodies. The same haunting music that followed Du's description of the valley being fertilized by blood and flesh throttles the soundtrack. The camera tracks across the room as the light from Gianni's candle exposes the long-deceased soldiers. Luca Finatti argues that this scene is the best of the film and compares its ability to remind us of our mortality to the sequence from Rossellini's *Journey to Italy* when Katherine Joyce (Ingrid Bergman) looks away from the petrified bodies at Pompeii. "The simple vision of these dead bodies makes a mysterious revelation, an epiphany that questions the conscience of those who watch and invites them to change their lives."[14] The moment is certainly powerful, but Olmi's invitation for viewer interaction is much more direct in the subsequent scene.

For Gianni, encountering death so vividly in the cave leads him to abandon the life of a scavenger and rekindle his relationship with Elsa. He attains work as a brick layer building homes, following the suggestion of his fiancée. Du turns up at Gianni's worksite and harasses the other construction workers. When the encounter threatens to escalate into violence, Gianni intervenes and pulls Du away from the site. The old man also berates Gianni, telling him that he has become a "sheep" and accepted his own slavery. As Du walks away, he bellows out a song that continues into concluding shots of the hills and the mountains surrounding Asiago, ringing through the valley as if the old man was disappearing and uniting with nature.

Gianni's decision to leave Du compels us to consider his choice. As a veteran himself, Gianni recognizes the disquieting psychological relationship, especially after the deaths of the men in the shack, between digging through the ground for remains of past violence and war. As a bricklayer, he is quite literally building the future of the nation. On the other hand, there is a freedom that Du represents in his union with the land that Gianni will not have as a bricklayer. Living as he does, the older man has no one to report to and remains unconstrained by the expectations of a society that will march forward offering material gain in exchange for an ever-increasing loss of personal autonomy. In their last meeting, Gianni sports a uniform that marks him as a servant of his new employer and that presages the dehumanizing effects of Italy's coming economic success. Olmi allows us to deliberate on a critical moment in Italian history, and by extension the direction of "progress" across the world, as Italy recovered from World War II and adopted a consumer culture. Olmi does not blame Gianni nor Italy for choosing a safer route, but through Du he does call attention to what has been lost from abandoning nature. The conclusion points to the ethical predicament Italy found itself in during the 1940s, which later transitioned into the political problems Italians were facing during *gli anni di piombo*.

The Scavengers' treatment of the dichotomy between traditional lives attuned with nature and the march of industrial progress foreshadowed many of the ideas at the heart of *The Tree of Wooden Clogs*. In its return to the *fin de siècle* period, the latter film reflects on the wholeness of its farmers' lives but concurrently focuses on their powerlessness in the face of oppression. It ponders the abuses that the farmers endure, rendering the viewers into spectators of suffering and prompting them to react. Olmi had been working on *The Tree of Wooden Clogs* for over twenty years and formed it from his own experiences and stories he had collected. As a boy, Olmi would visit his maternal grandmother's home in Treviglio, a small town in between Bergamo and Milan, an experience that he reports was like traveling back in time to the nineteenth century.[15] When Olmi's mother died, his grandmother moved in with him and continued to recount to him the stories of her life on a *cascina* (farmhouse), like the one seen in the film, when she was a child. Olmi combined his grandmother's tales with stories told to him by the Bergamese farmers who act in the film to shape the narrative.[16]

He prepared for the film while taking a lengthy hiatus of four years from feature filmmaking in the late 1970s following the release of *The Circumstance*. Most of his films since the early 1960s had received mixed or poor reactions at festivals and none of them had achieved the kind of widespread international critical acclaim that *Il posto* and *I fidanzati* had received. As mentioned in the last chapter, he had been supporting himself and his family by making short works for the *Carosello* advertising program, and other short films, on the RAI network and had effectively disappeared from the feature filmmaking world. It was a great surprise, then, when his three-hour saga on late-nineteenth century Bergamese farming life, which was originally planned as a three-part television series on the RAI, won the Palme d'Or at Cannes in 1978 and later the New York Film Critic's Circle Award in 1979.[17] Much of the critical attention Olmi and his film received was glowingly positive. It has also become a favorite work of realist-oriented filmmakers, such as Mike Leigh, who praises the film for its containing "the whole span of human experience."[18] However, at the time of its release many Marxist and far-left-wing critics within Italy continued to assail Olmi and his cinema because of the assumptions they make about his politics, often disregarding the films' calls for action in expressing their distaste for Olmi's averseness to showing his characters rebelling against oppression. As Jonathan Keates suggests, "[It] seems that Olmi's compatriots are more interested in his reluctance to toe certain approved political or ideological lines than in his merits as a filmmaker."[19]

A majority of the negative discussion surrounding *The Tree of Wooden Clogs* pitted Olmi's work against Bertolucci's nearly six-hour epic *1900* (1976). Although Bertolucci's Marxist allegiance resolutely frames his film and its portrayal of peasants, farmers, and wealthier economic classes, it never preaches didactically, but makes its position clear. Like Olmi's film, it also begins in turn of the century Italy, but continues through World War II. However, few similarities actually exist between the films beyond the eras in which they are set and their focus on peasants. Olmi's most vociferous critic was the Marxist novelist and cultural critic Alberto Moravia. Moravia felt that *The Tree of Wooden Clogs* advocates a retrogressive attitude of humble passivity. His article entitled "Ora basta, disse il cavallo" (Enough now, said the horse) accuses Olmi's film of employing humble hero character types he felt were common in canonical Italian literature. He then continues to offer his view of the film as reinforced by what he sees as Olmi's Catholic ideology. In his description of the film's events he ignores all evidence of the political connotations of the film's style. "The ideology of *The Tree of Wooden Clogs* is Manzonian" he writes; "that is it looks at farming culture as a model, with admiration and approval, attempting to adopt its vision of the world."[20] Olmi does look at the farmers with admiration and does not portray the Catholic faith in negative tones (although Don Carlo, the farmer's priest, is mostly helpless in aiding the peasants in their struggles). But he recognizes the limitations of the farmers' lives as well. The film resolutely demonstrates an awareness that progress is required to combat the treatment they receive from the landlord.

The film is episodic, not exactly in the manner of a film like Rossellini's

Francesco, giullare di Dio (*The Flowers of Saint Francis*, 1950), but in its telling of everyday events from the lives of each of the four families that live in the *cascina*. Whereas Rossellini's film combines several relatively disconnected narratives in the lives of St. Francis and his acolytes, Olmi interweaves the stories of his film's characters, cutting back and forth between the four households. The stories unfold through the entire duration of the film, which begins and ends with the Batistì (I will refer to the male characters as they are referred to in the film. For example, the husband and father of the Finard family is only called Finard by other characters in the film. Stefano, however, is referred to by his birth name). *The Tree of Wooden Clogs* is Olmi's most Flahertyesque and romanticist feature film in its patient observations and recreations of pre-industrial working lives and the worldviews such lives foster. After the opening scene with Batistì (Luigi Ornaghi) and his wife (Francesca Moriggi), the film proudly proclaims its intentions to recreate a past reality. The directness of the preamble, followed by Batistì weighing their priest's, Don Carlo (Carmelo Silva), recommendation to send Minec (Omar Brignoli) to school, immediately frames the film with a political eye. The film opens with a social problem the Batistì family seeks to solve themselves. But we soon see that the economic system they live in prevents them and their children from escaping their hardship filled lives on their own. By the conclusion, remembering that many of the actors themselves are farmers or ordinary citizens, we recognize that the film does not blindly indulge in nostalgia for the elegantly pastoral form of life humbly led by these people, but invites us to address similar injustices that we see in our present world.

However, we cannot deny that *The Tree of Wooden Clogs* adorns the lives of the farmers through the tranquil selections of Bach that color the families' emotions and spiritual ties to their work, the joy on the faces of the farmers during the evenings they sit listening to stories or singing, the laughter of the children, and the film's painterliness that seemingly vivifies the works of Vincent Van Gogh or Claude Lorrain. Before the film familiarizes us with any of its four principal stories we are immersed in this world by watching the farmers till dirt, harvest corn, the fascination the children have with a newborn foal, and then the alarming beheading of a goose.

Immediately following a shot of children joyfully jumping in the hay, a cut takes us to the courtyard of the *cascina*, and a large goose dashes across the screen. Children enter the shot, yelling, "Get her" until they corner the bird against a wall. One of the older boys hands the goose to Finard (Battista Trevaini). Initially, the capture of the bird appears frolicsome. Bach's music bridges the moment to the pleasant scenes preceding it. The children follow Finard over to a log stump, reassuring one another and expressing their fear that the animal may bite. Quickly, Finard lays the goose's neck

4. Revisiting the Past in the Present

Through Bach-accompanied images of the farmers working in the fields in *The Tree of Wooden Clogs*, Olmi urges us to reflect on the nature-based aspects of their lives that bring them peace (1978, RAI-Radiotelevisione Italiana).

across the stump, grabs a blade, and with a swift blow beheads the bird and then bleeds its neck into the dirt. When the farmer calls out for a container for the blood, a quick cut to the youngest Batistì child registers the boy's distress at witnessing death, simultaneously suggesting that this way of life encompasses his comprehension of the cycles of life and what it means to work and provide food to feed the family. This early sequence also prepares us to envision this world as less than ideal. It initiates a pattern of watching suffering throughout the work that prefigures the position of spectators within and outside of the diegetic world of the film. This is also seen in the pig slaughtering scene that the youngest Batistì child watches again with several other children. The camera's perspective and the editing structure in both scenes reflect Olmi's observational style, rarely moving into close-ups of the gutted pig or the faces of the farmers.

Olmi also presents us with the landlord's (Mario Brignoli) point of view of this world in a later scene, documenting the inequality likely sparking the riots witnessed in Maddalena (Lucia Pezzoli) and Stefano's (Franco Pilenga) trip to Milan. Olmi joins the viewer's perspective first with the curious Stefano and then with that of the landlord, who, removed from his family seems distant and withdrawn as he peers in through a window watching others enjoy music together. After shyly announcing his desire to court Maddalena, one evening Stefano and two other suitors join in the nightly gathering of the farmers at the *cascina*. In tightly framed shots, the peasant families huddle together in the congested room amongst the cows as they feed. Batistì hears music and then invites everyone to come outside and listen to the pipers they can hear playing at the landlord's house. Their satisfied murmurings comment on the performance as part of a Christmas tradition. Several close-ups display the parents holding their children peacefully alongside Anselmo (Giuseppe Brignoli), the widow Runk's father, with his granddaughter. Despite the barren and rough surroundings, we sense the warm affection shared by the humble families and their friends as they listen to the festive music under the night sky.

When Stefano walks home, he hears a Mozart composition from the landlord's house and he peeks beyond the gate to have a closer look at the home. Never venturing further than the shadowy yard to see the source of the music, the young man watches as the landlord glances inside of the window, with cuts back and forth between Stefano watching and the focus of his curious attention. Alerted by the dogs, the landlord demands to know who stands in his yard, but Stefano rushes off. The camera remains with the landlord and transfers us to his perspective of the inside of his luxurious home. The few moments of the film we spend with him, he is never vilified beyond instigating the investigation into the felled tree immediately before the film's conclusion. We do not see him treat anyone harshly or even give the command to evict the Batistì family. He is remote not only from the peasants, but also, the *mise-en-scène* indicates, from his own family and friends. Although curious and observant of the lives around him, like Olmi's other passive spectator characters, the landlord's detachment engenders his indifference to the farmers' welfare.

Through point-of-view shots through a barred window, the landlord's perspective shows us, a room of elegantly dressed people sitting in a large room and listening to a young man play a piano. Close-ups of their faces indicate a much colder atmosphere than that of the *cascina*. Olmi gives us no reason to dislike these people, but following the cramped quarters recently witnessed at the *cascina*, the *mise-en-scène* generates awareness of the abundant space at the landlord's home, highlighting the disparity between classes in this community. The contrast in lifestyles foretells what may fuel the rebels' anger in Milan and the economic and social inequality that would be readily apparent to the audience spoken to by the socialist in the festival scene.

Two of the families at the *cascina* withstand particularly arduous trials because of their poverty: the widow Runk's household and the Batistìs.

The widow Runk (Teresa Brescianini) struggles just to feed her many children and keep a roof over their heads. In one of the film's most compelling scenes that highlights our agency as spectators (which also reiterates the families' distinct blend of religion with nature and work) the Runk family's cow heals, possibly miraculously. M.A. Hall argues that this event "graphically illustrates the popular Catholic culture in which the Italian peasantry were both liberated and confined," suggesting that through a belief in miracles, the farmers expect something supernatural to save the Batistìs at the end of the film.[21] However, the film does not present this culture as in any way confining, but depicts the farmers' faith as self-affirming through their personal relationships with their God combined with their work. Though the passage itself abstains from displaying any kind of supernatural cause for the incident, the widow firmly understands the cow's healing as a miracle, and the depiction of the event, keeping with the rest of the film's style, also grants us that possibility.

Not willing to give up when a veterinarian instructs her to kill her valuable cow, the widow washes out a wine bottle, and walks hurriedly to the church, pleading to God aloud for his help and detailing in her prayer the dire circumstances she finds herself in since her husband has died. She returns to the cow's stall, grabs its horn to tilt its head back, jams the bottle into its mouth, and repeats the Lord's Prayer. Later in the film, a morning arrives when one of her daughters jolts out to the widow washing clothes at the creek to tell her that the cow stands. When the widow sees the cow on its feet she walks over to a picture of a saint on the stall's wall and kneels before it, offering her gratitude. But the sequence never confirms the widow's belief that the act was a miracle through the use of music, further discussion of the incident, or any conventional device such as a glowing halo or a vaselined lens. Instead, Olmi offers a bucolic image that illustrates the peasant's belief system without validating it. The absence of any religious authority, such as the priest, from this scene accentuates the personal faith of the peasants and their determination to work for God's blessings. But whether or not this incident can be attributed to an act of God, the widow's financial situation remains burdensome. Even with an event she may comprehend as a tender mercy of God, she will still struggle to feed her children. In context, the scene emphasizes the necessity for further practical action even in a world where God may occasionally intercede.

The hardships faced by the Batistì family are in many ways the centerpiece of the film. In the film's introduction, Batistì openly contests Don Carlo's instructions to send Minec to school because he and his wife are almost ready to welcome another child into their family and the boy could assist them with their workload around the *cascina*. When the family does decide to let Minec receive an education, the boy walks a few miles each day by himself in clothes inadequate for the harsh, cold weather of a northern Italian winter. One day when his clog splits in half at school, Minec tries to fix it by himself at first by unfastening the rope he uses as a belt and tying it around his clog to hold it together. His temporary solution quickly falls apart when he makes his way to the muddy road and he decides to remove his sock and shoe and walk home with one foot bare. The breaking of the clog occurs on the day Minec's new brother is born and when the boy returns home his father instructs him not to say anything to his mother about the incident. Night falls and Batistì puts on his cloak, with hatchet concealed, and heads to the side of the creek to obtain lumber. After selecting the tree he will fell, he starts chopping off limbs and branches from the upper half, constantly looking around to ensure he remains unseen. and gathers enough wood to craft a new clog for his son. Batistì returns home and after clandestinely looking out the window to ascertain if anyone has followed him, he cuts the wood for Minec's shoe while repeating prayers with his family. Clearly, he has gathered the wood secretly and without consulting with his wife because he fears the punishment of his landlord, and not because he expects any conflict between this action and his understanding of God's commandments.

As the film arrives at its climax, the landlord does not even exit from his carriage when he suspects that someone has chopped down a tree on his property without his consent. Instead, he sends the bailiff to investigate the scene. Our own observation of the punishment that the landlord and the bailiff mete out comes from the perspective of the other families who first discuss the implications of the incident with the tree and then witness the swift eviction of the Batistì family. As the film utilizes the families' point-of-view shots, Olmi underscores our own witnessing of this injustice. After Anselmo returns home with one of his granddaughters from selling his tomatoes in the village, a somber air permeates the widow Runk's home that compels him to ask what has happened. The widow tells her father of the eviction. The Batistìs must leave by morning with all of their possessions. Fear and a deep grief tinge their conversation about the supposed crime, leading to Anselmo's pronouncement that this means "taking the bread away from those people."

When the hooves of the bailiff's horse are heard, Olmi cuts to the Finard home, which is filled with the same uneasiness as the widow's. Neither family exits but observes the events from their own windows and doorways as the film cuts back and forth between both homes, establishing and displaying each family's point-of-view. They watch as the officer loads the landlord's animals that Batistì has cared for onto and behind a cart, Finard's wife lamenting, "Those poor people. They have nothing left now." When Batistì loads his few remaining possessions onto his own cart, we also view the disgraced farmer from the vantage point of the home of Maddalena and Stefano. The families do not even bid farewell to those departing, seemingly afraid and at a complete loss as to the appropriate course of action. As the family leaves in tears with no stated destination, the film casts shame on the other families for their lack of action and for simply watching people they have worked with for years turned out of their homes for nothing. By not doing anything they contradict the ethical principles of their background and existence as farmers who rely on one another for support in all aspects of their lives. However, the film does not provide a ready answer as to what their collective response should be. It demands a consideration of the film's examples of resistance to oppression that the farmers encounter outside of the *cascina*.

The film contains several potential, though deliberately obscure, responses to the abuse and hardship unfairly meted out to the peasant families. At Maddalena and Stefano's wedding the priest suggests the journey they will make on their honeymoon holds danger and warns them of people's "strange ideas." Immediately following their marriage, the newlyweds board a boat to travel by river to Milan.[22] Upon entering the city, the passengers spot a plume of smoke arising from their destination. Although many of them speculate that it may just be a bonfire, another priest aboard worries that it may be demonstrators. Besides the smoke seen while on the boat, the first impressions given of Milan reflect its commercialism. Peddlers rush out to greet them as they alight on land, and subsequent shots display men selling their wares as we hear prices negotiated and shouts of sales from the soundtrack. At a crosswalk across an alley, a group of soldiers leading young men in chains stops the couple in their tracks. Maddalena and Stefano look on with confusion and curiosity as the soldiers and prisoners walk by until the road clears and they can pass through. Seconds later, walking on another street, other pedestrians tell them that the soldiers have blocked the road ahead. Along their detour the commotion of the army racing by on horses and fearful exclamations of "they're going to shoot" force the newlyweds and other citizens under the shelter of a doorway until the battle concludes. The film offers us the naïve perspective of Maddalena and Stefano in the city, declining to provide information about the riot or the rioters. Names are not mentioned for us to associate the rebels with specific historical movements, and neither side is displayed in a particularly villainous light. As the scene unfolds, we only hope that Maddalena and Stefano will arrive safely at the nunnery where they will stay. Their wedding signifies a new hope for the families, partly because of the possibility that their exposure to the events in the city will open their minds to possible recourses in response to future hardships inflicted because of their low class status.

After reaching the nunnery of Maddalena's aunt, Sister Maria, they are encouraged to adopt a child into their new family. The adoption of the child is not a direct response to the rebels in Milan but acts as its own representation of bearing individual responsibility for the betterment of society. Martin Walsh writes in an excellent article analyzing Olmi's works up to 1971 that the director "focuses not on the evils of an unwieldy, stifling bureaucratic machinery, but upon the responsibility of each individual for his own life."[23] Olmi's films certainly do focus on the choices of the individual in the face of their own existence. However, the choices made by Olmi's characters also reflect a responsibility they sense in aiding those around them when they know of injustice or of another's heavy burden. The choice of Maddalena and Stefano to adopt the child reflects a motivation to perform a political act within their own sphere of influence.

Out of the four stories in the film, the Finard family's occupies the least amount of screen time but consists of a consequential event that appertains to the biblical parable of the talents and to audience responses to the rectifiable misfortunes of the peasant families. In Matthew and Luke, Christ tells the story of a master who gives three of his servants, according to their abilities, stewardship over some money, or talents, while he is away. The first two, who received more talents than the last, doubled the amount they were given while their master was away. The last servant hid his talent in the ground and the master chastises him for wasting his talent. This parable is adapted into Finard's story to reflect on how his greed and selfishness prevent him from productively utilizing his anger and unhappiness. In comparison with the rest of the farmers, Finard exhibits much more exasperation with his life and a general feeling of discontentment exudes from him in his interactions with his family. Olmi uses the town festival to link Finard's outrage to the historic struggle between classes.

The festival celebrates a miracle that occurred after a historic rebellion of local citizens against French soldiers 350 years ago. Don Carlo opens the festivities by recounting the incident's events from his pulpit at the church. Because three villagers threw stones at soldiers, General Lautrec of the French forces had decided to burn down the village. The townspeople headed to the church to plead in supplication to the Madonna, asking her to intervene on their behalf. A mural of the Madonna and Child in the church was said to have wept and when the General arrived at the church, the painting astonished him and he knelt in front of it, laying his sword and helmet down. The priest's summation of these events upholds his impractical stance on social change. Instead of highlighting the injustice that incited the peasants, he points to the remnants of this incident on an altar, stating that the armor and weapon remain there to this day to remind them of the dangers of the world.

In response to the passivity of the priest and others to the oppression and exploitation of the farmers, the film presents us with a kind of folk activism that has its roots in the inverted world of carnival. The children ride on a carousel; puppeteers, comic mimes and musicians perform shows; ritualistic contests take place; games are played, and the adult peasants drink heavily. The multi-day festival allows attendees to contest order and challenge, within a certain parameter, the roles society has designated to them. During the evening of the festival, Finard wanders into a crowd surrounding a political speaker on a raised platform. We see and hear the speaker at first distantly, framed in a long shot, reflecting Finard's separation from the speaker. The speaker calls for changes to create a true democratic society stating, in lines that will apply to Finard and the *cascina*'s families later, "Unfortunately, social progress moves forward slowly, blocked by those with fear, but above all those who call for it as a human right have not supported it with enough courage. Many remain in the background while only a few bravely move forward." Initially during the speech, Finard draws himself closer to the rabble-rouser and listens attentively, the camera cutting between close-ups of him and the speaker framed in a medium shot.

The speech does not seem to elicit any collective feeling from the large crowd that has gathered. However, those present cannot be said to be entirely indifferent, because their gazes remain fixed on the speaker; that is, except for Finard who spots a coin in the dirt during the speech. When he sees the money, he is bewildered that everyone surrounding him has failed to notice it. The camera crosscuts between the speaker and Finard staring at the coin. Convinced that he is not being watched, Finard slyly walks over and places a foot on the coin while pretending to give heed to the speech. Keeping his eyes locked on the speaker, he slowly bends down, removes his foot and places the coin in his hand. Having determined that it is indeed what he thought it was, he cannot contain a gleeful laugh as he walks away from the crowd.

Once out of sight he pulls up his cloak and races home to his horse's stall. He calms the animal down, picks up its hoof, and after removing debris, places the coin in the hole he has dug and packs his treasure with dirt, following the lead of the third servant of the parable of the talents. The title of Moravia's article, "Enough now, says the horse," derives from a later sequence when Finard checks to reassure himself that his money has stayed hidden and he discovers that it has vanished. Panicked, he digs through the horse's foot. He yells, swears, and spits at the animal as he hits it, accusing it of stealing from him. The horse reacts by chasing its master until it is pulled away by the other farmers from its target. Moravia complains that the horse actually revolts against Finard's abuse of him while the farmers remain passive because of their humility. The author's shocking misapprehension of the film led to his belief that Olmi was promoting a regressively apathetic worldview. On the contrary, the director has framed Finard as a character capable of using his fiery temperament as a talent to respond to the injustices of the farmers' situation. When he and the other farmers do nothing as the Batistì family is evicted from their home, Olmi associates their inaction with the potential apathy of the audience in their reactions to the film's conclusion. In reframing this seemingly halcyon historical moment set against gorgeous natural scenery by questioning why no one challenges a system that prevents these families from owning their own land and being completely self-sustaining, Olmi allows us to deliberate on contemporary unjust infractions against humanity's natural rights.

Twenty-three years after Olmi won the *Palme d'Or* at Cannes he returned to the festival with another history film that also scrutinizes lives trampled upon by society. In *The Profession of Arms*, even the life of a nobleman, no less one of the eminent Medici family, is expendable if it interferes with political interests and the march of progress. Olmi became interested in Lodovico de' Medici, more commonly known as Giovanni dalle Bande Nere (Giovanni of the Black Bands), while reading a surgeon's essays on Giovanni's leg operations after the knight was shot with a cannonball.[24] Olmi saw in Giovanni's story an opportunity to adapt an idea of Rossellini's regarding the increasing brutality of war resulting from the introduction of firearms.[25] In its portrayal of the passing of the Middle Ages into the Renaissance through the introduction of more powerful weaponry, *The Profession of Arms* takes up Rossellini's late mission of educating the masses on how civilization reached its current state. But as with his other historical films, Olmi interrogates how we understand the past to measure the worth of individuals in relation to systems that deprive people of sovereignty over their own lives. Olmi's imagining of Giovanni sets aside Giovanni's privileged status by returning to the director's characteristic time-shifting style, exposing the military captain's own intimate perception of his life.

The film does have brief intermittent explanations of the context, but it provides little exposition of the historical setting or many of the characters. This lack of information, combined with the mixture of the past and present with the fantasies, nightmares, and wanderings of Giovanni's deranged mind, make the film one of Olmi's most demanding works.[26] A familiarity with Giovanni's background does assist in unraveling the film's plot and the film's characterization of him as a tempestuous figure. Giovanni was the son of Giovanni di Pierfrancesco de' Medici (*Il popolano*) [man of the people], the great-great grandson of Giovanni di Bicci de' Medici, the founder of the Medici Bank and often seen as one of the inciting figures of the Italian Renaissance (to avoid confusion, I will use "Giovanni" hereafter to only refer to Giovanni dalle Bande Nere).²⁷ Giovanni was the cousin of Pope Leo X, and his wife, Maria Salviati, was the pope's niece through her mother, Lucrezia Maria Romola de' Medici. Giovanni's father died a few months after the boy was born and his mother passed away when he was only eleven years old. Before passing, his mother turned her son over to Maria's parents and he spent his teenage years under the same roof as his future wife.²⁸

Giovanni had a reputation for being a fierce combatant and as a youth was known to get into frequent conflicts with others, a tendency referred to in the film by Federico II Gonzaga (the Duke of Mantua).²⁹ Despite his affection for his wife, he was also a womanizer from an early age, another trait the film references through the nameless noblewoman we see Giovanni making love with.³⁰ But above all, Giovanni was recognized as a dedicated and effective soldier who earned the respect of Pope Leo as the *condottiero* (captain) of a group of mercenaries by recapturing Urbino during the Italian War of 1521–1526.³¹ When Leo died, Giovanni mourned the death of his cousin by placing black bands on his uniform, granting his troop their nickname (*bande nere*).³² After Leo's death, Clement VII undertook the papacy, and Giovanni still fought for the church but fell out of favor with the new pope because of enmity between Giovanni and Francesco Maria I della Rovere. The pope had befriended della Rovere and made him commander of all the Italian troops in preparation for the War of the League of Cognac, although della Rovere was the Duke of Urbino whom Giovanni had previously helped the church depose.³³ When a German group of landsknechts, a mercenary army of pikemen, led by Georg von Frundsberg moved through northern Italy on their way to sack Rome, Giovanni and his soldiers attempted to prevent them from crossing the Po river, but the captain was shot by a cannonball in an ambush.³⁴ Giovanni died after an amputation and became a folk hero for his bravery and resistance to foreign forces.³⁵ *The Profession of Arms* presents events ranging from von Frundsberg's journey through northern Italy until Giovanni's funeral, with earlier memories interspersed throughout the film.

A misleading group of initial shots following the opening credits give the impression that *The Profession of Arms* will be a war film. However, after a close-up of a helmeted head is followed by a shot of men lowering their spears in preparation for battle, an epigraph quoting Tibullus, a Roman poet of the first century, appears in the middle of the screen, bemoaning the inventions of weapons and their contributions to wars. The shot of the helmeted head in the background fades to black and the next shot fades in to the deathbed scene of Giovanni (Christo Jivkov) as Pietro Aretino (Sasa Vulicevic), an Italian writer and close friend of the deceased, gives a eulogy. Transitioning from shots promising a battle to Giovanni's death, the film immediately rejects the hagiographic mode of many biographical films, positioning the *condottiero* to be viewed as any other man.[36] Aretino's tribute, which is read aloud over shots introducing us to other nobility figures that play a part in the last week of Giovanni's life (including Federico II Gonzaga [Sergio Grammatico] and his cousin Loyso Gonzaga [Aldo Toscano]), is succeeded by a statement from Giovanni's stableman (Michele Zattara) that discredits the eulogy by referencing the role of political deceit in his master's death.

The delivery of these two declarations recall the sharing of letters between Giovanni and Liliana in *I fidanzati*, negating the distance between them. In the earlier film, the lovers were looking off camera as they read their letters aloud in the direction of their partner positioned on the other side of the screen in subsequent shots. However, in *The Profession of Arms*, Aretino and the stableman begin a pattern of the characters reciting their statements as they look into the camera, as if at the audience. Other characters later respond in the same manner to requests or in formal declarations they make. In most of these moments, the actors state their lines without emotion. The formal strategy behind these scenes echoes a plea behind the stableman's observation, asking us to recognize how we think of history as competing powers interact with Giovanni through these asides. To do this, the film enables us to observe the actions of those deciding Giovanni's fate in contrast to the ornate responses they deliver. Daniel Leisawitz writes of Olmi's use of letters in the film that "[The director] grants us an intimate view of history and of a personal story within that history through his artistic transmutation of these literary documents. This history is explicitly mediated, and through his depiction of the letters, Olmi clearly admits, indeed celebrates, such mediation."[37] Consequently, through the effects of these scenes, we see that Giovanni has become a pawn in his dedicated service as a soldier, and Olmi proceeds to measure Giovanni's worth as a man, rather than as a nationalistic hero as dictated by historical accounts.

After more letters and statements introduce several other key figures, including Francesco Maria della Rovere (Paolo Magagna) Maria Salviati (Dessy Tenekedjieva), and Georg von Frundsberg (Nikolaus Moras), in the events leading to Giovanni's death, the film shifts back in time to six days earlier. Aretino's voice-over reviews details regarding the invasion of Italy by von Frundsberg's landsknechts and Giovanni's intention to block their path to Rome. Aretino also summarizes some of the religious tension behind the war by mentioning the Germans' goal of hanging the pope with a golden rope that von Frundsberg keeps close to his saddle. Following this preamble, Giovanni stops at a camp in Gabbiana, where he dictates a letter to della Rovere outlining his strategy for dealing with the much more disciplined German army.

Giovanni's communications seem to fall on deaf ears. He receives no

4. Revisiting the Past in the Present 103

support from della Rovere and the noblemen who profess allegiance to the pope betray him. In between the dispatch of his letter to della Rovere and a response from Alfonso d'este, Duke of Ferrara (Giancarlo Belelli), to another letter, we see blacksmiths forging artillery and testing it on a row of armored suits. The Duke oversees the development of these weapons, and while he watches on as a cannonball passes completely through a suit of armor, a voice reads aloud a letter from the Duke to Giovanni. There is then a cut to the Duke seated in a stately room playing a violin while a servant reads the ornate statement expressing the Duke's regret that he is unable to assist Giovanni. At one point, the Duke interrupts the servant, and amends the letter to reflect his unwillingness to bestow upon anyone the weapons he has in his possession. However, the Duke does decide to share his weapons with von Frundsberg for political purposes. His disengagement from the communication with the captain initiates a pattern in the film of authority figures either willfully misrepresenting their feelings or having explicit intentions to betray Giovanni.

Federico II Gonzaga is just as duplicitous as the Duke of Ferrara and repeatedly lies to Giovanni and betrays him to avoid dealing with the havoc wrought by both the Italian and German soldiers passing through his territory. Matteo Cusastro (Fabio Giubbani), the Duke of Mantua's chancellor, advises Federico to permit von Frundsberg and his troops to travel through the Curtatone gate to relieve them of the armies' presence. To keep himself in the good graces of the pope, Federico then drafts a letter to Clement claiming that von Frundsberg and the landsknechts forced their way through. However, he then gives the order to close the gate to Giovanni and his troops to allow von Frundsberg more time to clear out of the territory. Giovanni and his troops bang on the gate, promising retribution for the betrayal. When Cusastro informs Federico of the captain's threats, he has to do so through a hallway because the Duke is undressing another noble's wife in his bedroom. Throughout the film, Federico appears lethargic, uninterested in his role and the impact his decisions make. When he is later notified by a messenger that Giovanni has been shot by artillery fire, he allows his chancellor to provide a response and exits to play with his dog. Later, to keep face, he visits Giovanni on his deathbed and offers anything at his disposal. The Dukes are antithetical to Giovanni in their lax commitment to their positions and they are indifferent to the outcome of the war as long as it does not endanger their situations. In displaying the perfidiousness of political leaders from the past by visualizing the contrast between their words and their deeds, Olmi stresses how little has changed over the centuries, specifically in regard to the causes and rationale behind wars and the complete disregard for the lives taken and shattered by them.

As Giovanni continues to pursue von Frundsberg, he is progressively awakened to the pointlessness of this war and the abuse he suffers from those in power. Because his communications with della Rovere and the pope to ask for resources and supplies have proved unfruitful, he enlists his wife, who is already on her way to Rome, to influence the pope to grant him funds so that he can pay his discontented troops. In her cold response, she relays the pope's promise that he will never forget the needs of the troops. However, money never arrives. Giovanni's cause is unsupported by the church despite his dedication to defending it and the pope from the forthcoming Sack of Rome that von Frundsberg has promised. Giovanni's troops, who rape women and steal from the people they are employed to protect, discourage the captain as well. As they await the Duke of Mantua's command to open the gate so they may chase down the Germans, the Italian soldiers break into a sacristy and plunder a wooden crucified Christ, "a Christ of the poor, of those that are hungry and cold," as one of the soldiers reminds his fellow combatants. Ignoring the sanctity of a relic from the church for which they are engaged in battle, the soldiers dismember the figure to build a fire while they jokingly warn each other that they should be careful or they will be punished in hell. Infuriated by the mercenaries' behavior, Giovanni grabs one of the broken wooden arms and beats a soldier over the head. Although such behavior, fundamentally in opposition to the alleged rationale of protecting the church, discourages Giovanni, his commitment to his duties never wavers.

He articulates this commitment as he lies on his death bed, interrupting the priest who is administering the last rites at his bedside to declare, "In these years of my life, I have always lived as a soldier, the same way I would have lived under the conditions of being a priest, had I worn your clothes." In this statement, the captain regretfully acknowledges what duty to his occupation has cost him. His life was unnecessarily sacrificed for a power struggle. Giovanni's profession, like that of so many of Olmi's other characters, has interfered with his ability to live freely. His duty as a soldier, and the expectations held of him because he was a member of the Medici family, has also obstructed him from forming a life with whom he chooses.

The film suggests the forced marriage between Giovanni and Maria was void of affection. They exchange letters during the film, but no passion exists between them. During their conversations, nothing succeeds in altering her expressionless demeanor. His continued communication with her, even facing his imminent death, is provoked more out of an obligation to his wedding vows than from romantic love. In the lengthy sequence in which Giovanni retreats to the residence of Loyso Gonzaga after his injury, he experiences a series of flashbacks and visions that opaquely review his life and relationships, opening his eyes to the distance between him and those he truly cares for. The walls of the room Giovanni rests in are

4. Revisiting the Past in the Present 105

Looking into the camera, Giovanni's unnamed lover (Sandra Ceccarelli) prepares to read him a letter aloud in *The Profession of Arms*. Despite their longing to be with one another, societal expectations have torn them apart (2001, Cinemaundici).

decorated with paintings featuring depictions of sex, violence, and demons. The images appear to frighten Giovanni and steer his thoughts toward a judgement of the value of his life. The first departure returns to a joust, hosted by a much friendlier Federico II Gonzaga, where Giovanni catches the eye of an unnamed, married noblewoman (Sandra Ceccarelli). She has appeared in earlier scenes, in flashbacks following a clandestine sexual encounter with Giovanni in a carriage, delivering a letter (looking into the camera) to her lover that laments the shame their affair has brought her, and riding with a chauffeur desperately tracking the captain while he battles the German troops. Wordlessly, at the jousting event they exchange longing glances and when a heavy wind rushes through the courtyard they withdraw to a room where they can be alone.

The film cuts back and forth between these reveries and visits from associates and treatment from medics. When the doctors determine that his leg needs to be amputated, Giovanni's gaze races around the room, resting on paintings featuring a snake, a woman's vagina, and an erect penis resting on a woman's leg as a man prepares for penetration. Horrified by the combination of the sexual images and the phallic connotations of having his leg removed, Giovanni recalls sex with the noblewoman in a carriage. In the middle of their ardent lovemaking, the film transitions to his wife, hanging up clothes to dry as the wind blows and reciting a letter expressing her regret that she is not wealthy enough yet to help take care of him. The recurring wind points to Giovanni's floating consciousness and its realization that he cares for Maria, but that he wanted to spend his life with someone else.

His feelings for the noblewoman are confirmed one evening after the amputation. His fevered mind envisions a pregnant Maria standing in front of his bed before a blazing fireplace. A cut is made from Maria back to Giovanni, but before returning to his point-of-view shot, we hear the voice of the noblewoman. Then when the cut is made back to the reverse shot, the noblewoman stands in Maria's place before an unlit fireplace. She narrates another letter to him, apprising him of her pregnancy and that she is sure that the unborn child is his. She pleads with Giovanni to write a letter to her husband so that he will spare the child's life. The sequence closes by returning to their entangled bodies in the carriage. Giovanni's repeated recollection of his trysts with his lover and the transformation of his wife into the noblewoman, direct his thoughts, during his final moments, to the person his heart truly belongs to.

Yet, as Giovanni is dying, the film also expresses his regrets for the end of his relationships with his wife and their only child, Cosimo (Andrea Iacopo Di Antonio). While the priest performs his last rites sacrament, and even after his death, the film continues to follow Giovanni's thoughts. Although we still hear the priest's prayer, he and his assistants have vanished when Maria enters the room, caressing her dying husband's face before she lays her head on his chest as she cries. The prayer carries on into the next shot of the soldiers preparing to dress the recently deceased Giovanni. When the prayer ends, the scene moves to an unspecified place and time. Giovanni, still alive and suited in armor, stares at his son who stands behind a barred gateway. They do not exchange words, but Giovanni begins to weep and closes his eyes before the film takes us back to the casting of his death mask and then to the funeral that opened the film.

The entire film has unveiled the artifice behind the opulent burial ceremony meant to embolden attendees to revere a hero who died in the service of his country and church. Guileless, Giovanni sacrificed his life for institutions and allies more than willing to cast him aside when supporting him was inconvenient. As the film's closing credits begin to run, Aretino narrates the continued march of the German troops that results in the 1527 Sack of Rome. The last words belong to the stableman who reminds us that after Giovanni's death an agreement was made between military captains that firearms would never be used again. Through *The Profession of Arms*' imagining of the love and life scarified by a soldier at the end of the Renaissance, and the recognition at the time of the need to curb the development of weapons capable of such destruction, Olmi contends that current, similar calls for peace and the condemnation of contemporary weaponry are not the results of more mature civilizations truly prepared to renounce all wars. Instead these weapons continued to progress until billions of lives could potentially be taken in a moment.

In 2014, Olmi made another anti-war film, *Greenery Will Bloom Again*, that also features soldiers sacrificed by indifferent superiors. The film was the only one of Olmi's features to be co-produced by the film school he co-founded, *Ipotesi Cinema*, alongside Cinemaundici and RAI Cinema, and was the director's fifth work to employ his son, Fabio Olmi, as cinematographer.[38] Marking the one-hundred-year anniversary of the beginning of World War I, the film is based both on the novel *La Paura (Fear)* by Federico de Roberto and on the letters and diaries of soldiers.[39] Although adapted from other's work and primary historical documents, the film had very personal significance to Olmi. In a coda at the film's conclusion, the director dedicates the film to his father who fought in World War I and later told his sons of his experiences. Olmi has implanted in his film the grim details his father tearfully told him of the war, of fellow soldiers and orders given that would lead to death. *Greenery Will Bloom Again* also has several significant connections with *The Scavengers*. It brings to life the preceding scenarios that led to Du's description of a valley, once littered with corpses, whose grass has attained its greenness by feeding on the flesh of dead soldiers, as gruesomely eluded to in the later film's title.[40] It also ends with a quote from Du: "War is an ugly beast that circles the world and never stops."[41]

Greenery Will Bloom Again centers on the beastlike, inhuman irrationality of war in its focus on a squad of soldiers commanded to follow through with senseless orders that are tantamount to suicide. The story likely takes place near the Austrian border, at the banks of the Isonzo river, where nearly 1.7 million Italian and Austro-Hungarian soldiers lost their lives.[42] Italy had been allies with Germany and Austria prior to 1915, when it suddenly went to war with them because of nationalistic and expansionist forces within the government.[43] However, Italian troops were not brimming with nationalistic devotion: most Italians were still tied to their local communities and traditions rather than those of the recently unified Italian state.[44] Not much effort was made to instill fighting pride in the soldiers. They were poorly equipped, their boots made of cardboard and wood, and often lacking weapons as they tried to hold their ground in makeshift trenches.[45] They were also led by a marshal, Luigi Cadorna, whose orders defied common sense. He insisted that "the superior is always right, especially when he is wrong."[46] Throughout Olmi's film, which reflects this history, the soldiers remain supportive of one another, but they have no patriotic illusions about the war or about the enemy.

The entire film takes place around and inside a snow-covered bunker held by a troop of unnamed soldiers. The fighting has halted to a standstill because of the snow. Unlike other World War I films, *Greenery Will Bloom Again* does not make use of scenes of line raids with soldiers rushing toward the enemies' trenches. Nothing demarcates either side's territory or boundaries. Rather the weather has bound the soldiers to their shelters, creating, through the confined *mise-en-scène*, a dreadful sense of ennui among the men. The film opens with a group of soldiers digging a path in the snow for the ration delivery team. The beautiful snowcapped mountains and valleys that surround the men render their entrapment in the bunker more unsettling. The soldiers often look outside longingly, at ground that does not bear the evidence of a catastrophic war. But, with one major exception, the snow neutralizes the variety of their natural surroundings, leaving the men uninspired as they grasp for hope.

In a poetic moment halfway through the film, a soldier does manage to draw inspiration from the view outside of a rifle hole. He tells a passing soldier that the daytime and nighttime animals speak to one another and also of a fox he consistently sees passing under a nearby larch tree. The passing soldier remarks that the tree looks unhealthy, but his companion rejects the observation by describing larches' singular trait of taking on a golden color during autumn. The passing soldier departs saying, "If only it were gold." And as the remaining soldier continues to stare out at the tree, it temporarily lights up, adopting a golden hue in a break from the rest of the film's drab, desaturated colors. The tree, though shorn of leaves, carries a promise of a brighter day. The idea of daytime and nighttime animals speaking to one another celebrates the natural harmony that exists outside and nurtures hope for reconciliation among opposing forces. Yet the soldier's sublime vision is shattered when the Austrians shell the bunker and the larch lights up in a blaze. An outspoken environmentalist by this point of his career, in this scene Olmi restates his exasperation with humanity's determination to destroy itself and nature along with it. The soldier who witnessed the tree's illumination, now stares blankly ahead, hopeless and helpless.

In a scene that pulls *Greenery Will Bloom Again* into the tradition of World War I films, from Renoir's *La grande illusion* (*Grand Illusion*, 1937) to Spielberg's *War Horse* (2011) and Peter Jackson's *They Shall Not Grow Old* (2018), that accurately represents occasional moments of camaraderie between soldiers on opposing sides of the conflict, one of the Italian soldiers, a Neapolitan, initially refuses to permit the bleak situation and surroundings to dampen his spirits.[47] As the ration team make their way up the mountain to the Italians, the Neapolitan, looking to the mountain under the sky for stimulation, serenades all of the valley with a song praising the beauty of the moon. When he concludes, the unseen Austrian-Hungarian soldiers applaud him in Italian with thick accents. He then asks them, in

A golden larch gives a soldier of *Greenery Will Bloom Again* hope until it catches fire during a battle (2014, RAI Cinema).

the Neapolitan dialect, why they cannot all sing together, proclaiming that songs are more powerful than bullets in reaching the heart. The Austrians do not join him but encourage an encore and he obliges. We never see them, nor hear them, after this incident.

As the film draws to a close, the bunker has nearly been completely destroyed and the Neapolitan soldier stares again at the moon from the rubble of the dugout. The lieutenant (Alessandro Sperduti), who has been promoted to provisional captain, orders the Neapolitan to sing again but the soldier refuses, explaining that he cannot sing when his heart is unhappy. Along with his refusal, although subtle, the regional distinctions in their Italian also marks the deficiency of national pride among the Italian soldiers. Without a unifying national pride, the soldiers recognize they have no reason for dying miserably in these mountains away from their families and trying to kill other men also likely feeling indifferent about the nationalistic purposes of the war.

The Italians' immediate superiors are unable to conceal their own disenchantment with their situation. When the major (Claudio Santamaria) arrives at the bunker with the lieutenant to issue a directive to the bunker's troop, he finds that the troop's captain (Francesco Formichetti) has fallen ill with a flu-induced fever. The captain forewarns his superior that because the flu has infected half of his men, they will not succeed in holding their position over the next few days. Although the major and captain are friends and embrace one another while asking about each other's families, the captain deduces that his friend has not made this visit to exchange pleasantries. Indeed, the major reports that division headquarters have identified a set of ruins from an intercepted map that they want the troop to occupy with a new outpost and communication line. The captain contends that this is a suicide mission ordered by people in an office who are ignorant about the conditions of the terrain, but he is reminded of the consequences he will face if he refuses to obey orders.

When the major enlists two men to serve as runners, the first is shot immediately after he begins his mission and the second places a rifle under his chin and commits suicide to avoid dying outside. The captain then renounces his position because he is unwilling to send any more of his men out to be killed. While the stronghold awaits a new captain, the major promotes the young lieutenant, under protest, to the newly vacated role. Unlike Giovanni in *The Profession of Arms*, none of these soldiers hold delusions about their occupation as soldiers. The men, not even in the presence of those carelessly sending them to their deaths, are hopeless, knowing that they face imminent death either by following orders or for disobeying them for a cause they have no commitment to.

Anticipating a raid, the sergeant (Domenico Benetti) suggests that they line all the men up at the edges of the dugout at the rifle holes. Regrettably, instead of attacking with a raid, the Austro-Hungarians bombard the shelter again, this time destroying the perimeter of the bunker where the soldiers have assembled. Many of the men die in the assault and the sergeant weeps, blaming himself for the losses suffered. Desperate to assign some kind of meaning to their misery, some of the men turn to God while others curse him. As the healthy soldiers tend to the wounded, one of the men prays over those who have fallen, spurring the response of another soldier that God can hide now and that no one knows where to find him, not even the pope. The God-fearing soldier replies that "God is wherever you look for him," but his companion is dismissive. "God didn't listen to his son on the cross. Why would he listen to us?" In a review of the film in the Roman Catholic daily, *Avvenire*, the reviewer likens the soldiers in this scene to Job, noting their affinity with the biblical figure's own bewilderment as to why he was so harshly afflicted.[48] Olmi is consistent in making his characters primarily responsible for their agency, and insisting that they cannot blame God for their own or others' decisions. By allowing God's conceivable intercession in events that do not require human agency, as with the widow Runk's cow in *The Tree of Wooden Clogs* and the stirring vision of the glowing larch experienced by the soldier earlier in this film, Olmi's cinema concedes that God may exist but that the desolation and injustice that Olmi's films depict are only preventable by human action, transferring responsibility to his characters and to us.

Part of this responsibility lies in recognizing the humanity of the soldiers. Often in Olmi's films, the director chooses to leave many of the characters nameless, but in *Greenery Will Bloom Again*, this tactic takes on additional significance through a specific character who accentuates the neglected individualities of the soldiers. Along with the rations that arrive at the beginning of the film, a sack of letters arrives and a soldier calls out names as some of the men eagerly grab their mail. However, one soldier, credited as *Il dimenticato* (Niccolò Senni) or the forgotten one, stands aside the mail caller, staring desperately at the envelopes as they are flipped through, waiting to hear his name. We do not encounter this character again until after the shelling.

Near the film's conclusion, looking outside of a peep hole, the forgotten one hears the wind batter against the bunker's wreckage and calls out to see if anyone is there. After a series of shots transitioning between the scorched snow outside and reaction shots of the soldier's face through the peep hole, we hear a soldier calling out names again to deliver mail and a cut returns us to the forgotten one standing alone, facing the right side of the screen. Then, following a close-up shot of the mail being thumbed through, the film mirrors a shot from the earlier mail call scene, tracking across a line of men waiting to hear their name. But in this instance, no one answers, and as the names continue to be read out the film cuts to a close-up of the forgotten one's distraught face. The deliveryman ceases to call out the names and another cut returns to the long, profile shot of the forgotten one. This time he sets his rifle against the wall, takes off his helmet, turns and addresses the camera. He then recounts a story of his lover, who has not even sent him a postcard, that he found in bed with another man during his first leave in six months of service. One of Olmi's peripheral figures, the forgotten one's story and speech to the camera are pleas to redeem him and the other forgotten soldiers from obscurity, to prevent others from becoming indistinguishable names among a list of fallen soldiers.

In the film's closing moments, two other soldiers appeal to us as they look into the camera, both repeating the forgotten one's petition to be remembered. The first is the provisional captain, who reads aloud a letter to his mother explaining to her the trauma that soldiers like him will have experienced when they return home. In an extended close-up, he tremblingly voices his concern that veterans will be unable to forgive, expecting that the war will rob them of their humanity. Between the provisional captain's letter and the next soldier's address to the viewer, Olmi splices in documentary footage marking the stages of the war, progressing from battle scenes to medics hauling away the wounded from the battlefield and then to enthusiastic crowds welcoming soldiers home. But the last of these images, before we return to the shelter, is of a broken cross barely standing above an unmarked grave that sets the stage for a somber entreaty from the original captain's attendant. He reminds us that the grass will grow again over the battleground and none of the events or suffering that occurred there will seem real, implying that the history of this tragic farce will be completely ignored and forgotten.

Olmi commemorates World War I by reminding us of the individual lives that were taken, beckoning us to imagine the nameless individuals of the film as real individuals when its characters turn to us for compassion. The idea that those who are unable to forgive lose their humanity suggests that societies continue a perpetually destructive cycle when they refuse to examine the historic tensions that precipitate wars. Like Olmi's other history films, *Greenery Will Bloom Again* endeavors to make history palpable, to make its significance on the present relatable. These films tag the perennial systems and abuses that have reappeared in different forms over time to prevent individuals from living self-directed lives. In three of these films, Olmi highlights that one of the ways in which those in power at the national and local levels have historically prohibited self-directed lives is through their staking of claims on the natural world. In *The Scavengers*, *The Tree of Wooden Clogs*, and *Greenery will Bloom Again*, nature elicits hope in the individual in the potential for a better life or the promise of a peaceful existence, though the characters are eventually cut off from it by those in authority or by the direction of society. We will now turn to Olmi's fables and parables, featuring protagonists that occasionally succeed in escaping the governance of entities representing such authorities.

5

Exemplary Realities
Olmi's Fables and Parables

Since its development as a medium, the cinema has featured fairy tale and fable films that have sought to engage with the less fantastic worlds of their audiences. As Kristian Moen confirms, many early film theorists, filmmakers, and stars "engaged with the potentials of cinema to show fairy tales and transformation in ways that resonated with a changing social and cultural sphere."[1] And this tradition has only strengthened in the medium's recent past. As many have observed, the past few decades have given rise to a profusion of fairy-tale-related films around the world, what fairy-tale scholar Jack Zipes has labeled a "cultural tsunami."[2] Zipes concludes that this "tsunami" has developed in the twenty-first century in response to "the utopian longing of audiences who need stories to help them position themselves in relation to the disturbing and relentless changes that continue to occur and threaten to engulf them."[3]

Although not discussed in any of the many books and articles scrutinizing this recent phenomenon, many of Olmi's late works have purposely sought to assist audiences in reframing their worldviews with films analogous to fairy tales that address current issues and angst from a distance with fantastic or magical settings and characters. In the last thirty years of his career, since the release of *Long Live the Lady!* in 1987, Olmi has mostly turned to fables, parables, and religious subject matter in his fictional features while continuing to magnify the bonds between individuals, their trades and nature. Luca Finatti argues that these films "enable the director to propose 'models' of humanity, ... giving form to ideals, possibly utopias."[4] The "models" Olmi's fables and parables offer are characters similar to the protagonists of Olmi's other films in the responsibility they feel toward their loved ones and families. The characters in Olmi's fables and parables certainly also experience the transformations central to the genre, but as usual, the director is most interested in transforming his audience's conceptions of reality and of how they live in their environments. In the conclusion of these films, the characters often make critical decisions that reflect their moral progression. Although these conclusions follow in the tradition of literary fairy tales, fables and parables by featuring morals, the films do not promote them as uniform solutions. The morals are often imprecise and certainly not Aesopian.

As with his earlier films, such conclusions epitomize Olmi's stated artistic objectives to have his viewers take responsibility for the realities they perceive from the screen. "The public wants to evade reality because any reality portrayed on the screen demands that the spectator take responsibility for it.... Most films subvert culture because they encourage evasion of responsibility. In my view, society must be made of responsible men, for those who do not take responsibility for their own lives are ripe to be led by a dictator."[5] This is a commitment to achieve the ideal of a Bazinian "total cinema." As with his other films, Olmi has shaped his fables and parables to leave them open to personal interpretation. He has shared that he is partial to fables and parables because "[they] are a way to understand reality by extracting it from its context and making everything emblematic. [They] condense all the knots, texture, everything that is hidden in real life. [They] are formed from exemplary realities."[6] These films venture beyond the strictures of realism in the Italian present and past toward romantic visions of China, Paris, and fantastic Italian locales set in indefinite eras, all bearing a mysterious aura slightly askew from the real world. Olmi's fairy tale related films delve into these settings, not as an escape from reality, but as a way to engage with it, our environments and a moral examination of our lives.

Although as early as 1983, with *Keep Walking*, Olmi moved away from realism, his true shift toward fables and parables occurred after he was struck with a severe neurological disease, Guillain-Barré syndrome, in June 1984 that completely paralyzed him for a brief period and prohibited him from operating a camera in the future.[7] A project he had been nurturing based on his childhood memories of Milan during World War II, that would later transform into his only novel, *Il ragazzo della Bovisa*, fell through and Olmi began to wonder if his filmmaking career was over.[8] Eager to prove his abilities while he was recovering, he sat at his typewriter and produced the story that would become *Long Live the Lady*.[9] The illness brought Olmi to a contemplation of his life and his career decisions, including his time working in the Edisonvolta offices as a clerk before he became a filmmaker, the same experiences which inspired *Il posto*.[10] Many have commented on the film's resemblances to Olmi's second film, including the director himself who has gone so far as to call *Long Live the Lady!* a remake of the earlier work.[11] The film's protagonist, Libenzio (Marco Esposito), shares with *Il posto*'s Domenico a quiet, observing demeanor, both characters unsure of what to make of all the rules and regulations of

5. Exemplary Realities 115

the life-crushing institutions and systems that have them in their grasps. Several moments in *Long Live the Lady!* are directly lifted from the earlier film, such as the scene when the six tenderfoot attendants anxiously await instructions from a head waiter, which reproduces the awkward moment in *Il posto* when Domenico and other young people stare at one another in expectation of a company supervisor. The institutions at the heart of both films terrify us through their potential to stifle life out of the workers. But in the later film, Olmi has transformed the representation of this subjugation into a weighty allegory, symbolizing the snares societies set to entrap individuals into conditioned roles.

Nearly the entirety of the film takes place inside of a remote castle, naturally eliciting comparisons to Kafka's unfinished novel, *Das Schloss* (*The Castle*), in its setting's metaphor for an absurd, untouchable power structure.[12] From the outset, *Long Live the Lady!* immediately primes us to approach it with a discerning eye, ready to decrypt its weighty symbols. When the opening credits roll across the opening sequence, a subtitled note informs us that "events and persons in this film are not all imaginary," playfully indicating that we should feel free to see the operations of any power structure we wish in the ridiculous banquet for the powerful that will be held at the castle.

The film begins in nearly the same narrative position as *Il posto*, with Libenzio and five classmates, two boys and two girls, at the crossing-point of assimilating themselves into the working world. They have just arrived in a foreign and unfamiliar location to commence their new lives. A jeep, full of food for an illustrious dinner, and with the lady's (Sandra Sabbatini) throne affixed to its roof, transports the young people from a nearby train station to the castle's gated estate. As the vehicle pulls up to the castle's entrance, the driver directs the waiters to find out where they are wanted, initiating the increasing confusion they will experience as they seek to make sense of the castle's workings and its unspoken guidelines. After a grouchy superior spots them and separates the boys from the girls, the camera reinforces the austere, prison-like qualities of the setting by framing one of the boy's apprehensive glances toward his girlfriend through barred windows.

The grim air of the castle and the brusque treatment they receive from their new bosses leave the new waiters intimidated and uncertain of what to expect from their new employer. As they are taken to room after room to await instructions from a head waiter, who will eventually expound upon the honor of serving as an attendant, the young people try to convince themselves that they are somewhat fortunate to work at the castle. After their usher finally escorts them to see their supervisor, the camera momentarily rests with her as she wipes a tear from her eye, as if she feels guilty for acting as an accomplice to the fate that now awaits these young people.

While the neophyte workers stand at attention and watch the head waiter finish listening to a piece of music on the other side of the room, the film uses its first flashback. Unlike many of Olmi's other non-linear works, the time shifts that occur in this film are only flashbacks and do not mix in possible or imagined futures. The tick-tock sound from a clock in the head waiter's room and the sight of Christ's nailed feet from a crucifix on the wall sparks a childhood memory in Libenzio. A child's voice quietly chanting "tick-tock" accompanies a graphic match cut to a classroom where an elementary school-age Libenzio sits rubbing his feet, the cut matching Christ's feet with the feet of the boy. Libenzio moves his shoes against a bar under his chair in time with the ticking of the clock. He lays his head against his wristwatch to listen to its ticking. As he whisperingly repeats its noise, his teacher looks at him and hisses "silence," and the child, astounded, sits up and stares back at the teacher before the film returns to the head waiter's room. The memory initiates the film's allusions to the methods utilized by societies to maintain hegemony through inseminating perpetually subordinated identities into individuals from childhood.

A few moments later, following the head waiter's insistence on the dignity of their profession, we see Libenzio and his friends at a training school for waiters, watching slides of various opulent table settings. In another flashback later in the film, we return to the school and watch an instructor reviewing the many pieces of a table setting and the exact order in which the waiters should place them. The school's firm instructions on how to behave as a waiter play over a montage sequence of the waiters disobeying these guidelines and either quickly correcting themselves or being punished, as in one instance when the instructor commands them not to blow their noses in the dining hall and a folding wall encloses upon Libenzio when he disregards the rule. The instructor's recitation of these rules transitions into a scene at a church where a priest reminds Libenzio, as a child, and a group of other children, not to commit impure acts. The same priest makes another appearance in a separate flashback after the waiters at the castle are asked to give their names. Libenzio stands in front of the other children and the priest explains that the boy's name derives from the Latin word "libare" or "to toast," signifying that he is a bringer of "nectars and libations," as if he was fated to serve the gods or those superior to him. The symbolic implications of these scenes are easily applicable to the way many hegemonic systems reinforce class status in individuals from childhood, their adult educations and into their careers. The system figuratively threatens to exterminate Libenzio, as in the scene when the wall closes in on him, if he seeks to emerge from his predetermined caste as a servant

5. Exemplary Realities 117

to the powerful or break their rules of decorum. This type of sequence is what leads Marcia Landy to classify Olmi as a Gramscian filmmaker in his frequent outlining of the social conditions of the world for a discerning audience.[13] These scenes reflect Libenzio's journey into a critical awareness of the cultural influences that have guided his path and exemplify how we can also thoughtfully interpret how similar forces have affected our own situations.

Libenzio first becomes conscious of a means of escape from his life of servitude and the castle when a supervisor asks him to gather liquor cages from a cellar pantry. After grabbing a pair of cages, he spots a waiter's bowtie on the ground. Before he can investigate it further, his supervisor calls out to him wondering why he is taking so long. After his supervisor reprimands him, he asks Libenzio to fetch more of the cages. But when Libenzio returns to the pantry, the bowtie has vanished, its outline visible in the dirt. Perplexed by its disappearance, he searches the room and spots a locked door, placed a few feet above ground level, behind the cages. Although the culprit left no traces behind, it appears as if someone quickly gathered the bowtie to conceal clues of a possible escape route.

Libenzio keeps the possible exit in mind as he and the other waiters prepare for the banquet in honor of the lady. The lady and her guests are all mysterious figures. Their names and titles are not known but a loudspeaker informs the help preparing for the evening's events that the dinner's attendees are "illustrious figures from the financial, political, scientific, and cultural worlds." They are a multiracial and multinational group, decked out in fine apparel and representing the international elite class of global decision makers. They all appear accustomed to the rituals of the banquet, something that evidently occurs regularly as inferred from their comments about their assigned positions at the table "this time." None of their relationships to the lady are made clear. Nothing about the guests, the strange rituals associated with the dinner, and the reason for its, or the lady's, importance is shared with us or the waiters. David Shipman suggests, because of Olmi's gentle ribbing of the castle's host and guests that he "clearly loathes," that the film and its meal are most clearly inspired by Buñuel, "whose film on a dinner party was teeming with detail, not always scabrous."[14] It is unclear which film Shipman references, as several of the Spanish director's films (*El ángel exterminador* [*The Exterminating Angel*, 1962], *Le charme discret de la bourgeoisie* [*The Discreet Charm of the Bourgeoisie*, 1972] and *Le fantôme de la liberté* [*The Phantom of Liberty*, 1974]) prominently feature lavish meals. In any case, Olmi, who rarely includes the ruling and wealthy classes in significant roles in his features, does seem to have been influenced by Buñuel in his own visual characterization of the absurd formality of upper class eating habits.[15] In *Long Live the Lady!* and Buñuel's films mentioned above, the dinners are ridiculous farces, devoid of any real meaning, except to those who seek to solidify their social standing. However, Olmi expresses much less acrimony toward the diners in his film. Buñuel's dinners offer him the chance to lampoon the wealthy, whereas for Olmi the dinner chiefly serves as a microcosm of the world that Libenzio longs to escape from.

As the staff wait for the final preparations to be completed, the cooks' boisterous swearing rings from the kitchen (where they boil a monstrous Fellinian fish and prepare other odd dishes) into the dining hall. When a senior member of staff chastises them, the cooks abuse him with some creative profanity about his sister. The cooks, like the young waiters, show signs of vitality and freedom absent from everyone else at the castle. They have yet to submit themselves to the castle's rigorous code of conduct, which noticeably has a hold on the majority of older characters.

The banquet previews the pettiness of the adult world through its demanding set of rules. Once the head staff have deemed the dining hall ready, they allow the guests to enter the room and stand behind their designated chairs to await the lady's arrival. Several of the guests feel insulted by their positions at the table and one even has the audacity to move his seat and refuse the senior staff's entreaties for him to return to his allotted chair. Another guest failed to show up and because the lady does not tolerate unoccupied seats, one of the servants, to the chagrin of the attendees, removes his gloves, dons a pair of glasses and fills a chair at the table. The rules also dictate that babies and children cannot attend the dinner. The staff detains them in a room with nannies and clowns who struggle to meet the needs of their charges. A huge Neapolitan mastiff, Grifo, rests outside of the children's room, apparently to frighten the kids into staying put. The parents themselves refuse to leave the dinner to attend to their children because they fear making a bad impression, even when one baby shows signs of a fever.

Any threat to order is unwelcome in the hall, the unruliness of youth seemingly most of all. When the lady finally joins the dinner party, we understand why. She is an old woman fitted in black from head to toe with a dark veil over her face. She makes no facial gestures, does not consume any food, speaks to no one, and looks at her guests through a small pair of binoculars. To communicate with her guests, an elderly man constantly stands at her side and somehow interprets her desires and thoughts for the guests and staff. She is death personified, entirely deficient of feeling and energy. Libenzio's gaze wrests itself away from the ghastly sight of the lady and rests on a beautiful, young red-headed woman. The sight of the girl evokes childhood memories in Libenzio of a painting featuring an angel in a field playing with children. The girl's presence at the banquet, and Libenzio's association of her with the innocence of his beloved childhood angel,

5. *Exemplary Realities* 119

abates his anxiety about the dinner and his new position. As the possibility of a romance with Antonietta made office life more endurable for Domenico in *Il posto*, a similar hope carries Libenzio through most of the evening.

Eager to distract themselves from the dullness of the meal (which lasts for nearly fifty minutes of screen time) while the lady stares them down with her binoculars, the guests comment on the slightest variations in the behavior of those sitting around the table, or occasionally exaggerate the qualities of the unappetizing dishes placed before them. They exchange remarks on the simpleton who wears a white breastplate and on another man caught stealing a table decoration from the person seated next to him. The guest who attracts the most attention is the belligerent diner who refused to comply with the seating arrangements. He has seated himself on the end of one of the arms of the u-shaped table, away from his original position next to the lady at the table's center. He plays with his food, flirts with the married woman seated to his right, blows smoke rings and then extinguishes his cigarette in his soup, and even sticks his tongue out at the lady. He is the sole attendee to show signs of subversion toward the lady and challenge the lifelessness of the banquet. But his demonstrations of rebellion prove to be just for show, as he ultimately bows respectfully to the lady and accepts her invitation to visit her that night following the dinner. Despite its meaningless and vapid formality, the attendees exhibit no actual signs of wanting to break away from the event because merely being in the presence of the lady grants them at least the semblance of power.

Before the waiters serve dessert, a lengthy intermission pauses the proceedings; there is a wordless, abstract video presentation of what appears to be a business report. The servants retreat to the hallway to take a break as electronic beeps, matching the movement of graphs and charts in the video, echo through the dining room. During this recess, one of the staff notices through a security camera that an unexpected work van has pulled up outside of the castle. Libenzio's father (Alberto Francescato) has come to greet his son. The supervisor grants two minutes to the waiter to visit at the foot of the castle. Libenzio, who has barely opened his mouth during the entire film, remains tightlipped with his father. A quick flashback hints at the reason for their reticence to interact warmly with one another. At a graveyard scene, Libenzio's father declares that the boy will now live with his grandmother (Giovanna Vidotto), indicating that Libenzio's mother died during his childhood. The flashback then moves to a meal at the grandmother's home as she instructs her grandson how to say his prayers and cross himself properly, information that the boy's father mockingly dismisses as only fit for those who wish to enter the priesthood.

This flashback, the earlier memory motivated by seeing Christ's feet and Libenzio's fervent interest in the angel from the painting, all suggest that Libenzio was possibly diverted from a career in the church. Besides feeling abandoned by his only remaining parent, his belief that he was coerced into abandoning a vocation that he was naturally inclined to explains Libenzio's resentment toward his father. As they visit at the castle, the father does not hide that he has only stopped by because he was in the area and he was reminded by Libenzio's grandmother to go see his son. Although not completely without parental figures, in many ways Libenzio fulfills the role of the orphan in folk tales and children's literature who, as Melanie A. Kimball writes, "are at once pitiable and noble. They are a manifestation of loneliness, but they also represent the possibility for humans to reinvent themselves."[16] Similar to Cinderella and other orphaned characters from fables and fairy tales, Libenzio finds himself without family or friends at the bottom of the social ladder as a servant. However, no fairy godmother comes to rescue him from his destitute life. He has to secure his own path out of the oppressive castle.

At one point during the evening, Libenzio's superiors send him back to the pantry with the liquor cages and he notices the door above them has been unlocked. Cautiously prodding open the door, he sees a garage full of vehicles with an exit out of the castle. Although he does not brave a getaway yet, two events convince him to use this escape route later. A few moments before dinner is served, the lady summons Libenzio's red-headed angel to communicate with one of her interpreters. The girl stands next to the lady, who compliments her on her beauty and tells her that nothing in life will be unobtainable to her. Libenzio watches the brief conversation and continues to stare at the girl until she exits the dinner. Immediately before she leaves, shots of the angel in the painting intersect with extreme closeups of the girl's face, leaving the impression, combined with the comments of the lady's interpreter, that she may as well be a heavenly being, inaccessible to Libenzio because of his class. As she silently departs, she returns his gaze coldly and Libenzio closes his eyes as if to dismiss from his mind all hopes he had placed in her. Without the idolized figure of the girl anchoring him to the castle, nothing deludes him about a possible happy future there.

That evening, a disturbing nightmare of several shadowy castle employees strangling him finally provokes Libenzio's flight from the castle. He quietly grabs his clothing and bags and rushes to the cellar. Someone has locked the door again but this time they left the key behind. In the process of grabbing the key from the top of the door and unlocking it, Libenzio's bowtie falls down and lands underneath one of the liquor cages, leaving a trail for a future jail-breaker. The change of scenery to the exterior of the castle provides us with a palpable sense of relief, as the flashbacks are the only sequences that have taken place beyond the castle since the waiter's arrival at the beginning of the film. Near the castle's outer walls,

Libenzio hears gun shots fire and, anxious that they may be in response to his impromptu departure (though they appear to be for a hunting party), he quickens his step and scurries into the forest. Dashing in between trees, he hears a dog barking in pursuit. In a clearing, Grifo the mastiff catches up to Libenzio. Hopeless, Libenzio yells for help, calling out to his mother, and throws his bags and himself on the ground before curling into the fetal position. But instead of pouncing on the boy, the dog lays down next to him. Libenzio lifts his head and after observing the dog's submissive manner, pets him. A final subtitled note closes the film, in the spirit of happily ever after, confirming that the dog did not bite the boy and was just waiting for Libenzio to run again so that they could play together.

In comparison with *Il posto*, *Long Live the Lady!* closes on a much more optimistic note, albeit just as inconclusive and directed toward interactive responses. The conclusion mimics the happily ever after coda, but its effect is not equivalent. Libenzio has broken free from a life of thankless, menial work, but he has not ended up with the red-headed girl from the castle, nor does he have a stable direction for the future. At the conclusion, Olmi also uses the common feature of fairy tales, fables and parables of providing symbolic obstacles (e.g., the dog, and the castle in this film) that, through fear of them, naturally suffocate ideas of confronting them. Like the dog, a figure representing society's enforcers, these seemingly unconquerable symbols prove malleable to human will when fear and other emotional and mental impediments. are subdued.

In *The Legend of the Holy Drinker*, obstacles emblematizing guilt and regret thwart the attainment of spiritual peace. Although the eponymous holy drinker Andreas Kartak (Rutger Hauer) never completely overcomes his vices (alcoholism, lust, slovenliness, etc.) and his feelings about the events that have shaped his destitute life, Olmi does not condemn Andreas for his shortcomings, nor does he cause us to question Andreas's honorable intentions and devotion. It is a redemption story, but one that is about the attainment of personal redemption rather than seeking forgiveness from peers or society. If he does seek forgiveness from God, it is only by arriving at a reckoning of his life in which he reaches a state of "perfection" in the beatitudinal sense, in which he learns to love himself and others.[17]

Olmi reports that when he read the story, Joseph Roth's novella resonated with his mood at the time.[18] While in physical therapy in Sabaudia recovering from the neurological disease that paralyzed him, and writing the script for *Long Live the Lady!*, Olmi was approached by film producer Roberto Cicutto to adapt Joseph Roth's novella about the last weeks in a soul-searching, alcoholic, homeless man's life.[19] The production would be atypical for Olmi and resolutely confirmed that the director was moving in a new direction from the fiction films he made prior to his illness. There are several specific features that immediately mark this shift in the film on its surface. It was the first of Olmi's works to be shot completely abroad, filmed in Paris at many of the specific locations identified in Roth's novella. Furthermore, Olmi had previously only worked with one major star, Rod Steiger, in *A Man Named John*. In *The Legend of the Holy Drinker*, Olmi casts four major international actors (Hauer, Anthony Quayle, and French actors Dominique Pinon and Sandrine Dumas) and gave the film an additional sheen by recruiting from Hollywood Italian émigré Dante Spinotti as his cinematographer (who also shot Olmi's next feature, *The Secret of the Old Woods*).[20] Only one of these changes became a permanent characteristic of Olmi's future work (most of Olmi's late works feature professional actors in lead roles), but they all denoted a stark contrast with the films that defined his career in the 1960s and 1970s.

The Paris of *The Legend of the Holy Drinker* is itself fanciful and lends a fable-like tone to the city of Roth's novella. Roth, an Austro-Hungarian Jew, exiled himself to Paris in the early 1930s, making it his home before he died of alcoholism just days after completing *The Legend of the Holy Drinker* in 1939. For the author, the city's cosmopolitanism appealed to his divided identity as both a Jew and Austrian and even his interest in Catholicism.[21] Olmi's film retains this sense of cosmopolitanism, but additionally renders the city magically atemporal, similar in some ways to the city of Woody Allen's *Midnight in Paris* (2011). The novella is set in 1939, but Olmi's Paris fuses elements ranging from the early 1900s to the 1980s. For example, Andreas rides contemporary subways, but he and the majority of the characters wear pre–World War II clothes. Moreover, the bars he visits and the vaudeville performances he attends have an early-twentieth-century air about them. The diegetic music of this world and of the soundtrack contribute to this temporal mélange as well. Polka music and José Padilla Sánchez's "Ça c'est Paris" ring through the film's dance halls while Stravinsky's compositions accompany other scenes. The timelessness of this Paris calls attention to some of the city's perpetually celebrated qualities, for its general open-mindedness and as a home throughout the nineteenth and twentieth centuries to émigrés like Roth and Andreas. The film's setting embraces Andreas, and its enchanted streets authorize the occurrence of the miracles and visions that direct him from pauperdom into an acceptance of himself as a virtuous individual, one worthy of beatifying himself as a saint when he dies.

To redeem himself and seal his sainthood, Andreas must pardon himself not only from the guilt he feels about his drinking and other mild indiscretions, but he must also address the regret he feels about his life and the journey that has led him to homelessness. The film introduces us to Andreas as he descends a flight of stairs to a boardwalk along the Seine.

His clothes and downtrodden bearing reveal his destitute state. His face is scruffy and pale with a touch of purple discoloring his lips. A well-dressed elderly man (Anthony Quayle) stops Andreas at the foot of the stairs and asks him in French where he is going.[22] The elderly gentleman shares his conviction that God has placed them in each other's paths. After cautiously observing that he notices Andreas has fallen on hard times, the elderly man asks how much money he can donate to help. Andreas suggests a small amount, twenty francs, but the elderly man insists on giving him 200 francs. Andreas asserts that he is a man of an honor and it would be difficult to accept such a great sum because, as a drifter, he is not easily found and would not know how he could repay his would-be benefactor. But the elderly man ignores Andreas's reluctance, while acknowledging that he is a man of honor, and stuffs the money into his shirt pocket. The elderly man then shares the story of his conversion to Christianity after reading the story of Sainte Thérèse of Lisieux, leading him to renounce his former life and humble himself by sleeping under the bridges. He asks that if Andreas feels the need to clear the debt, once he can afford to do so, that the money be given to the priest of Sainte Marie des Batignolles, which houses a small statue of Sainte Thérèse. Upon Andreas's oath that he will repay the money, the old man expresses his pleasure again in their meeting and quickly departs.

Though strange, the encounter does not initially possess a mystic quality, but as the film continues this meeting's preternatural aspects become increasingly apparent. Andreas meets his benefactor on one more occasion, though we never learn his name, nor why the story of Sainte Thérèse meant so much to him that he was willing to sacrifice everything to validate his conversion. The elderly man's mysteriousness prompts us to wonder if he may be a figment of Andreas's imagination, if the entire film is a narrative produced by Andreas's fevered mind, or if he is himself the apparition of a saint (or a manifestation of Sainte Thérèse) that incites Andreas to take an inventory of his life before he passes on. The elderly man may just have recognized in Andreas a lost soul who could have benefited from the deathbed pledge of his beloved Sainte Thérèse and acted as a proxy for her. Thomas R. Nevin contends that Thérèse (one of only three women to be awarded the title of Doctor in the Catholic Church's lengthy history due to her singular theological perspective) had an action-based spirituality, hoping to make the world her heaven, "not among her beloved family and all the saints but here, on terra firma."[23] As she was dying, she promised to do good on earth, to aid the wretched, inciting many of the adherents who read her autobiography to claim that Thérèse had performed miracles on their behalf.[24] The widespread belief in these miracles play a crucial role in the events leading to Andreas's death and atonement.

The elderly man's gift in the name of Thérèse has immediate effects, triggering Andreas's recollection of who he is and what has happened to him. Keen to keep his word to pay back the saint when he can, Andreas sets his belongings down under a nearby bridge and unpacks a tin box to fetch some paper and a writing utensil to write down Thérèse's name and the location of her statue. In doing so, he happens upon a watch that provokes memories of the object's personal significance to him. In this flashback, a sequence of Andreas's parents giving him the watch at a train station is sandwiched between shots of him sitting in front of a train window pensively looking at the watch in his hands and then outside. In later flashbacks we gather that Andreas has immigrated to France where he moved in order to find work as a miner. In most regards, Olmi closely follows the events of Roth's story, but his adaptation inserts his free-flowing time-shifting style, which alternates between memories, the present, and imagined events. This extends the novella's succinct summary of the past into opaque montage sequences that intersect with Andreas unpacking his history throughout the film. These moments extend the effects of the multi-temporal Paris of the film, engaging us in both witnessing how tragedies and failures transform Andreas over time and also in pondering how they and their enduring consequences can be confronted.

These painful recollections continue the next morning when Andreas, after spotting his disheveled face in a café mirror, treats himself to a shave. Staring into another mirror from the barber's chair, Andreas mentally returns to his arrival in Paris, fresh-faced and holding himself out of the train window with an open future in front of him. Several shots follow of Andreas greeting a woman and her husband, which ensuing flashbacks and events reveal are a couple with whom he had a close relationship that ended tragically when, defending himself, he accidently killed the husband.

The reawakening of Andreas's misfortunes is offset by non-supernatural miracles, events that initially allow him to become a functioning member of society again and to directly confront his past. Eventually, these events remind us of falling manna from heaven as they perpetually lift him back up when he is on the brink of sinking back into desperation. When he returns to the café, an obese patron (Joseph De Medina) offers him a two-day job as a mover. This fortunate incident sets Andreas temporarily on his feet again. But now that he has some money in his pocket, he is lured back to his vices. He visits his favorite bar, the Tari-Bari, inebriates himself, and finds prostitutes to satisfy his reawakened libido. But the film does not malign Andreas by sanctimoniously pitting his benefiting from charity against his buying sex or his alcoholism, nor does it separate his vices from the part of his honorable character that is resolutely determined to return the donation he received to Thérèse. Rather, these aspects of his character are intertwined with his coming to terms with his experiences and with who he is.

Because of both a renewed sense of pride and his humble appearance, even after cleaning himself up once he has left the street, Andreas goes to pains to demonstrate his qualities as an honorable man. At meals and when he drinks with friends, he consistently requests that he pays the bill or returns the favor of a drink with buying another round. But

With a smile on his face and oblivious to his future homelessness, Andreas (Rutger Hauer) looks forward to his future from a train window in a flashback from *The Legend of the Holy Drinker* (1988, Cecchi Gori Group).

he still comes up short of his goals for how he would like to be perceived by others. When he goes into a shop to buy a wallet, the shopkeeper instantly shows him cheaper, traded-in items based on his appearance. In a later scene, his boxing friend, Daniel Kanjak (Jean-Maurice Chanet), demands that Andreas accept two suits that he does not want.

He also fails to pay back the donation as soon as he can. At the time he received the funds Andreas stated his intentions to return the money on a Sunday during mass, which happens to be the day after he receives full payment for his work as a mover. He eagerly wakes up with the church bells and rushes to the church of Sainte Marie des Batignolles, but he just misses morning mass. He resolves to wait for the next mass at midday in a nearby café. He drinks several glasses of wine while waiting and then runs, stumblingly due to his drunkenness, out the door when a waiter alerts him that midday mass is beginning. But as he exits a woman passing by in a taxi calls out his name. It is Karoline (Sophie Segalen), the woman from the couple that he met after he arrived in Paris. In his drunken state, her face and voice rouse images of his time with her that have a sudden, melancholic effect on him. He tells her of his appointment with Thérèse, but she, thinking he intends to meet another woman, convinces him to break it and come with her to a restaurant so they can talk. We then see more disjointed images from their time together, silent except for Stravinsky's "Suite No. 1," that suggest, but do not detail, Andreas's tragic relationship with Karolina and her husband.

These disruptions to Andreas's plans to visit Thérèse, and his other interactions with old and new acquaintances, function as a kind of final confession before his death. But it is himself, and not a priest, who will grant absolution. In many regards the characters who interact with Andreas before his death resemble the ghosts of Dickens's *A Christmas Carol*, guiding a lost soul through different stages of time to self-realization. The flashbacks these reunions stimulate here, and in all of Olmi's cinema, operate as a reanalysis of a character's relationships with their loved ones. However, in *The Legend of the Holy Drinker* they also form a re-evaluation of Andreas's life that will eventually release him from remorse and self-loathing.

The incident with Karoline's husband weighs heavily on Andreas. She is not angry at him at all, but instead asks what he has been doing. He is forthcoming about his homelessness but stays upbeat, adding that he has started working again. They do not discuss the past, but another group of shots from the development of their affair are spliced into their dinner. A closeup of Karoline's face that concludes the temporal interlude is followed by a matching shot at the restaurant that highlights her transformation. She not only bears no grudges toward Andreas because of the inadvertent death of her husband, but she appears content and much better off financially then she was before. In medium shots of them at the table, *chiaroscuro* lighting divides the frame and Andreas is isolated in darkness on the left, and on the other side of the table Karoline sits bathed in light from the window, dressed in white. The *mise-en-scène* implies that Karoline is an angelic figure, presenting herself as a guide to lead Andreas out of the darkness.

Andreas is willing to confront the trauma and the hardship his affair with Karoline has caused him but spending the evening with her uneasily dancing and making love, and how she has apparently moved past the tragedy, does not release him from the pain of his memories. The next morning, while riding toward the Tari-Bari bar on the metro, his mind races back to the death of Karoline's husband. He then wastes the entire day drinking and heads back under his bridge to spend the night. His inability to shake himself from his past arrests his rehabilitation.

A nighttime visit from Thérèse (Dalila Belatreche) as a child renews his commitment to the saint and to lifting himself out of the gutter. Andreas opens the used wallet he purchased a few days earlier and finds a thousand francs inside. Exchanging the money for smaller notes in a bar, he spots a poster featuring a former friend and classmate, Daniel Kanjak, who has become a champion boxer. Andreas easily tracks down Kanjak, who kindly pays for a hotel room for his old friend when he discovers Andreas is homeless. After they spend the night out on the town, Andreas cheerfully enjoys the luxuries of the hotel that embolden his pursuit of a beautiful young dancer, Gaby (Sandrine Dumas), sleeping in the room next door. After waking up next to her, Andreas has a fantasy of another life, where he,

5. Exemplary Realities 127

well-groomed and in fine clothes, lifts a glass to her after a performance. Wearing a new suit gifted to him by Kanjak, Andreas acts out his dream for a day, passing hours away frivolously together with Gaby, riding in carriages around the city and carelessly philandering. But sadly, when the next Sunday morning arrives, he realizes that she has pickpocketed the remainder of his money and he is again unable to pay his debt.

Even in the otherworldly settings of his fables and parables romance is rarely allowed to blossom in Olmi's cinema, and when it does it is often fleeting and never serves as a solution to the characters' predicaments. For Andreas, the relationship with the dancer in particular acts as a distraction to his redemption because of its basis in material abundance. Gaby's reaction to his confession that he needs to pay someone back is to look through his coat and steal his money and then to beat him when he mentions his debt is to some girl named Thérèse. Her attraction to Andreas stems from her misconception that he is a man of means. She shows no signs of interest in his emotional and spiritual state nor in helping him relieve himself of the pain from his past.

Sitting in the café across from the church after learning that he has been robbed, Andreas finds 200 francs that he had set aside in the small envelope on which he wrote Thérèse's name. Though he has no other money, as the bells call for mass to commence he exits the café for the church. However, a former co-worker and friend, Woitech (Dominique Pinon), walks into him just outside of the door and a warm embrace gives way to memories of earlier, happier times together. Woitech accompanies Andreas inside the church, but he begs his friend to lend him the francs meant for Thérèse so that he can pay off a loan shark. Because of Andreas's love for his friend, he does not upbraid Woitech for lying to him when his friend buys several glasses of wine and funds a rowdy night at the Tari-Bari.

During an intense rainstorm in the morning, broke once more and near the bridge he sleeps under, Andreas is approached again and offered more money by the elderly gentleman who originally lent him 200 francs. Andreas details the efforts he has made to pay his debt to Thérèse, but the man insists he does not recognize Andreas and hands him another 200 francs. Cold and wet, Andreas bunkers down for the rest of the day and the evening in the Tari-Bari to wait out the storm. As the evening wears on, his face takes on a purple tinge and his eyes become baggy as the effects of a rapidly developing illness take their toll. Drunk and suffering from sickness, he notices an elderly couple that have also taken shelter in the bar. At one point, falling in and out of sleep, Andreas looks up and the elderly couple have metamorphosed into his parents. He tearfully stares at them, and they return his gaze, as he holds out his hand offering them the watch they gave him when he left home. Their interaction is cut short when Andreas wakes up once more and the elderly couple have vanished. Realizing it is Sunday morning again, Andreas gathers his things but leaves penniless after the bar owner demands payment of his tab.

Perhaps with the faith that another miracle will materialize and he will finally be able to give Thérèse her money, Andreas, still ill, breathlessly dashes to the church but arrives again just as mass is concluding. Despondent, he begins to walk away from the church before a policeman places his hand on his shoulder. The sight of the policeman prompts a flashback, which informs us that Andreas has previously been expelled from France and that he illegally remains in the country. But instead of asking for his documents, the policeman hands him a wallet that he believes Andreas dropped as he ran. Andreas walks into the café and is in the process of explaining to Woitech the incredibly good fortune that just befell him when he assumes that he sees Thérèse, in the form of the girl who appeared to him under the bridge, in the café. Although also named Thérèse, the girl explains that she is just waiting for her parents to finish mass. Andreas kneels before her, tearfully expressing his astonishment that she has come to him even though he has failed to visit her so many times. The girl refuses his money and offers him the little pocket change she has on hand before dismissing herself to meet her parents.

When the girl departs, Andreas collapses and Woitech, a bartender, and a couple of men in the café determine from Andreas's appearance that he is dying. They carry him into the sacristy of the church where the priests and altar boys change clothes. They place him on a throne in the middle of the room and everyone reverently stands around him in a circle. A point-of-view shot from the throne catches sight of Thérèse peeking into the room, preceding a reverse shot of Andreas desperately holding out the 200 francs to her as he closes his eyes and dies. The film then fades to black and the novella's final lines appear on the screen to close the film: "May God grant us all, all of us drinkers, such a good and easy death!"[25]

Recompensing Thérèse, Andreas absolves himself at death of a debt that epitomizes the disappointments of his life and his methods of coping with the pain they caused him. The film alludes to the spiritual magnitude of the debt through a series of emblematic figures and events (the elderly man, Thérèse, Andreas's watch, the chain of "miracles" and the resurgence of his past through uncanny meetings with former friends) that Olmi urges us to disentangle in relation to assessments of ourselves. Olmi yokes our readings of the film and the piecing together of his time-shifting style to our interpretations of these symbols and our ability to empathize with Andreas through our own remorse. Finatti contends that the girl Thérèse and the elderly man are incarnations of God that summon Andreas back to a righteous path.[26] If this is true, God does not infringe upon Andreas's responsibility and right to survey his life and judge it himself. And in this respect, Andreas is Olmi's ideal character. As with the protagonists of Olmi's other fables and parables, Andreas exemplifies Olmi's romanticist philosophy of the necessity of individuals developing their own appraisals, rather than their societies, of God, of their moral standing, and of the value of their lives and work.

Another of these characters in Olmi's next film, *The Secret of the Old Woods*, also experiences a transformation of his existential perspective. However, in this instance, it is in relation to his views on the purpose and vital significance of the natural world. Although the source novel by Dino Buzzati follows the generic conventions of fairy tales and fables set in the forest, intrinsically marveling at the seemingly mysterious and magical woods of the story, Olmi brings environmental concerns to the story's forefront. Through the film's frequent, reflective shots of the breathtaking scenery, filmed in the Dolomite mountain range in northeastern Italy, of Colonel Procolo's (Paolo Villaggio) inherited tract of land, Olmi urges us to experience nature and evaluate its importance. Olmi's frequent highlighting of the non-human world in the film implements one of the "approaches" of ecocinema, as described by Paula Willoquet-Maricondi, by "contemplative[ly] ... foster[ing] an appreciation for ecosystems and all of nature's constituents—air, water, earth, and organisms."[27]

Buzzati and Olmi had been working on developing a science-fiction film together in the early 1970s that was repeatedly shelved while the director worked on other projects. But in the 1990s, many years after Buzzati's death, Olmi settled on adapting one of the author's novels that touched on some of the same themes of the earlier work.[28] While casting the film, he deliberated on having Marcello Mastroianni, who had long wished to work with him, fill the lead role but finally gave the part of the colonel to Paolo Villaggio. Retrospectively, Olmi regretted the decision because he felt that Villaggio was more of a "mask," "like [Roberto] Benigni," than an actor like Mastroianni.[29] Despite Olmi's misgivings, Villaggio gives an understated performance that highlights the absurdities of the colonel's conceited belief that the forest is his to exploit as he sees fit. Villaggio was beloved in Italy for the ten films centered on his comic creation Ugo Fantozzi, described by Peter Bondanella as "the ultimate obsequious underling ... who cannot accomplish anything without cutting an embarrassing, pathetic figure."[30] In *The Secret of the Old Woods*, Villaggio plays against the submissive persona of Fantozzi in his portrayal of the colonel as an obdurate authority figure, evocative of the Fascists in power when Buzzati wrote the novel. But he still cuts a droll, ridiculous figure, having his orders and pride constantly undermined by the animals and the spirits of the woods. Villaggio's performance allows the film to forego a sentimentalized climax in which the colonel would come to a dramatic realization that he has abused nature. The colonel does see the error of his ways in the film's closing moments, but because of Villaggio's restrained portrayal this faint transformation leaves us reflecting on what specifically led the colonel to change his heart.

Refraining from following the characters' trains of thought and without spending much time affixed to the unspectacular activities filling everyday lives, *The Secret of the Old Woods* seems like one of Olmi's most conventional films. But the reduced focus on the humans and their social responsibilities and positions complements the eco-centered structure of the work and its redemption of the natural world. The film's frequent, poetic use of shots of wooded mountains and misty valleys, and its personification of trees and animals, consistently reminds us of the non-human life that makes up the world. From its outset, the film treats the old woods as a collective entity, a character with its own temperament, needs, and desires.

The film commences with a ceremony in front of a mansion in the forest, honoring the recently deceased cavalier Morro and his respect for the woods surrounding his home by unveiling a statue of him carved from a fir tree. Morro would not authorize anyone to cut down trees or to profane the area that means so much to the local villagers, and yet the official leading the event states that the choice to carve the cavalier's image out of a tree was made to memorialize Morro's unification with the forest. But Morro is not pleased with the blasphemy that has been carried out in his name and an approaching thunderstorm expresses his displeasure from beyond the grave, forcing the ceremony's attendees to rush back home. Following shots of mist weaving through the forests of the Dolomites, we hear Morro pronounce his own wishes for his estate. His synthesis with the woods and the surrounding area assists in establishing the natural world as a character, although following this introduction the forest's other inhabitants express themselves collectively. In his statement, Morro leaves some of his estate (his home, a tract of land, including the area known as the "old woods,") to his nephew, the colonel, but he bequeaths the rest of his property to his young grandson, Benvenuto (Riccardo Zannantonio), an orphan whose care is also entrusted to the colonel. The cavalier implores the colonel to spare no expense or effort in preserving the sanctity of the forest.

The passing down of the old woods from one generation to the next typifies humanity's temporary stewardship over the environment that future eras will inherit. The colonel is representative of decision-makers who squander the world's resources for profit. Dismissed from the armed forces, the colonel trades in his uniform for clothing more suitable for working in the outdoors, but he does not abandon the habits and perspectives that he gained through his military service. He brings his domineering and non-compromising attitude to the old woods, rejecting his uncle's

5. Exemplary Realities   131

wishes. Upon his arrival at his new home, he takes issue with the mansion's nature-themed decoration and its reliance on a magpie (voiced by Micaela Giustiniani) stationed in the yard as a sentry. He redecorates the home with his military paraphernalia and promises that radical changes will be made around the house. When a group of local foresters request to show the colonel the old woods, he considers them inferiors, shocked that they are informal enough to lack rank among themselves.

The forest pushes back against the colonel when he states his intentions to cut down trees in the woods. During the colonel's tour of his new property, one of the foresters challenges the colonel, refusing to shut his mouth when commanded. The forester, whom we come to know as Bernardi (Giulio Brogi), is actually the leader of the wood's spirits, and he tells the befuddled colonel of the founding of the old woods. Many years ago, a bandit, Giacomo (Luciano Zandonella), cultivated a bare plot of land and transformed it into a forested sanctuary that shielded him from his pursuers. Raising his voice, Bernardi continues to tell the story before disappearing in the forest and shouting that cutting down the trees would be a crime. He threatens the colonel with his declaration that the bandit could return at any moment to reclaim what is rightfully his.

The incident in the forest commences a back and forth struggle between the colonel and the old woods, each side strategizing on how to gain the upper hand for control of the area. The friction between the stern military leader and his adopted home recasts Olmi's investigation of freedom, and its association with nature, and the subjugation of complete liberty required by civilization's innate regulations in *The Scavengers*. In the earlier film, the historical moment preceding the boom, when the majority of Italians moved away from lives spent working in and with nature, was revisited as a watershed moment for the nation. The skill to interpret the natural world as a living being with feelings and moods was essential to work, a relationship that also pinpointed an individual's place in a cosmic order. The shift in labor meant sacrificing freedom and existential balance in the name of progress. However, *The Scavengers* does not infer that the widespread diaspora of the Italian labor-force endangers the environment. In *The Secret of the Old Woods*, the colonel's wish to conquer the forest completely by monetizing and privatizing it, and compelling its animals and natural forces to obey his commands, imperils the old woods' existence. His uncle had also deforested other areas of the property, but Morro decided to preserve the old woods because he recognized what its survival meant. Strictly dedicated to the single-minded principles from his life spent in the military, the colonel cannot see the forest for the trees as he fails to perceive the value of conserving nature.

Irritated with the seemingly chaotic and unorderly habits of the forest and its relationship with his home, the colonel also aims to order his living space and assert his authority. When the magpie squawks in the middle of the night to announce a visitor, who happens to be the elusive Giacomo circling the house, the colonel sees no one. After being kept up all the night, the colonel storms outside with a gun and while shouting underneath the bird's tree that he will shoot it if it does not stop its signals, he accidently fires the weapon and fatally wounds the magpie. Dying, the bird withholds whose presence he was announcing, leaving the colonel oblivious as to who has begun to shadow him, though we soon discover who it was. The spirit of Giacomo is an elderly, shabbily attired alpinist and was likely a distant figure standing at the outskirts of the unveiling ceremony of Morro's statue at the beginning of the film. The colonel never acknowledges Giacomo's presence but the ghost, and frightened rumors from the villagers, pique his curiosity and inspire him to research the history of the old woods in local records. A book written by a former abbot that visited the area apprises the colonel of the origin of the forest's spirits. Evidently, the spirits of the trees of the old woods materialize into animals and people, but if someone cuts down a tree, the life of the animal or person that holds the tree's spirit is extinguished.

The colonel brushes aside the dire warnings of the damage he will cause with his plans to deforest the old woods. His selfishness and greed obstruct him from including the retention of the integrity of the old woods' ecosystem, and its long-term benefit for himself and eventually for his nephew, in his vision of an orderly estate. He sabotages the plans of the

The woods' souls watch lumberjacks fell trees in *The Secret of the Old Woods* (1993, Penta Film).

spirits to make a defensive alliance with the unruly wind spirit, Matteo (voiced by Omero Antonutti), by releasing it from confinement in a sealed cave and acquiring its services to protect his encroachment upon the forest. After having removed all forcible opposition to his scheme to monetize his new property, he observes hired lumberjacks at work and notices a group of elderly men, attired in brown and grey suits, watching the felling of the trees.[31] The spirits of the trees manifest themselves to protest their removal and subsequent death. The scene progresses into a kind of funeral with Bernardi issuing the last rites by leading the recitation of a lay about a celestial forest for Sallustio, a soon-to-be felled tree's soul. In a last-ditch effort, Sallustio turns to the colonel and asks if he will consider issuing a counterorder to save the tree's life. The colonel pridefully replies that he has never given a counterorder as Sallustio suddenly disappears. In this scene, through his use of elderly men as representations of the tree's spirits, Olmi links *The Secret of the Old Woods* to his other films' depictions of the waning Italian agricultural lifestyles and the corporatization of Italy. Olmi's representation of nature had logically progressed, at this point of his career, from revering the earth with astonishment at its beauty and its generative power in his Edisonvolta films to fearing for its future as the pursuit of profit has increasingly altered nature's ability to nurture life.

Through the colonel's nephew, Olmi imagines a younger generation providing a possible solution to fears of environmental degradation as children in the film experience nature and gain a respect for it. The abbot's book also informs the colonel that children, because they lack certain preconceptions, can perceive the forest's spirits even though they remain invisible to nearly everyone else who does not believe in the magic of the old woods. The children of the film have a connection to the forest that allows them to communicate with it telepathically. One evening, the forest summons Benvenuto and some of his friends from a military school near the old woods for a nocturnal concert directed by Matteo. No one tells the children of the recital. They just know that it will happen. Under the moonlight, they huddle together with the spirits and enjoy the melodious choral music. Dante Spinotti's stunning shots of branches swaying and bathed in moonbeam as they react to Matteo's concert convey the harmony that pervades through the forest, even creating a sacred space out of the old woods. Attended by the spirits in animal form, the children wander rapturously around the woods in a state of spiritual elation. Even the colonel briefly relishes the music, but he ultimately breaks the event up, scattering the animals and Matteo when he bellows at the children to return to their school.

The colonel has an uneasy rapport with Benvenuto. His nephew owns all of the land in the surrounding forest that does not belong to him, inspiring him to fantasize about the boy's death. In one of the most sinister moments in all of Olmi's work, the colonel asks Matteo to close the door during a meeting so they may discuss the boy and a murderous plot off-camera. Their original plan involves bringing Benvenuto to the mansion and then leaving him out in the forest alone overnight under the pretense of measuring the woods. But this fails to kill the boy and as time passes, the colonel begins to harbor a fondness for his nephew, the spirits, and the forest.

After the forest is saved from a bug infestation by Matteo, Benvenuto falls gravely ill on his own. Initially the colonel shows little concern. But one evening his shadow has an argument with him and leaves him because he is no longer the man he once was. This symbol of the loss of his soul spurs the colonel to visit Bernardi to ask the sprits to intercede and save the boy's life. But even when his nephew's death seems imminent, the colonel maintains his composure and hesitates when asked to leave the old woods alone in exchange for the boy's life. The colonel ultimately replies that the spirit knows better than he does what he will do, and he returns home and sees his shadow again behind him.

Benvenuto recovers, but shortly thereafter Matteo lures him outside to ski downhill, apparently as a backup plan to murder the boy after he has overcome his illness. The wind whispers to him and pressures him to conquer his fears and ignore his headmaster's warning that he is too high. When he accepts Matteo's promptings, the camera alternates between his point of view and shots of him joyously rushing down a mountain. By mimicking the thrill of a skier's first-person experience dodging obstacles and weaving around trees, the film rekindles our own wonder for the natural world. Following the aesthetic strategy of the scene of Matteo's concert, Olmi stresses in this moment that an appreciative experience of nature is the primary criterion for grasping its indispensable worth.

The colonel does not show signs of being capable of similarly delighting in the old woods' magnificence. But as the film concludes, his egocentrism does not stand in the way of him recognizing that his worldview is outdated. Benvenuto's skiing scene ends before the boy reaches the bottom, leaving us unsure of his safety when Matteo tells the colonel that he has perished in an avalanche. The announcement incites the colonel's first display of emotion. Upset, he gathers a shovel and excitedly runs to the largest pile of snow he can find and starts digging. A forceful winter wind blows through the forest, making the already bitter cold unsurvivable. As the colonel dies, the spirits of the old woods, in the form of humans and animals, encircle him. Matteo tells him that Benvenuto did not die and he was only trying to bring the colonel cheer when he lied about the boy's death. The colonel presses Matteo to swear that the boy is fine but ignores it when it asks him when his heart began to warm toward his nephew.

5. Exemplary Realities   135

Like Andreas, only in death does the colonel's life enable a spiritual transfiguration. The colonel has undergone a reconfiguration of his philosophical underpinnings that motivated his decision to give up destroying the life of the old woods. His concerns have pivoted away from himself and his desire for wealth and power toward his nephew and his future, which is directly connected to the health of the natural world. The result of his choice is a death with honor attended by an endless line of soldiers marching past him. The colonel raises his hand in salute to the troops and freezes into a statue, matching his uncle's wooden effigy at the front of the mansion. Because of Villagio's restrained acting, which Morando Morandini compares to a Kabuki performance, his masked facial expressions limit our identification with him and his journey to altruism and ultimately environmentalism.[32] As he is commemorated in the film's conclusion, we have to fill in the spaces his performance has left to discover what has motivated the love for his nephew and nature that has guided him to his *volte-face*. Olmi achieves in *The Secret of the Old Woods* what he intended with Rod Steiger's mediator figure in *A Man Named John* by successfully setting the stage for us to vicariously relate to a subject through an impassive hero, rendering the film into a possessive experience.

Singing Behind Screens uses two similar mediator figures to immerse viewers into a mythological China. Neither of these mediators are the lead, but they act as surrogates for Olmi as he presents his self-aware, orientalist imagining of the nineteenth-century pirate queen, the widow Zheng.[33] Olmi first came across this intriguing personage through Jorge Luis Borges' *Historia universal de la infamia* (*Universal History of Infamy*), a collection of short, fictionalized accounts of historical criminal figures. However, it was not until he read Yuan Yung-Lun's epic poem of the widow's story, which reminded him of Christ's parables, that Olmi felt inspired to make a film about her.[34] The allure of a pirate story set in a mythical China appealed to Olmi, who saw *Singing Behind Screens* as a follow-up to *The Profession of Arms*, through the idealized image of a world where complete forgiveness of wartime atrocities was possible.[35] To create this self-reflective, romanticized parable, Olmi made a pantomime fairy tale version of the widow's story, setting sections of the film on a brothel stage as a play and the rest of it on the waters of the Yellow Sea (actually the Bay of Tivat in Montenegro), with the action on stage reenacting and corresponding with the raids and battles on the ocean.[36] He chose this method because it gave him greater freedom to project a figmental China where this story could take place. "Since it is a tale, the Chinese reality must be evoked through a tale-like interpretation of this reality. It's China as seen from a Western point-of-view. The only thing I could do to put myself in the mindset to recreate China was to not go to

China. I had to recreate China by using bits and pieces of a landscape that alluded to China but was not China."[37]

In the formation of his fanciful China, Olmi filled the roles of his Chinese pirates with actors of various Asian ethnicities, including the widow herself, who is played by a former Italian architecture student, Jun Ichikawa, of Japanese descent.[38] If the film had been more successful, it may have raised the same kind of controversy that surrounded the then-forthcoming American film *Memoirs of a Geisha* (2005) for its casting of Chinese women in Japanese roles.[39] But the director's deliberate orientalism quashes the charges that were raised against that film. Olmi underscores his Western vision of China as a Brechtian collage made up of pieces that he fits together in a fantasy with tenuous links to history, fact, and even ethnicities.

Singing Behind Screens is Olmi's most sensual film, with plenty of female nudity on display and shots that also gaze on sexualized male bodies. Olmi uses this sensuality to entice us into his China, exoticizing its entryway through the bordello. The film's whorehouse is a mysterious place that caters to the sexual fantasies of its patrons but also offers moral instruction by way of plays performed in the middle of the building. Prostitutes make their living in small compartments placed around a stage, shaped and decorated like a pirate ship. This unusual setup allows the whorehouse to also advertise itself as a "cosmological institute," luring in both sex clients and customers seeking enlightenment.

The first mediator, a young Italian man (Davide Dragonetti), is one of the latter. The film introduces us to him as he enters a cab in an unspecified city and hands a Chinese driver a business card, asking to be taken to the institute. The driver laughs mischievously when he looks at the card, aware of the shocks in store for the boy. Upon arrival at the institute, the young man questions his escorts to find out where he is, but they insist that he has arrived at his intended destination. When he is ushered into his compartment and sees other tenants disrobing in adjacent units, the young man becomes increasingly uncomfortable. Meanwhile, on the stage an old Portuguese pirate captain (played by former Spaghetti Western and Italian comedy star Bud Spencer), acting as both the narrator of the film's play and a commanding officer in the scenes that take place on the Yellow Sea, delivers a prologue that briefly unfolds the history of Chinese and female pirates. The captain is the film's second mediator and as he begins the play, Olmi cuts between the arrival of the young man, scenes from a silent Italian pirate film (*La bella corsara* [*The Beautiful Corsair*, 1928]) and a striptease introduction of the exploits of another historical female pirate, Mary Read (Carlene Ko), on the stage. When the captain transitions to the widow's story, she enters the young man's compartment, gives him an elixir,

5. Exemplary Realities 137

and removes his clothes before the film returns to a love scene between the widow and her husband, Admiral Zheng Yi (Makoto Kobayashi).

In the arrangement of the stage's and the performers' relationship with the audience, and cutting back and forth from the sea to the theater, Olmi has literally adapted the alienating Chinese theater that Bertolt Brecht so admired, a theater where "the audience forfeits the illusion of being unseen spectators at an event which is really taking place."[40] Acknowledging the problematic Western stereotypes of East Asia, including his own, Olmi initially indulges in blatant orientalist titillation to seduce us into the story, setting the stage for an erotically charged swashbuckling adventure of the high seas along the lines of the *Pirates of the Caribbean* (2003–2017) franchise. But it quickly becomes apparent that the film has no intention of arousing us and that it has dispensed with the swordfights and peg-leg captains common to traditional pirate films.[41] The widow's crew, which historical records report once amassed to 70,000 pirates, has been whittled down to a few dozen marauders to keep with the low-key tone of the events in the film that build up to the story's serene conclusion.[42]

At its core, the widow's parable is about the potential of love as a bond between lovers, as a source of anger when it is taken away, and as the origin of forgiveness. The captain begins the story with the happy marriage between the two pirates Zheng Yisao, the widow's married name, to her husband, Zheng Yi, the commander of a huge pirate fleet. She is devoted to her spouse and they have a loving rapport. However, they keep this contentment to themselves. They have an extremely destructive relationship with society. The film deromanticizes their lives by specifying the damage they cause and the lives they disrupt. During a coastal raid commanded by Zheng Yi, the film first adopts the projection speed of *The Beautiful Corsair*, deceiving us into expecting exciting sword fights and plank walks. Abruptly, the film resumes a normal projection rate and an imperial servant's voiceover announces a royal edict to government officials describing the pirates' pillaging of poor coastal villages, massacring of innocent civilians, and kidnapping of young girls to sell in Macao as prostitutes. Olmi limits the violence in this scene, and later raids, to cannon shots fired from the ships on the villages, choosing not to convince us of the pirates' depravity by immersing us in it. But the descriptions themselves are jarring enough to remove whatever misconceptions we may have invested in the widow initially. The scene brings back to light some of the more heinous crimes that have been expunged from recent depictions of piracy in popular culture.

The government does not remain blameless either, which is equally at fault for destroying the lives of its citizens in an effort to save money. Just to prevent the pirates from profiting from stolen goods, the government's initial response to the damage wrought by the fearsome couple and their crew is not to protect its citizens but to have eight hundred villages destroyed and move the villagers inland to begin an agricultural life. They then give Zheng Yi a peace offering through the honorary title of "master of the royal corsairs," to prevent further attacks. This alliance angers a cartel of businessmen that had partnered with Zheng Yi and had capitalized on his plunder. They decide to seek revenge by having his food poisoned and killing him. The widow is distraught with grief, but instead of resigning herself to a lengthy mourning period, she dons her husband's clothes and declares herself the new admiral before her crew.

In this section of the film, Olmi is at his most Brechtian, instructing us how to watch his film while removing the orientalist camouflage that he has used to cloak the widow's parable thus far. After Zheng Yi's death, the Captain stands before the theater audience and tells them that they will now learn the consequences of the murder, reminding them as they consider this story that "the theater, ladies and gentlemen, holds up a mirror for you to observe men's behavior and the value of things." When the widow pronounces herself as the new admiral, the film briskly oscillates between the ship at sea and the young man awaking in his compartment at the theater. At the moment that the widow fires a pistol at the ship's bell to ring in her dominion over the ship, in several shots, collectively lasting less than two seconds, the young man is whisked from the theater and onto the ship, cowering in fear before he is transported back to the safety of his compartment. The charms of the widow's beauty at the bordello has worn thin and the horrors effectuated by the pirates has transcended the screen and has become imaginable in his world. The orientalism used to characterize the widow has disappeared and she has mutated into a monster. The scene shatters the illusion of the theater, alienating us from the lecherous world that the young man, and we, settled into. But the purpose of the film's alienating effects is not to completely deny all empathy with the widow and her story. Olmi utilizes them in order for "an observing, watchful attitude [to be] cultivated," as in Brecht's theater.[43] Although this world has now been uncovered as a mirage and has descended into a much more ominous tale than the captain advertised in his introduction, the hope the captain expresses that the audience will learn something from this story remains in place.

The widow's womanhood is central to the morals that can be drawn from this parable. Several scenes and brief moments foretell the transformation that will occur at the film's conclusion because of attributes ascribed to her femininity. In spite of her viciousness, once the widow takes command of the pirate fleet she demonstrates a degree of comity toward the other pirates and even toward their prisoners. She institutes fair regulations, dividing the booty among the pirates and threatens death by hanging

5. Exemplary Realities 139

to those who rape women. Her kindness toward the prisoners is marked as a gendered action by the captain who reacts to the boldness of her leadership with the comment, "For a woman she has the balls of a real man." She shows signs of tenderness when she recites nature-infused poetry about her sad and lonely state in a scene where her caressing of a moonlit pirate's body revives memories of her promises to her husband that they would grow old together. In another scene she covertly exchanges smiles with one of the children the fleet has kidnapped. But her subordinates do not question her because of her softheartedness or because of her womanhood. She is as determined and unrelenting as her late husband in her leadership.

Denouncing both the government and the cartel that killed her husband, the widow wastes no time in setting sail to resume villainous attacks on merchant and government ships and villages along the Yangzi river while trekking inland. Consequently, the government sends Admiral Kwo-Lang (Li Xiangyang) with a direct order to kill her and not offer her clemency. The widow handily defeats the Admiral and although she grants him an honorable death by allowing him to perform *seppuku*, or *hari-kari*, the government accuses her of murder.[44] In response to the defeat, the emperor (Chen Xuwu) appoints his cousin Ting Kuei (Sultan Temir Omarov) as the new admiral of the navy and they both ride out to surround the widow's fleet with the imperial navy's armada. A number of ships surrender to the navy and rumors circulate among the pirates of the generous pardon (including food, wine, and even state pensions) they could also receive by turning themselves in.

When the widow's crew spots smoke aboard the emperor's ship, they believe that the supposed deserters have carried out a secret plan of attack. However, the smoke is actually issuing from a smokestack because the captain's ship is a steamboat, which terrifies the pirates and is identified by the Captain as a kind of "modern devilry." But after ostentatiously exhibiting their fearsome firepower, instead of threatening the pirates directly or slaughtering them without warning, the navy flies dozens of kites over to them with the message "punishment and forgiveness" painted on their wings. The next morning, more kites land around the widow's ship with various fragments referencing a fairy tale about a butterfly escaping from a celestial garden that it shared with a dragon. The messages summon the butterfly "to return to the flowers of the celestial garden," prompting the widow to ruminate overnight on the appropriate course of action.

As the sun rises the next morning, the widow has a silent vision of her husband, adorned in the royal robes he was wearing when he was poisoned. The specter of her husband serves as the final impetus in her choice to accept the emperor's offer. Although Olmi does not assign any specific interpretation to the husband's appearance, his presence reminds us of the

The widow Zheng (Jun Ichikawa) kneels before the emperor, awaiting his pardon in *Singing Behind Screens* (2003, Cinemaundici).

betrayal that he suffered when he made his own deal with the government, but it also prods her memories of the love that she still holds for her husband. Following her handmaiden's suggestion that she should not bring her sword if she is going to accept the emperor's offer, the widow sets aside her pirate admiral's gear and drapes herself in regal, traditional Chinese feminine attire. She throws her sword into the sea, and Stravinsky's "Firebird Suite" triumphantly attends her as a royal convoy rows her to the emperor's ship. At his ship, the emperor lifts her bowed head and pithily applauds her decision with the statement, "Forgiveness is more powerful than the law." Back in the theater, the young man listens to the Captain deliver an epilogue describing the harmony the widow's choice secured. Men could return to their work while "women's voices regaled the day singing behind screens."

It is possible to interpret the conclusion as conservative if we understand that the widow has returned to a more traditional role and the closing lines as indicative of her own future status, but this reading is not supported by a close examination of her interactions in the film. Throughout *Singing Behind Screens*, the widow is always the guide or the decision maker even prior to her husband's death. In the theater she coaxes the young man into relaxing and enjoying the play. When the government hands over the honorary title to make peace with her husband, it is the widow who parleys with them while her husband lies in bed. Even in her lovemaking scenes, the widow remains in control by being either on top or holding her husband's head in her lap. And at the conclusion, she is not intimidated into leading the pirate fleet out of their nihilistic pursuit of violence and plunder because of a fear of death. Olmi's staging and fabulization of the actual, chronicled peaceful surrender of the widow urges us to approach her and her realization of peace with a skepticism that can only be countered by the application of what we inscribe on the film with our own memories and impressions of love. Considering her choice to surrender, it seems that she makes the decision out of the love she possesses for her crew, a love, as suggested by the film's flashbacks that she cherished for her husband and has transferred to those under her command.

Singing Behind Screens is Olmi's only feature with a story centered on a woman and in it he promulgates his stated views on women's roles as leaders in society. "If women have, as protagonists, the [natural] task of regeneration [of life] … they have that same primacy in the knowledge of love that men … do not have. This is the reason for which, in difficult moments of history, it is women who become the protagonists."[45] Olmi puts forward the widow as an example of the singular type of leadership that a woman can contribute to a society. The emperor's steamboat signals that China has entered a new era that, guided by love, the widow assists in transforming into one of tranquil unity.

A more familiar, troubled era circumscribes the events of *The Cardboard Village* and its story of a group of illegal African refugees seeking sanctuary in a foreclosed Catholic church. Olmi codes the film with biblical allusions to make a parable about the meaning of faith and religion in the face of humanitarian epidemics such as the refugee crises that still beleaguer Western Europe. *The Cardboard Village* was born out of another project, a documentary on the cultural remnants of Christ in Mediterranean cultures.[46] But an injury to Olmi's leg kept him in bed for several months, leading him to reconsider his next film and its scope.[47] Olmi had declared that *One Hundred Nails* would be his last fictional feature in 2007, but decided that another fictional production, in which he could bring the Mediterranean's traces of Christ to him, would allow him to adapt his documentary project to his impaired mobility.[48] He wanted to shoot *The Cardboard Village* in a theater, but was forced to shoot at the Palaflorio sport stadium in Bari in order to construct the film's church.[49] His plans to shoot in a theater were not motivated by a wish to reuse the theater as a reflective device as in *Singing Behind Screens*. Without using any external shots of the church, or any natural lighting through its windows, the church becomes disassociated from any specific building and dislocated from any specific community. The only trait that locates the church in Italy is that all of the non-refugee characters speak Italian. Because of the film's undefined location and the transformation of the priest, it fits into the discussion of Olmi's fables and parables more easily than it does among the religious films that will be discussed in the next chapter.

The church of *The Cardboard Village* has long been abandoned by its parishioners. In the film's opening shot, from the position of the church's cross in the apse, the camera looks down upon the church's priest (Michael Lonsdale) as he bows at an altar. From an omniscient, Godlike perspective, we are placed in a position to judge the priest according to the events that follow. The priest prays aloud to God, bemoaning the church's fate and also expressing his wish to remember everything as it is before repo men storm into the church and claim all of the church's religious paraphernalia. Exasperated, the priest puts on his robes and calls to heaven "*Kyrie eleison*" and "*Christe eleison*" ("Lord, have mercy" and "Christ, have mercy") as if he is reciting prayers during a mass. The sacristan (Rutger Hauer) constrains him and begs him not to embarrass himself. The ritual the priest makes of the despoiling of the church marks its conversion from a house of worship into the space that will be used by the refugees as a shelter. The progression of the priest's attitude toward this space and what his religion is, beyond the symbols and icons that have been stripped away, is followed throughout the rest of the film. Likening the refugees to biblical figures and situations, Olmi seeks to give new life to the spiritual and moral lessons of the Bible by having us deduce what precipitates the priest's transformation.

To highlight this transformation, Olmi directs Hauer and the actors portraying the refugees to give detached interpretations of their roles, leaving Lonsdale with the film's most emotionally expressive performance. Because the majority of Olmi's films feature non-professional actors, their performances are typically muted, but only in *The Cardboard Village* do actors express a minimum amount of feeling as they interact with others. Recalling the use of actors in the films of Robert Bresson, who directed with the belief that "the actor's acting throws the eye" and always received restrained portrayals from his performers, with the priest Olmi highlights where the deciding agency lies in consideration of the refugees' lives.[50] Olmi uses the refugees' inexpressiveness, as Paul Schrader writes of Bresson's actors, to "convey a reality which is not limited to any one character."[51] He minimizes the details of their background, beyond that they are African and at least some of them are Muslim, to a few clues that do not allow us to ascertain any specifics of where they are from.[52] In doing so, Olmi removes all stereotypes we may have of them and invites us to consider their humanity by cloaking them with events from Christ's life, such as the flight to Egypt and Judas' betrayal, to appeal to Western moral foundations.

Only after they arrive does the priest even become aware of the refugees' existence. Aging and unwell, he has requested the church's permission to live out his remaining days in the abandoned building. The loss of the items that defined the church for him, and the lack of attendees that forced the shutting down of the building, have left him in a state of spiritual angst, irresponsive to the plight of others. As he sobs in his kitchen, shots of a shipwrecked boat on an empty beach play on a TV set with the volume turned off, signaling a disinterest in the suffering of others.

After the sacristan has locked all the doors and left the priest alone, the priest walks into the chapel, places a group of small figurines, representing the crucifixion of Christ, on the bare altar and gives a sermon to the empty pews. He confesses that even when his masses were well-attended, he felt an emptiness that he now recognizes as doubt. Despairing, the priest follows the admittance of his uncertainty by whispering "Christ is silent," as if his faith has been shattered because God did not rescue the church from this fate. Immediately after the priest voices his loss of hope in the church and God, Olmi shifts the film's focus to the refugees, implying that the principles of the faith that the priest cherished can find root again in helping people who are in desperate need of aid.

When the refugees and their escorts break into the back of the church, some of them are breathless and the roar of a helicopter we hear confirms that they are being pursued by authorities. Other refugees knock on the door of the church's small apartment to plead for medical aid for a severely injured man. The priest starts to call for an ambulance, but the refugees tell him that if emergency services come they will be deported. The priest is kind to his guests but he does not yet grasp the desperation of their situation and how much they need him. He offers his guests towels for the wounded man and the little food that he possesses. When the priest asks the leading escort, a Christ figure who is an engineer at the "Institute of Astrophysics and Cosmology," what drives him to help these people so much, he responds, "You are a priest. You should know better than me."

It is not until one of the female refugees, who in her blue hijab resembles the Virgin Mary, gives birth to a child in the church's storeroom, that the priest's understanding of faith becomes more action based. As the priest opens the door to reveal the newborn infant, the visual presentation of the child recalls traditional paintings of the nativity with light from the open door enveloping the baby in a column and contrasting darkness filling the rest of the room. The priest instantly approaches the altar in the back of the chapel, kneels before the small figures he recently placed there and softly intones the Christmas carol "O Come, All Ye Faithful" in Latin. As he sings, the film cuts to several closeups of the small, crucified Christ figure. After he associates the images of the refugees' suffering and the infant's birth with the life of Christ, he gains a new sense of responsibility for them. When the sacristan visits him later, demanding to know why the priest has given sanctuary to the refugees (who, the sacristan asserts are "different from us, they cannot be like us"), the priest replies with a question asking about what it means to be "us." The priest's rejoinder to the sacristan's insistence that he is putting "us" at risk by helping "them" is to insist that when being

In *The Cardboard Village*, echoing visual representations of the infant Christ, Olmi envelopes the refugee baby in light (2011, Cinemaundici).

charitable places "us" at risk is when there is the greatest need for charity. Having developed a Levinasian response toward the other, the priest has lost the solipsistic conception of his faith and acknowledges his moral duty to shield the refugees after he has come face to face with them and recognized their humanity.

His interaction with the refugees has re-emboldened his faith and appreciation of Christ, but in a manner that allows him to address his doubts by directing his admiration and worship of Christ toward prioritizing Christ's teachings on love over the symbols, rituals and dogma of the church. When the immigration enforcement services knock on the church's door, the priest confidently dismisses them with righteous indignation despite their threats of legal action. He maintains that the building's original consecration as a church overrides whatever state ordinances challenge his ability to accord sanctuary to whom he deems worthy of protection. When they break into the church later with the help of the sacristan and a Judas-like escort, who promises to betray the pacifist engineer, the priest denounces them with scripture and chases them out of the church with his umbrella. Afterward, alone in his room he stares at the crucifixion scene he has hauled back to his bedside table. Through voiceover, we hear a confessional prayer he makes to the Christ figure, admitting that he cannot feel pity anymore for Christ because God feels too distant. The vacuity of the icons that earlier filled his chapel has become apparent to him in comparison with the fulfillment he receives in taking care of those desperately in need.

The priest's relationship with a local doctor (Massimo De Francovich), who survived a holocaust concentration camp as a child, also indicates the shift of focus in his faith. Although the doctor has serviced the area for some time, he first meets the priest when he stops by the church to look at the injured refugee. The priest greets the doctor by reminding him that in the distant past they would have worked together, referencing historical correlations with the treatment of patients' physical and spiritual wellbeing. But the doctor insists that the two occupations have always performed different duties. He is an agnostic who has abandoned his faith after searching for God through prayer when he was younger and unsuccessfully trying to contemplate the possibility of God's existence as an adult. Though he leaves without saying goodbye when the priest presses him about why he has stopped praying, the doctor returns to the church later when he hears the priest is unwell. After assuring the doctor that he is only suffering from old age and a seasonal illness, he confides in his new friend regarding an episode that occurred when he was a young priest that still pains him to recall. Tearfully, he shares his regret over not holding a glance longer with a woman he was attracted to, a small moment that he feels may have altered his life and his beliefs about the essential value of love. Concluding this story, the priest shares his recent resolution regarding the importance of love and that doing good does not require someone of faith. He makes this admission to clarify his earlier statement about the similarities of their professions and to persuade the doctor that he holds no self-righteous prejudices toward non-believers. The priest's confession revisits a common characteristic among Olmi's characters in several of his other films, such as *Il posto*, *I fidanzati*, and *Legend of the Holy Drinker*, in which Olmi uses flashbacks and flashforwards to silently express similar regrets over relationships. The priest's reassessment of the missed opportunities in his life points to a confidence that giving into such love, even in the form of longing and heartbreak, can lead one to express love to others through charity.

The refugees are undergoing their own religious struggles among themselves. Though some of the women wear hijabs, it is not clear if all of the refugees are Muslims and since the film never identifies their country of origin (beyond being an African nation) we have no basis upon which to develop assumptions about their religion. But they all seem to share a belief in God and the majority of them oppose contention between religions and interpretations of God's will that support violence. However, a handful of them are planning a terrorist attack. Since their arrival, one of the female escorts, a prostitute, cares for the expectant mother, treating her tenderly because she appeared ill. The prostitute only becomes aware of her patient's pregnancy when she unwraps a packet of baby clothes that the woman has brought with her. She does not even know this woman's name but tending to her needs through small acts of kindness (placing a coat on her when she shivers, making a bed for her out of items in the storeroom, etc.) has engendered feelings of love. When one of the other women instructs her to kill the new mother because she gave birth out of wedlock, "in sin," the prostitute refuses, disputing the command as a perversion of God's law. As with the priest, service has led to compassion, trumping dogmatic interpretations of God's will and religious extremism. Earlier in the film, underneath the makeshift tents that have been constructed among the chapel's pews, the same female refugee that ordered the death of the new mother is seen unwrapping a large explosive device. She and a small group of her supporters argue with the engineer about the necessity of violence in ending the situations that impoverish them and bring wars and famine to their country. The extremists, the Sadducees and Pharisees of the film, do not foresee a world of peaceful unification with other religions. The engineer contends with them, arguing that words can change the world and that there is reason to be optimistic for change, a perspective shared by the majority of the refugees.

Many of the desperate men and women at the church place great hope in the newborn child, whose mysterious, immaculate birth marks him as the film's second Christ figure. In the scene when the immigration enforcement services break into the chapel, they coerce the refugees into naming the boy's father. They can only reply that the baby is a "child of Africa." All that remains of the child's father is a mysterious notebook, with a cover featuring the Disney character Tigger, from the *Winnie the Pooh* adaptations, which washed up on the shore alongside the shipwrecked boat that transported the refugees. The notebook contains a creation story similar to that taught by the three Abrahamic religions but focuses on the untamed Garden of Eden and its life-supporting qualities, as a mother to all the peoples of the earth. Fleeing from whatever disasters plague their homeland, the refugees aspire to return to the idyllic utopia described in the notebook, a "return to the life of essence, to the truth of needs" that Olmi saw vanish in Italy during the 1950s and 1960s and stresses that humanity needs to adapt in some form again.[53] Indeed, the world depicted in the notebook shares many qualities with the societies envisioned by the attendees of the Slow Food movement's conference that Olmi recorded in his documentary *Terra Madre*. The movement suggests that the developed world look to underdeveloped, agriculturally centered nations for necessary instruction on how to combat climate change, poverty, famine, and other global problems by returning to environmentally sustainable farming and food production. This idea is specifically reflected in *The Cardboard Village* through one family of refugees, who share that they made the trip to establish a better life for their son but now see that the West will not be a safe place for them to start a new life. They decide to turn back with faith that Africa will have a new beginning.

As suggested by the Bible-like scriptures found in the Tigger-decorated notebook, the nativity in the church, and the search for an ideal environment for their families to live peaceful lives, children press the refugees to hope for a better future, whether in the developed world or in Africa. In both worlds, religious zealotry and antagonism toward the other threaten everyone's future, as represented in the film through the intolerance and bigotry of the sacristan and the hatred of the West that fuels the prospective African terrorists. While those refugees not returning to Africa leave for their next destination in the West during the film's closing moments, the notebook is burned, the terrorists prepare to carry out their plan of attack, and the engineer opens the now empty church to the police who are on the verge of arresting him. The compassion-based religion based on love cultivated by the priest and the majority of the refugees is symbolically defiled as the police shatter the church's glass windows when they arrest the engineer. The parable closes by reprimanding the West for failing to follow the basic tenets of the Judeo-Christian ethics that lie at the foundation of Western civilization. As with most of the other fables and parables in this chapter, love is the key to both individual and collective salvation in *The Cardboard Village*. It has shifted the way the priest and the prostitute think about God and the way they worship him. Olmi closes the film by leaving us to contemplate where love could be applied elsewhere in this situation and our own moral reaction to the refugees' needs. For Olmi, love is the ultimate panacea for the heroes of his fables and parables. Love is gained in these films through varied combinations of unifying with friends, family, a sense of God or a natural order, and nature, the factor that binds all of these components together. He fully elaborates upon these beliefs in his films directly investigating faith, Christ, and religion.

6

Christ and Religion According to an Aspiring Christian

Scholars and critics often brand Olmi as a Christian or religious filmmaker, regularly defining him by remarks similar to Elliot Stein's in *The Village Voice*, which surmise that "Olmi is an unrepentant Catholic."[1] And although such categorizations in themselves have not precluded Olmi from receiving the kind of renown that his work warrants, they certainly have given some influential voices reason to question his merits as a filmmaker, as in the case of Alberto Moravia's unwarranted criticism of *The Tree of Wooden Clogs*.[2] Deborah Young observes, "In Italy, the critics have begrudgingly admitted that Olmi is a major director of his generation, adding points for his supposed 'peasant' origins, and subtracting them whenever his faith becomes explicit."[3] Such stigmatization of religious belief is problematic in its assumptions about the merits and worth of Olmi's cinema based on his perceived faith, but it is doubly wrongfooted in the presumptions it makes about his beliefs based solely on the subjects of some of his films, rather than giving dedicated attention to how Olmi depicts these subjects.

In the last few decades, Olmi repeatedly referred to himself as an "aspiring Christian," an appellation he assigns himself because he has not yet reached a level of commitment where he feels comfortable calling himself a Christian.[4] "I have never been a man of faith, in the sense that I have not been able to reach a state in which I could say 'great, from now on I believe and nothing more will come that will shatter my condition.' My faith has never been like this and it's still not like this. I am constantly in search of faith. Every now and then I experience flashes in which I feel the quiver of a total faith, but a moment later I find myself in a state of continual rumination."[5] This is not the statement of a fervent believer, but the disclosure of one who, like many, finds his faith vacillating between belief and uncertainty. Clearly, for many years the vast majority of those who have written about Olmi's faith have misunderstood it and his reasons for making films with specifically religious subject matter.

However, Olmi also frequently discussed his admiration for Christ, whom he claimed he was obsessed with.[6] "I have always felt as if Christ was with me with his breath on my neck."[7] Christ's teachings of love were fundamental to his worldview, and it would not be an exaggeration to consider them as one of the central inspirations for all of Olmi's films. But rather than strengthening his religious devotion, Olmi's interpretation of Christ distanced him from the Catholic Church. During the reign of Pope Benedict XVI, he wrote a furious book-length open letter to the church, accusing it of having abandoned the teachings of Christ. "The example of Jesus of Nazareth, a carpenter and master, can still help us rediscover the joy of how to spend the precious gift of our existence. But you, ancient church, that has erected many altars to Christ, seem to have forgotten him. Even you!"[8]

Olmi embraced Pope Francis's policy changes and goals of alleviating poverty and highly regarded certain figures of Catholicism's recent past (such as Pope John XXIII and also the subject of his recent documentary, *Vedete, sono uno di voi* [Look, I am one of you, 2017], Carlo Maria Martini, a progressive cardinal) but he insisted that there are other "secular popes," such as leaders from the Slow Food Movement, Vandana Shiva and Carlo Petrini, whose guidance is just as vital for the world's wellbeing.[9] As seen in his films, involvement with, and caring for, the natural world is integral to Olmi's spiritual worldview. In Olmi's cinema, a life spent appreciating nature's beauty with family and friends, accrued naturally by the farmers and manual laborers of his films, cultivates spiritual wellbeing and love. In his works specifically exploring religious subjects and figures, those who strive to understand God in accordance with their experiences, respect the earth and all of its creatures, and choose to live in harmony with those around them, instinctively possess the altruism and compassion that Olmi associates with Christ.

The life of Pope John XXIII (born Angelo Giuseppe Roncalli) readily aligns with this perspective as depicted in *A Man Named John*. Harry Saltzman, best known as one of the founders and early producers of the James Bond franchise, felt motivated to do something to commemorate Roncalli while in Rome during the pope's death and he eventually approached Olmi to make a film of his life.[10] In an effort to avoid making a straightforward hagiographical biography of the pope, Olmi introduces a mediator figure in his film, played by American star Rod Steiger, to witness the major events in the life of the pope without taking on his physical appearance or wearing religious attire. During the pope's childhood, children do re-enact formative moments from the pope's life while the mediator observes the scenes and comments on them, but after he reaches adulthood the mediator dispassionately delivers a voiceover and dialogue with lines often directly taken from the pope's letters and his published diary, *Il giornale dell'anima* (*Journal of a Soul*), during the major events that lead to Roncalli becoming pope.[11] (Below, I will often use "Angelo" and "the mediator" interchangeably).

The mediator does not emote or project a personality, but he moves from being an observer of scenes in the pope's life to standing in for him and delivering his dialogue. Olmi's experiment with the mediator, and the film itself, were not well received by critics nor by the director himself. This was his first and only major international production and was his only work prior to his fables and parables to cast stars (Steiger and the Italian actor Adolfo Celi).[12] He could not accommodate himself to the system of the film's production. "Saltzman did everything he thought would help me. He gave me a troupe of thirty people, but that only disgusted me. I would walk into the hotel lobby in the morning to find them all waiting for me.... After a week, I understood that nothing was working properly. I felt like a man who has fallen out of love with a woman and doesn't know how to get rid of her."[13]

The finished product exhibits some of the problems Olmi experienced attempting to merge his style with the demands of a major studio biopic. In some sequences, Olmi's tendency to elide information about narrative events prove too confusing when combined with the film's review of so many of the incidents and people in the pope's life. For example, the scenes with the Bishop of Bergamo (Celi), which are included to highlight his influence on the future pope, reenact a defining moment in the pope's life, and features an important conversation between them, but their bond is not established in the way that Olmi so deftly implies the strong emotional pull Giovanni feels for his father and Liliana in brief moments of *I fidanzati*. Additionally, *A Man Named John* occasionally has an institutional tone that does not match the rest of the film's stillness and its tranquil approach to its characters. This is especially true in the lengthy introduction and conclusion's use of choral and organ music and archival footage of crowds of devotees surrounding the pope to adopt a reverential attitude to Angelo Roncalli while the rest of the film stresses his ordinariness. However, this is not a "hagiopic," a film about a religious subject that Pamela Grace defines as upholding values such as "blind faith, chastity, extreme forms of virtuous suffering, and the superiority of one religion over all others."[14] In spite of Olmi's misgivings about the production, the film does succeed in looking beyond the pomp surrounding the recently deceased pope to reveal an ordinary man whose farm-bound childhood instilled in him the spiritual values that shaped his decisions as the head of the Catholic Church.

Following the film's eleven-minute introduction of "the good pope,"

6. Christ and Religion According to an Aspiring Christian   151

and its explanation of the role and purpose of the mediator to the audience, with a sudden cut the film plunges directly from hymns and images of the pope and the Vatican to the jazz-infused mundane reality of the mediator. His car sits behind a truck in bumper-to-bumper traffic on a highway congested by a fatal accident. The clash of the transition between the cloying presentation exalting the pope and the unpleasantness of the mediator's world detaches Angelo Roncalli's childhood from the overwrought spectacle that preceded it, preparing to deflate the persona of one of Catholicism's most transformative recent figures into a humbler, plainer individual. The mediator weaves around the accident and arrives in the pope's small hometown, Sotto il Monte (which was later renamed Sotto il Monte Giovanni XXIII), as night falls. Going into the town, the mediator has to hit the brakes when a donkey-pulled-cart gets stuck in the road, a moment that recalls a near-collision in *I fidanzati* when a horse-drawn-carriage nearly runs into a car. As in *I fidanzati*'s Sicily, Sotto il Monte is also a location that had mostly evaded industrialization halfway through the twentieth century.

The town's center, in the film's contemporary present of the early 1960s, possesses a quaintness that makes the film's time traveling to 1881, the year of the pope's birth, nearly unperceivable. Following several establishing shots of the town, the mediator looks around and hears a noise that guides his attention to the Roncalli's home, a *cascina* similar to the one occupied by the farmers in *The Tree of Wooden Clogs*. Indeed, Olmi's later reconstruction of his own memories and the stories of his grandmother in *The Tree of Wooden Clogs* resemble the scenes in Sotto il Monte because the town is also located in the province of Bergamo, Olmi's birthplace and near the home of his grandmother. The director was well-acquainted with the roots of Roncalli's early life and the kind of environment that would mold the compassionate worldview that endeared the pope to so many.

Before he begins to narrate and interact with the life of the pope, the mediator watches on as family members carry a pregnant woman, Angelo's mother (Rita Bertocchi), to a bed as she goes into labor. Even at his birth, the pope, who was the fourth of thirteen children, spends his childhood surrounded by the close circle of his extended family.[15] Olmi characterizes Angelo's early life by the intimate ties between the family members, connections that are nurtured by their lifestyle as farmers. Such positive depictions of traditional institutions like the family in a film about a religious figure, and his aversion to making more overtly political films, clearly feed the erroneous public image of Olmi as a conservative Catholic filmmaker who made films about submissive characters. However, the film makes clear that Angelo's religion and strong family have not rendered him into a passive figure.

The family patriarch, Uncle Zaverio (Antonio Bertocchi), together with all of the other adults in the family, gather round the newly born infant and immediately evaluate the baby's health while discussing his fitness for baptism. From the day he is born, church, family, and work are the three pillars of Angelo's moral foundations. We see Angelo (Fabrisio Rossi) at age four, watching others working in fields and mills, attending religious processions, playing with farm animals, and reciting prayers together with his family. In a determinative moment of the boy's religious perspective, Zaverio carries Angelo up the stairs and places him in a crib at the foot of his bed before reading to him from the book of Revelations about the second coming of Christ. Listening to his uncle describe Christ's return accompanied by angels, the boy stares up at a small crucifix affixed to the wall. In all of Olmi's religious films, and in keeping with his own stated interpretation of his religion, there is no suggestion of the supernatural in this scene, no miracles that presage Angelo's papacy or that mark him as different from any other farming peasant acquiring a religious sensibility. Olmi centers the pope's childhood on the humble circumstances that feed Angelo's religious imagination, a theology, like that held by the farmers of *The Tree of Wooden Clogs,* that does not rely on, but accepts, a God of miracles who intercedes on behalf of the faithful. For Olmi, this kind of faith comprehension is what renders the pope into a man of determined social action.

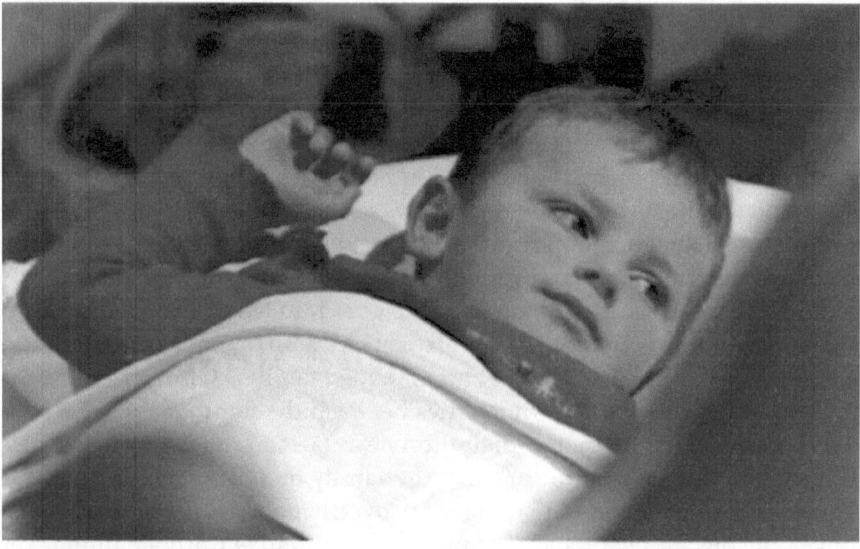

As a child, Angelo Roncalli's religious understanding is formed at the foot of his Uncle Zaverio's (Antonio Bertocchi) bed in ***A Man Named John*** **(1965, Sol Produzione).**

At seven, through another formative experience, Angelo (Alberto Rossi) learns the values of decency, honesty, and trust. A mischievous child with a face besmeared with food and dirt stains, Angelo causes trouble with his fellow altar boys. One day playing soccer, they stumble into a pumpkin patch. The boys, including Angelo still in his altar boy robes, rush through the field and seize pumpkins to take home with them. Carrying a fruit one-sixth of his body size, the boy proudly hauls his loot into the Roncalli's family dining room. Upon learning the owner of the patch did not give Angelo the pumpkin, Zaverio tells his nephew he does not want it in his house and that the boy should immediately take it back to its rightful owner. Returning the fruit, Angelo answers the pumpkin farmer's questions about why he has brought back the stolen property, who his uncle is and if he has been baptized. Later, the farmer brings a sack full of pumpkins to the Roncalli home and unloads them in front of Angelo. He then asks the boy to tell his uncle that "pumpkin Matteo" has stopped by and that he considers Zaverio a gentleman. Such moments imagine Sotto il Monte as an Edenic society, its farming community serving as a moral instruction ground for Angelo before he leaves the confines of the small town for the much harsher realities that greet him after he has entered the priesthood.

Some biographers of the pope have framed the development of Roncalli's active altruism as a reaction to national and churchwide shifts. Greg Tobin's history of the pope's life presents Roncalli's study at the seminary in Bergamo as a major inspiration for his later social awareness. Tobin argues that because he was in the city, Roncalli witnessed part of the national Catholic response to Pope Pius IX's call for social action by Catholics in Italy. "Catholics both clergy and laymen, set up soup kitchens, fought for the rights of the working class, and organized unions."[16] Olmi's film does not situate the development of the pope's philanthropy within the zeitgeist of *fin-de-siècle* Italy. As he grows older, Angelo's mother recognizes her son's predilection for religious service at church and ruefully agrees to allow him to study to enter the priesthood. But life at the seminary proves confusing for the boy and only when he returns home for a local festival is he able to comprehend the significance of the service-based theology that his childhood prepared him for. When Angelo returns home from the seminary, the mediator, who assists others in setting up decorations and lights for the festival at a local church, interprets the pope as an Olmian character who has gained his sense of social duty through personal interaction and relationships. The mediator speaks to the local priest and expresses concern over having wasted the afternoon by not practicing his typical religious observances and studies. Humbly acknowledging his own lack of a formal education in comparison to Angelo, the priest assures Angelo that he is making good use of his time and he advises him that the highest priority a priest should have is the care and joy of those over who he has been given stewardship. Accepting this advice and applying the ethics he learned as a child to his budding theology, the mediator returns to work, raising the church's chandelier in unison with the church's parishioners.

The prioritization of service to others is reiterated when the church sends him to Rome at age eighteen and Angelo reflects on God's purpose for his life as a priest, the ideas that he wants to study and the goals he wants to set for himself in his future service. He discerns that love is a common feature among all the thoughts that he contemplates regarding his future. Immediately after a voiceover conveys these introspective musings, the mediator watches a shopkeeper button together a priest's cassock for display in a shop window. Shots of his father, mother, and Uncle Zaverio working outside are injected into the scene. Like so many Olmi characters, Angelo finds his mind racing back to his loved ones after he has been separated from them. Staring at the cassock that materially defines for many Catholics what a priest is, he remembers his family working and their poverty. His intuition tells him that while working on the farm with his loved ones as a boy he has already learned that the most vital and true aspect of the priesthood, of service to God, should be loving and serving others.

His resolution to these principles is given further reinforcement, especially toward advocating for the rights of the working class and the poor, when the church assigns him to serve as a secretary to the Bishop of the Diocese of Bergamo, Monsignor Radini-Tedeschi, a man also deeply committed to challenging social injustice. Contrary to the wishes of the Vatican at a moment when links between Italian trade unions and the church was deeply controversial, during a strike in Rancia the bishop not only ensures the strikers have food to eat, but openly supports their actions and cites his backing of the workers as a Christian obligation.[17] The bishop shares with Angelo his aims to actively oppose prominent notions that the church aligns itself with the rich and the powerful. At the outbreak of World War I, the bishop falls ill and dies. Moved to confront his own mortality as his friend and mentor passes, Angelo covenants aloud to Christ that he will sacrifice his life for God. With his last breath, Tedeschi joins his prayer asking him to include the cause of peace in his offering. Angelo's life between World Wars I and II is defined by how he keeps this promise. The film's final third contrasts his ascent to new positions of power within the church to the rise of fascism in Germany and Italy through archival footage of acclamatory crowds cheering fascist victories.

As the film traces the future pope's journey to begin his appointment as an apostolic delegate, the mediator sits on a train headed for Bulgaria, reflecting on the Latin phrase *"obedientia et pax"* (obedience and peace) that Roncalli has included in his apostolic coat of arms. While the

6. Christ and Religion According to an Aspiring Christian   155

voiceover expresses his wish that these words define his life, the mediator looks out the window, cueing a montage of Bulgarian farmers and peasants working in fields and riding in carts, re-emphasizing Angelo's association of peace with his family and his childhood. This is confirmed as he travels from village to village by horseback to visit the scattered Catholics across the mostly Orthodox country, and worships with people in their churches. From his humble accommodations in one of these villages, Roncalli again acknowledges his debt for his worldview to his family in a letter he writes them on his fiftieth birthday. While he reads the letter aloud, inserted shots of his family praying and working together illustrate his assertions that the virtues he gained as a child are more valuable than anything he learned in school to prepare him for his mission to ease tensions between faiths in the country and to develop the local churches to meet the challenges of modernity.

As the film nears its conclusion, he finds himself in opposition to church administration or other leaders during his assignments, leading him to identify and sympathize with workers and other downtrodden members of society as he searches for peaceful solutions to problems caused by World War II and bureaucracy. While working in Istanbul to address issues between the new secular Turkish republic and religions, he takes notice of a nighttime practice of Turkish fishermen at the Bosporus strait in Istanbul. In the waterway, the fishermen gather to illuminate their boats with lights of different colors and strengths as they fish. One night as he watches them work in the rain, he expresses his aspirations to attain their level of diligent dedication to feeding their families in his own work for the church. In scenes like this, and others in Paris and Venice when Roncalli similarly voices his solidarity with members of the lower class and disgraced individuals who his fellow clergy members have cast aside, Olmi finds in the pope's story a man whose perspectives on life, work, and philanthropy were analogous to his own. The film abruptly heads into its conclusion following his appointment in Venice and only uses a few minutes of archival footage to review his brief tenure as the pope. These final moments, like the introduction, are ill-suited to the rest of the film. However, notwithstanding these flaws and problems with the film's pacing, Olmi manages to configure a convincing vision of what inspired the pope's identification with the poor and working classes, determining his status as one of the most important figures in modern Catholic history.

In the early 1980s, following the great critical success of *The Tree of Wooden Clogs*, Olmi had additional leeway to bring a more contemplative religious-themed work to the screen, beyond the influence of a major studio, with another work made in collaboration with RAI Television. *Keep Walking* was a long-nourished project inspired by Olmi's childhood belief that the three wise men were duplicitous. He had long questioned why Christ had to flee from his manger after the arrival of the wise men and concluded that they were either "opportunists or traitors."[18] As Brent Landau suggests, the wise men's history leaves open this kind of interpretation because of the limited details and brief space given to the most well-known record of them in the New Testament's Gospel of Matthew, which gives the wise men "no specific country of origin [or] number or names."[19] Besides consulting Matthew's account, Olmi looked to other mentions of the biblical figures in the Apocrypha, the writings of Al-Masudi and stories attributed to Marco Polo to look for inspiration in converting his childhood suspicion of the three wise men into a film about religious hypocrisy and finding spiritual contentment through simple means.[20] He decided to bring his interpretation to life not through a recreation of first-century Jerusalem and Bethlehem but by filming in and around the small Tuscan town of Volterra.[21] On set he encouraged actors to "leave behind their everyday clothes but ... bring with them their spiritual, cultural, and psychological make-up."[22] After finishing a theatrical cut of nearly three hours made for an out-of-competition premiere at Cannes and a brief run in cinemas in 1983, Olmi was unable to complete his original plan of editing a two-part, four-hour version of the film for television when he was suddenly struck by Guillain-Barré syndrome.[23]

The theatrical edition of *Keep Walking* is a complete work, only missing extended backstories of some of the pilgrims that Olmi intended to add to the longer television version.[24] Mimicking the structure of scripture, the film imagines a number of allegorical events that could have arisen on the wise men's journey to find Christ. However, no specific mention is ever made of Bethlehem, Jerusalem, Herod, Mary, Joseph, or Jesus Christ. Olmi has purged from the film any specific biblical locations and has only kept the traditional name of one of the three wise men, Mel (Alberto Fumagalli). In doing so, he both thwarts audience expectations of a Hollywood biblical epic and makes the story and its investigation of faith more immediate and open to analysis.

The film's narrative follows Mel, and his foul-mouthed, altar boy-like assistant, Rupo (Antonio Cucciarrè), as they lead a group of pilgrims to find the savior announced by a new star. Olmi introduces us to these characters and the rest of the cast as they put on their costumes for the film in a backstage area. As an offscreen loudspeaker announces that the show is about to commence and that the performers are all normal people filling the roles of soldiers and pilgrims, the separation between the actors' personalities and that of their characters is diminished. Already inhabiting their characters and adopting their names in the costume room, Rupo swears as he struggles with his costume before Mel condescendingly commands

6. Christ and Religion According to an Aspiring Christian   157

him to light the lamps for the opening night sequence. Circling the backstage area to locate the lamps, the young boy greets his friends and playfully mocks an actor for staring too long at himself in the mirror. In a final act of preparation for the performance, and to initiate the audience into the story's diegesis, Mel and Rupo prepare a bowl of incense outside in front of a star-studded sky painted on an animal skin. At its outset, the film resembles a cinematic mystery play or pageant with an unpretentious, communal sense of participation, allowing Olmi to highlight the importance of personal interactions, and the love that forms from them, as the true keystones of Christ's teachings.

Though seemingly sincere in his belief and his wish to aid others in their worship of God, the foundation of Mel's faith is rooted in a strict observance of Mosaic law and his blind dedication to it leads him into sanctimony and self-righteousness. As a priest, Mel can perform intricate rituals, recite scripture, search for meaning in the alignment of the stars, but he is not yet prepared for the kind of religious life compatible with the ideas prioritizing love that will spring from the god whose arrival he awaits. Olmi leaves the veracity of, and motivations behind, Mel's prophethood open to interpretation. His claims, especially after the appearance of the nativity star, seem suspicious, yet his prophecies do lead his followers to find an infant that some of them accept as their savior.

The priest has a warm affection for Rupo but finds himself constantly chastising the boy for his irreverence, disobedience, and questioning of the importance and meaning of scripture and rituals. To the boy's frustration, Mel consistently responds to Rupo's questions by replying that he would not understand the explanations, asking him to blindly obey. However, as exhibited in the story's first sequence, Rupo's sweet tenderness compels him to not accept many of Mel's strict, dogmatic rules and laws that contradict his own moral sensibility. While Rupo and a friend capture a lamb in the wild that they hope to keep as a pet, two soldiers pursue a young woman who seeks sanctuary with Mel. Mel successfully hides her and has an assistant prepare a fire for a sacrifice to cleanse her of her sins. When Rupo and his friend see the resulting smoke from afar and infer what their new lamb may be used for if they take it home, they hide the animal among some shrubs. However, their efforts are undercut by another assistant who brings the lamb to Mel.

As he looks at the lamb placed on the slaughtering table while Mel reads the plodding prayer, Rupo begrudgingly recites a psalm for a few moments and then slams the scriptures to the ground and storms off. Mel yells after him that he is committing sacrilege, but the boy shouts back that the lamb did not commit any sins and suggests that if someone needs to give up their life it should be the woman. Overtaken by rage, Rupo climbs up a nearby hill and continues to swear at Mel and the other assistants while he grabs fruit and hurls it below at them. The boy's love for the animal leads him to question Mel's religious authority, observing in his anger, when the priest cites God's request for the lamb's life, that the Lord didn't ask for anything until the woman arrived. Later, Rupo tells Mel that he no longer aspires to read in the temple or to serve the Lord. Here, he shows the first signs of his keen comprehension of his religious impulse and his firm resolve to challenge beliefs that do not correspond with it. As Dean Duncan observes, "Rupo is not quite an angel, nor is he perfect in behavior. He is, however, whole, or sufficient, perfect in innocence and sweetness, courage and faithfulness."[25] Allowing his heart to govern his actions and determine his relationships with others leads to displays of anger at times but ultimately compels the boy to follow the spirit of the law above its letter and prepares him to come of age spiritually as they search for God.

As with the strikingly earthly ambience surrounding the baby Jesus, Mary, and Joseph, the star that sets Mel, Rupo, and others on their journey to find a savior is not accompanied by angels nor hymns from on high. A loud rumble, similar to the roar of an airplane, accompanies a blinding light that blazes across the sky awaking Mel and causing a stir in the nearby city. The vague portrayal of the incident does not allow us to specifically identify what everyone has actually seen. It could be a miraculous star, or it could be a comet exerting enough gravitational force on the area to cause the rumble. It is certainly interpreted differently by Mel and Rupo. Gathering in the city with everyone else after the appearance of the mysterious light, Rupo runs through the streets shouting that the light is a symbol of peace. The star's manifestation, occurring at a moment when Rupo contemplates leaving behind the life of a celibate priest while he speaks with a beautiful girl, has filled him with optimism. That he interprets a bright light of unknown origins as a symbol of peace indicates that its appearance has expanded his understanding of what is possible, granting him confidence in his future. However, his impression of the star is only briefly shared with us and his voice is one among many of the cries ringing the air. Yet, they are important to consider in contrast with the gloomy pronouncements of "God's will" delivered by Mel.

Those assembled in the city quickly turn to the priest for his reading of the incident. As the crowds follow him to the king's chambers, he denounces the idols of other religions and issues stern warnings to those who would turn away from his god. He is asked why he has broken with his habit of silently praying in his temple and suddenly become so outspoken about his beliefs. He responds that because man cannot understand God, God has chosen him as a messenger and that the star in the sky symbolizes the Lord's arrival on the earth. Mel's inspiration for these prophecies

6. Christ and Religion According to an Aspiring Christian 159

remains suspect because he seems to be crafting together God's decrees as he speaks. Possibly stimulated by Rupo's outburst when he was preparing to sacrifice the boy's lamb, during Mel's rambling speech before the king a point-of-view shot focuses on a pair of bloody pig heads and he suddenly denounces the practice of animal sacrifice. If he does act as a mouthpiece of God, specifically a forerunner of Christ, his method of explicating God's will does not convince us and something vital is lost in translation. Mel's delivery, tone, and message do not portend Christ's peaceful message as suggested by the teachings contained in the Sermon on the Mount or his insistence that the two most important commandments are based on love.[26]

Nevertheless, Mel's somber representation of God intrigues many of the city's inhabitants and they accept his offer to follow the star to locate God. Their journey runs for half of the film's three-hour length and has a disjointed structure that meanders from sequence to sequence. In an insightful analysis of the film, Luca Finatti argues that because of its unusual structure in comparison with the director's other work, *Keep Walking* offers a unique opportunity to consider the construction of time in Olmi's cinema.[27] He argues that this specific section of the film is able to accomplish what Olmi's time-shifting editing style achieves in many of his other works because of the "fragmentation of the story itself into many episodes, releasing them from a temporal dimension of liner and casual succession."[28] He concludes that the film has "an epiphanic structure," one that creates an experience that enables revelation for the viewer.[29] Finatti's insights illuminate how Olmi uses the extensive duration of the journey itself in film time, and its apparent disconnectedness, to frame the film's complex approach to Christ and religion. The pilgrimage's episodes are a series of preparatory experiences to meeting Christ that offer space for reflection. Reading the pilgrims' journey to find God in this manner corresponds with the film's contrasting of the practical religion of Rupo and many of the pilgrims with Mel's harsh, and possibly deceptive, construal of God's will.

We see Rupo and several of his traveling companions' relationships with God manifest themselves as organic, stemming from their contemplation of enduring affliction and experiencing joy with others rather than from threats of hellfire and fear of the unknown. However, not everyone making the trip has spiritual motivations. A pair of elderly swindlers cause trouble throughout the journey, taking advantage of every opportunity to fleece money from believers by collecting offerings from the pilgrims or gathering relics to sell when they return home. One man turns back immediately after starting the pilgrimage, apparently feeling he has done enough to appear pious before friends and relatives. But the majority of those traveling have genuine intentions of making some kind of transformational discovery. A diverse set of personalities, often representing different types of believers, make up the rest of the ensemble of pilgrims that join Mel and Rupo. Soldiers sent by the king, a noble woman, families and individuals on quests for meaning, all meet the priest outside of the city.

Love often opposes Mel's smug, holier-than-thou religious exhortations during the pilgrimage. Before they depart, the girl who spoke with Rupo at the moment of the star's arrival, gives him a small, gold earring. Both of them, accepting the gift as a clear token of her affection, and in typical Olmian fashion, remain silent to allow themselves to relish the feelings they share for one another. In a later sequence, Mel finds the earring and first accuses Rupo of stealing it. Upon ascertaining that it was given to him by a young girl, he asks Rupo to read a relevant passage of scripture aloud that he praises as wisdom that has guided generations. Just from the selection of these verses, Mel communicates to Rupo not only that he empathizes with the suffering caused by the pangs of youthful affection, but that he also understands the importance of loving relationships between people, something that he does not typically demonstrate in his public religious persona. This moment points to a probable motivation for the priest's pivotal decision to choose saving the lives of the pilgrims over staying with the infant savior and possibly dying with him and his parents.

Soon after they depart, the group spots an armed soldier atop a nearby hill. Expecting a dangerous encounter, Mel looks to the sky and loudly asks God if he is protecting the pilgrims. However, the solider only intends to announce the marriage of his master and invite the pilgrims to throw flower petals to greet the newlyweds as they pass by. Mel continues to look like a fool by self-righteously suggesting that the couple is lucky to receive the greetings of "a man of God" and then lengthily detailing the purpose of their journey. Although Mel forces Rupo to read a psalm as the couple passes, the pilgrims give them a warmer greeting with the petals and loud cheers. Because Mel's ostentatious displays of devotion do not supply the spiritual nourishment sought by the majority of the travelers, they find it elsewhere through the friendships they gain on the journey. The sight of the happy couple induces the noble woman to confide with some members of the caravan about the failures of her love life. Later, she announces that even though they have only been traveling for a few days, she has already forgotten her previous life and marvels at how familiar her traveling companions seem to her. Like Olmi's farmers and laborers, his pilgrims' faith is bolstered by the support they gain from their community as they endure struggles together in nature.

The film does not cast judgement on some of the pilgrims, like the noble woman, who is obese, and an elderly couple and their son, when they choose to stay behind, especially during a steep mountain ascent, and not complete the pilgrimage. Others tire and suggest stopping for a while,

6. Christ and Religion According to an Aspiring Christian

One of the three wise men, Mel (Alberto Fumagalli), leads pilgrims up a mountainside path in *Keep Walking* (1983, RAI-Radiotelevisione Italiana).

infuriating Mel who upbraids them for not grasping that their god is not like the idols they may have previously worshipped. They cannot reach him anywhere. A nearby hermit overhears Mel's shouting and challenges the stern, inapproachable deity that Mel preaches to his followers. The hermit explains that he awaits a god who will be his friend and that will not force him into subjection. As evidenced by the relationships they have formed and the lessons that their lived experiences on the journey have forged in them, the pilgrims also hope for such a magnanimous god who will love them and understand them.

During this pilgrimage, Mel does not receive power from on high to perform miracles and lead his followers to their destination. Even after joining forces along the way with the two other wise men and their caravans, Mel cannot divine the precise location of the infant Jesus once they arrive in Jerusalem. After the wise men pay homage to Herod, the king of Judea, two women cautiously approach one of the pilgrims and disclose to her the star's location, which will guide them to Christ and his family in Bethlehem. The people of the city hesitate to speak openly about the birth of Christ because they fear Herod would try to kill the baby if he felt his power was threatened.

Following the instructions received from the two women, the caravan travels to Bethlehem where they surprise Joseph, unassumingly humming outside of the ruins of a castle. Upon verifying that Joseph's distant ancestors were kings and that his wife has recently given birth to a baby boy, Mel breaks into rapturous prayers and kneels before the dumbfounded father and asks him to take the caravan to their lord. Although puzzled by their claims, Joseph leads the elated pilgrims to the manger that houses his wife and child. No halos hover above the family's heads nor do heavenly lights shine down to confirm the baby's divinity. This is a peasant family in humble circumstances, but they do not appear destitute nor disheartened by their conditions. Mel's point-of-view shots, close-ups of the baby's hand grasping the air from his crib, and the reaction shots that follow them, express his captivation with the child's innocence before he affirms that they have found the savior. Rupo's lamb is included among the gifts they bestow upon the child, foreshadowing Olmi's expansion upon the animal's traditional and metaphorical association with Christ in the conclusion's brief adaptation of Herod's massacre of the innocents.

Some of the pilgrims murmur doubts because in addition to having an infant proclaimed as their god, his destitute surroundings and his crying connote to them that he is just an ordinary baby, powerless to even lift his own family out of poverty. Others, such as the woman, now dying, who sought Mel's protection at the beginning of the film, give offerings to Rupo as a token of their belief and hope in the baby's divinity. The wise men themselves do not debate the child's status, quickly and unconvincingly confirming their belief in him and acknowledging the doubts of some of their followers before moving their conversation to the threat they agree that Herod presents to them and their caravans. At their evening sermon, the silhouettes of two distant soldiers catch Mel's eye and later, during his prayers, he has an experience that urges him to gather together the leaders of the caravans. He tells them of a vision that occurred as he drifted off to sleep in which shadows materialized into an angel in his tent and commanded him not to return to Herod, as asked to do, but to flee home. The other wise men profess that they experienced the same vision.

Olmi presents Mel's vision enigmatically, leaving open the possibilities that Mel is a blatant fraud, a prophet, or something in between. Shots of Mel praying alone are juxtaposed with point-of-view shots of a lantern's flickering flame casting dancing shadows across the interior of his tent. He then steps outside and spots the same silhouettes he saw earlier, before he sees an entire brigade of soldiers marching toward the caravans' camp. Though no angel appears on the screen, and Mel gives a misleading description that his experience may have been a dream when he was clearly not sleeping, the film suggests that some type of divine inspiration may have led to Mel's

6. Christ and Religion According to an Aspiring Christian   163

realization that Herod's soldiers were approaching. The scene poses questions about the nature of divine revelation, the abuse of religious authority, religious hypocrisy, and the problems of submitting oneself completely to faith and God even at the cost of one's own life or the lives of others. If Mel actually believes he had a vision and that the baby they found is the savior of the world, he has chosen to literally abandon his God, or possibly to allow God to fend for himself, in favor of saving the lives of his followers, likely motivated by the love he feels for them. But the troubling possibility remains that he has concocted the vision only to save himself, that he uses his religious authority to manipulate and control others for his own self-interested purposes.

During the return journey, one of the pilgrims (who earlier witnessed the priest lay aside for himself a sack full of the offerings of precious goods that the pilgrims intended for the savior) accuses Mel in front of the caravan of deceit and fabricating the vision that ordered them to abandon the child. Mel quietly confronts the pilgrim after the soldiers detain him, and the defiant young man accuses the priest of knowingly deserting God when they had an obligation to stand with and defend their savior. Mel retorts that he is no soldier and that his accuser is no hero either or he would have spoken up before they left Bethlehem. Distressed while overhearing the conversation, one of the soldiers commandeers a horse and rides it to Bethlehem. A field strewn with the dead bodies of women and children greets him, the result of Herod's campaign to find and kill the child. It is a brutal scene that indicts Mel for his cowardice, but also confirms that he likely saved the lives of his followers. As the soldier looks around the field, he hears the cry of Rupo's lamb, which stands alone in Christ's stable, distinctly empty of bodies. The lamb's presence serves both as a suggestion that the baby and his parents may have safely escaped, and as a symbol of the principles of Christlike love that have survived despite corrupt religious leaders such as Mel. The ending reflects Olmi's conviction in the fundamental values of Christ's teachings and the potential for his adherents to practice them outside of the bounds of institutional religion.

In the early 1990s, Ettore Bernabei, ex-director of RAI Television and a longtime friend of Olmi, approached the director to contribute a film on the book of Genesis to a series of biblical adaptations produced by Bernabei's company, Lux Vide, that would be broadcast on television stations around the world.[30] Olmi agreed to participate upon the condition that he could make a film on his own terms, a work informed by his memories of his illiterate grandmother narrating Bible stories to him.[31] Olmi received approval and shaped his film as the retelling of the first nine chapters of Genesis to a child by his grandfather (Omero Antonutti).[32] Milly Buonanno notes that Olmi's adaptation, the first of the series, received the lowest ratings of the entire project, "considered the largest international co-production in the history of television."[33]

Filmed in Morocco with a cast of local, non-professional actors, with the exception of Antonutti who plays both the grandfather and Noah, Olmi's film stands out among the rest of the series' conventional adaptations of the Bible. Yet, in setting us up to view the film from a child's perspective by beginning the film with a Moroccan boy interpreting the Bible's creation myth through his environs and their latent mysteriousness, Olmi's film accentuates what many of the Hollywood biblical epics and other Old Testament films only hint at in their attempts to capture, in the words of Adele Reinhertz, "the vastness of space, with pans across deserts, mountains, and skies."[34] Olmi's *Genesis: The Creation and the Flood* ignites awe and reverence for the natural world, sparking the fundamental questions of existence and seeking out the intrinsic worth of religion.

Genesis progresses from a child listening to his grandfather's stories, to frightening, prophetic images of our war-torn contemporary world, and finally into a fantasy in which the grandfather fills the role of Noah. Olmi interweaves scenes of the grandfather's family listening to him in different settings with recreations of the episodes from the Bible that he recounts to them, which are often populated by members of his audience. From the film's pre-industrial setting, as the grandfather reviews the creation of the world and its destruction, time becomes increasingly malleable. But unlike time-shifting in the majority of Olmi's other films, *Genesis*'s free-flowing transitions between temporal eras and fantasy are not solely motivated by characters' familial and social ties. Here, they also visualize the formation of the shepherd family's attempts to grasp the eternal from the world around them, to give shape to God.

As the film opens, following a pair of shots of twilight-hour skylines, Olmi guides us into this atemporal setting with a child telling his mother in the darkness that he is afraid. His mother assures him that she is nearby as the image slowly admits more light, revealing a tent's interior. At the developmental stage of childhood, the boy asks the kind of questions, such as "will I be able to open my eyes after I shut them?" when he is going to sleep, that very young children mull over as they form a basic comprehension of the seemingly unfathomable experiences and things their senses present to them. Moving between temporal and fantastic landscapes, this impressionable perspective frames our own view of the film as we follow the child's location of his place in the universe before moving on to the grandfather's establishment of the family's moral grounding with his stories. Dissimilar from Mel in *Keep Walking*, the grandfather does not lay claim to any religious authority as he speaks. He leaves it to us to arrive at an understanding of God and the creation myth.

6. Christ and Religion According to an Aspiring Christian 165

A grandfather (Omero Antonutti) holds his curious grandson in his lap as they stare out at the landscape, and he tells the boy the creation story from the first book of the Bible in *Genesis: The Creation and the Flood* (1994, Lux Vide).

Replying to one of the grandson's queries, the grandfather tells the boy that he, like all children, are like Adam, as God will "reveal his glories openly to the young and innocent," before placing the child on his knee outside of the tent and describing the seven days of creation. While the grandfather details the creation of the earth day by day, shots alternate between the child and images that occur to him as he absorbs his grandfather's words and assigns meaning to them visually, proceeding from day and evening shots of the surrounding landscape to local animals and birds. The grandfather's voice-over pauses after detailing the creation of animals in the middle of the sixth day, and the scene shifts to a peaceful moment on another day when the boy plays with sheep in front of the tent and his family. Dark clouds shadow the ground before the grandfather resumes his story with the creation of man, forcing the family under the tent when a storm breaks. But the boy dashes outside in the rain and cups a handful of water that he pours into his grandfather's hands, tasting leftover drops by licking his fingers. Interpreting the creation myth, moments of sensory experience elucidate the boy's conceptualization of man being formed from dirt. In the context of the myth, the shot of the grandfather's hands holding the water seems to anticipate the molding of a man from clay, infusing the story of the creation of Adam with vivid, tactile significance. In these scenes in which Olmi envisions the process of giving purpose and shape to existence in lives spent in partnership with the earth, the director uses his experiential style to imagine what informs the worldview of the manual workers and laborers that his films hold in such high esteem. The shepherds of Genesis are cut from the same cloth as the farmers of *The Tree of Wooden Clogs* and *A Man Named John*, the dam-builders of Olmi's Edisonvolta films, and the Sicilians of *I fidanzati*. Their lives are whole because having a relationship with the earth not only provides them with the means of their survival, but also because its cycle of seasons and its maintenance of life give impressions to them of a universal order that sustains them and has given them life.

Olmi does not dramatize these stories with actors giving emotional or expressive performances. Rarely does anyone but the grandfather speak. Primarily, the stories are expressed through the tone expressed by the stunning scenes of nature and the characters contemplating and making sense of the world. Accompanied by a subdued score from famed film composer Ennio Morricone, Olmi underscores the shepherd family's innocence prior to the grandfather's account of the garden of Eden with scenes of the children playing with animals and watching the wind blow flowers.

Dark, moonlit shots characterize the garden of Eden scene, suggesting the ignorance of Adam (Sabir Aziz) and Eve (Haddou Zoubida) before they eat from the tree of knowledge of good and evil. The depiction of the event in the film does not adopt the common doctrine of most Christian traditions regarding Adam and Eve's choice to eat the tree's fruit, exemplified by Augustine's statement that "We are subject to the death of the body, not by the law of nature, by which God ordained no death for man, but by his righteous infliction on account of sin; for God taking vengeance on sin, said to [Adam], in whom we all then were, 'dust thou art, and unto dust shalt thou return.'"[35] The grandfather's story does not judge Adam, although when he shares that Adam and Eve have eaten the fruit, the story of the incident moves some of those listening to tears. It is a transformative challenge to be removed from the paradise of the garden of Eden, but over the course of the film Adam and Eve's choice ultimately is revealed to open up love and life to them, rather than leading to the punishment of a vengeful God. In Olmi's *Genesis*, jealousy, revenge and war cause misery, not God.

God initially tells Adam and Eve that they and their offspring will suffer because of the decision to eat the fruit, but he also acknowledges that they have become like him in their capacity to discern good from evil, now possessing the ability both to create life and to take it. During the remainder of the film, learning to treasure this ability, through loving one's family,

6. Christ and Religion According to an Aspiring Christian 167

the earth and its creatures, brings both the biblical characters and the shepherd family closer to God and to the happiness and peace that Eden represent to them. Contrarily, isolation and failing to respect the utility of the non-human world breeds a jealousy of others and resentment against God. Of course, this dichotomy begins in the film with the story of Cain and Abel. Eve greets Cain's birth as a gift from God, a consequence of her ability to understand love after eating from the tree of knowledge of good and evil. But her firstborn son avoids the company of others and resultingly fails to feel such love.

Cain is a farmer who works in the field, unlike his younger brother, Abel, a shepherd. The Bible's account of the story does not specify why God rejects Cain's offering and favors Abel, nor provide any rationale for why the older brother murders his sibling. In a mostly silent sequence, Olmi fills in the gaps, observing Cain's resistance to nature and his developing jealousy over Abel's perceived happiness. Cain works alone in the field, forgoing the use of animals to help him in his labor. The tools he uses to dig in the soil are inefficient, and while struggling with his work, he spots a large rock and quickly grasps its potential to assist him. Not dissimilar to the apes' realization of the multiple uses of a bone as a tool in the opening sequence of Kubrick's *2001: A Space Odyssey* (1968), Cain soon devises other uses for the rock beyond digging holes. He kills a sheep and uses its skin as a bag to water his crops, which Olmi immediately contrasts with Abel chasing after a lost member of his flock to rescue it. Abel integrates himself with nature, gratefully accepting the gifts it provides him and seeking to learn from it, as in the moment when he listens attentively to the whistling of the wind and then imitates its sounds with his flute. But Cain struggles to take inspiration from the world like his brother, unable to harmonize with it.

Olmi imagines God reacting to the brothers' offerings through their separate interactions with nature before the grandfather arrives at point of the story when the murder takes place. In the representation of God's rejection of the elder brother, Cain experiences a series of hardships at the hand of nature in the form of wild pigs and torrential rainfalls that destroy his crops. Despairing at his misfortune alone in a cave, Cain speaks with God, and God asks him why he is so angry and does not attempt to bridle his thoughts. During their conversation and after the murder of Abel, Olmi cuts to a jaded-looking elderly man sitting alone in a mud brick home, suggesting Cain's harboring of a lifelong guilt for his crime after God protected him from vengeance seekers. The murder, which occurs one day when Cain hears his brother playing his flute and rushes forward to bash Abel's head in with his rock, replays in the elderly man's mind prior to the camera resting with him as he wallows in regret. Olmi's version of this story makes Cain and his crime relatable, reflecting on him as an anxious figure unwilling to accept his hard luck and lashing out at God and then his own brother when he cannot bear the injustice of his circumstances. However, Olmi suggests that the murder was completely preventable through the visual comparison he makes between Cain's aloofness (demonstrated through point-of-view shots of Cain watching and listening to Abel from afar) and the shots of the shepherds' and Noah's families sitting tightly together at various points of the film.

Olmi reinforces this reading of the story following the forging of a sword by one of Cain's ancestors, Lamech, who announces that he has murdered a man and raises his weapon defiantly as if to challenge all those who would seek vengeance on him. As the grandfather reflects on the evolution of weapons and warfare in this creation myth, he and his family migrate across the desert. Momentarily deviating from the Bible to provide his own commentary on its stories, the grandfather instructs his family that the world suffers from a cycle of violence that constructs its history. He condenses these struggles into an analogy of people traveling along separate routes and none knowing securely that they are on the right path as Olmi frames two caravans, moving in opposite directions, in the background, supporting the film's proposal that alienation breeds suspicion, creates otherness, and ultimately leads to violence. As the film continues into the story of Noah and the flood, these traits become associated with the ancient cities that Adam's descendants develop, forbearers of the metropolises of Olmi's boom and post-boom films.

After introducing Noah, the film breaks away from the linear progression followed in the book of Genesis and watches the evolution of society in these cities. The grandfather sermonizes that basic values, such as loyalty and honesty, have vanished while avarice and corruption spread rampantly. After he repeats God's comments on humanity's increasing depravity, shots of a nocturnal dancing scene in the film's unspecific past are interrupted by grainy, video footage of a modern dancing club. The partygoers from the club move to the same music and rhythm as the ancient dancers. The footage then cuts to an overhead tracking shot of an unidentified city at night before shots of contemporary warfare discontinue the scenes of celebration. As he reminds his listeners of God's promise to destroy those who do not respect creation, the grandfather's narration is interspersed between troubling scenes of bombs dropping, oil fields burning, and bombed-out cities. His face is framed in a close-up shot, looking out into the distance as if he can foresee these calamities, a natural continuance of the violent tendencies sparked by mistrust and greed in his own day.

When considered alongside Olmi's other depictions of city life, the denunciation of the cities in *Genesis* seems especially severe. But as his other films demonstrate, and as he has stated in interviews, Olmi only criticizes cities because so few of their inhabitants stop to consider the wholeness and simplicity of previous lives. "I don't want to go back and lose what industrial society has given us. At the same time, I don't want to lose a certain kind of man. In a former era, when farmers seeded the earth, they didn't understand the chemical process that made their crops grow, but they worked from a faith that gave them responsibility for their lives."[36] Olmi's condemnation of the two eras' cities in the film underscores that he sees the wars and environmental calamities facing humanity in the present as moral consequences of irresponsible societies who, in pursuit of wealth, have blindly thrown aside many of the spiritually affirming attitudes toward mother nature held by previous generations.

Through Noah, Olmi presents the corrective to these situations and the sins that lead to them. He is effectively the savior and Christ figure of the story that the grandfather presents, both in his literal preservation of earth life during the flood and also through the example his life provides. After he issues the Lord's denouncements of city life, accompanied by shots of city ruins, the grandfather pronounces God's blessings on those who "eat from the work of their hands" as we see Noah happily gardening with his family. The film's favorable depiction of Noah's pastoral life suggests that his close relationship with the world is the reason that the Lord selects him and his family to build the ark and survive God's pledge to destroy all life on earth. Accordingly, instead of seeing or hearing God speak to Noah when the grandfather narrates their pact, Noah's attunement to the environment alerts him to the approaching disaster. Afloat on a flimsy raft in the sea, as fierce winds and a dark, overcast sky bear down on him, Noah lays himself flat on the raft's surface to avoid being blown overboard. As if he has understood the severity of the flood by reading signs from the environment, in the next scene Noah directs his family in the construction of the ark.

When the storms preceding the flood brew, Noah's family is brought to a standstill as they contemplate the magnitude of the imminent catastrophe the world will soon face. It is at this point that they look around them and see the animals in need of safe haven, prompting the grandfather's recitation of God's wish that the family take aboard the ark two of every type of living creature to preserve them through the flood. In Olmi's cinema, God is one with nature and if he interacts or speaks with people, as in the miracle of the healed cow perceived by the widow Runk in *The Tree of Wooden Clogs*, it is through their interpretation of nature and not through paranormal manifestations. Here, Noah and his family can save lives not because of God's divine intervention, but because they have an inherent sense of how to listen to nature and take action themselves.

Although the grandfather outlines in his story the amount of life lost during the flood and the dire situation Noah faced, he also includes that the

Lord does not neglect to take care of Noah and his family. Once the flood begins and Noah and his family have drifted asea in the ark, they gather, frightened, below deck and sit around warm coals and listen to Noah read scriptures in which God informs his followers that they can offer a heart of thanksgiving in place of an animal sacrifice to thank him. Following these words, Noah circles the ark and lights lanterns spread across the ship, setting the tone for the new era that will follow the deluge. As the rains cease and the flood subsides, the family takes pleasure in tending to the animals before the ark rests on the mountains of Ararat. As in the biblical account, Noah sends out a raven and then a dove to bring back proof of dry land. When the dove returns with an olive branch, Noah prepares for the family's return to an earthbound life by working in the ark's garden. In Noah, Olmi fashions a figure whose environmentally dependent lifestyle forms the basis of his spirituality, whose ability to have faith in his readings of nature makes him capable of being a prophet. His continued dedication to maintaining a farming lifestyle motivates God's promise to never again eradicate earth life as he has done during the flood.

One Hundred Nails features a more explicit Christ figure who also finds that a simpler lifestyle spent in nature is a path to spiritual fulfillment. Olmi announced that this would be his last fiction film and he would only make documentaries for the remainder of his career.[37] Though Olmi later changed his mind about making further features, *One Hundred Nails* feels as if it would have been an appropriate final work for the director in its story of a professor renouncing academic life and retiring to live on the banks of the Po River before completely disappearing. Olmi describes the film as his own interpretation of the Gospel of John, with the Christ figure not only teaching a new philosophy to his disciples but learning from humanity before he departs.[38]

The inspiration for Olmi's conception of a contemporary Christ figure arose from two sources. Olmi reports that the film's jarring, iconoclastic opening, featuring the discovery of a library full of books nailed to the floor, formed through an experience he had watching the news coverage of the war in Kosovo in the late 1990s. As he watched footage of a beautiful library that had been destroyed in the warzone, his thoughts moved to the people who were being killed and the lives destroyed.[39] He looked at the books in his own house and asked, "Why do you stay nailed there and not rebel against all of this tragic profanation," generating a mental image of books nailed down that remained with him.[40] Olmi first presented the river Po as a symbol of Christ, a sustainer of life, in 1992, in his poetic documentary, *Lungo il fiume* (Along the river), exploring the beauty of the river accompanied by verses read from the Bible and music from Haydn.[41] But *One Hundred Nails*' Christ figure's abandonment of society to join a small riverside community was specifically motivated by a visit to the Po Olmi made while the film was in development.⁴² A group of elderly men who spent their days by the riverside befriended Olmi and offered him wine, leading the director to adapt this environment and its inhabitants into his film.⁴³

Driving the story of *One Hundred Nails* is the mystery of not who committed the act of vandalizing a university library by nailing one hundred of its books to the floor with nails, but why. The film's investigation of the professor's (Raz Degan) bizarre behavior is less anti-intellectual and anti-religious than it is interested in exploring the contrast between the ostentatious observation of cultural and religious values in institutional religions and the actual cultivation of community and spiritual unity through shared experiences and friendship amid nature. Olmi stresses this reading of the film by beginning with an epigraph by the philosopher Raymond Klibansky reading, "Books, even though necessary, do not speak by themselves." The quote's application to the film is immediately apparent in its opening scene. A custodian opens up a university library in the morning to discover books nailed to the floor and he anxiously calls the carabinieri claiming that a great slaughter has occurred. Through this uncharacteristically controversial scene, Olmi assaults the cultural prestige given to books, questioning how it is possible that this custodian, and the priests and professors who will reiterate his horrified exclamations, can compare the loss of objects to the loss of human life.

As more details about the crime emerge, Olmi's challenge to the cultural roots of civilization investigates how institutional religions do not possess the values that they claim to uphold. Through a number of noir-like flashbacks following the discovery of the crime, we discover that a group of priests and a monsignor (Michele Zattara) oversee the library and we witness their conversations with the professor that immediately preceded the crime. Olmi alters the motivation of his distinctive time-shifting editing in this sequence, with flashbacks prompted by the monsignor's passion for his books instead of love for other people. Recalling the events of the previous evening to the carabinieri, during the flashback the monsignor treats the books as if they are his dearest acquaintances, telling the professor that when he leaves the library he feels like he betrays his "friends." Standing in as a representative of the Catholic Church in 2007, two years into the divisive papacy of Pope Benedict XVI, the monsignor's self-imposed exclusion from any kind of social life that would put into practice the principles of love taught by Christ marks the church as pharisaical; so caught up in implementing strict interpretations of dogma that it has completely set aside the fundamental teachings of its purported founder. In the context of this condemnation of Catholicism, the nailed books, with the nails driven entirely through the books to affix them to the floor, are easily associated with the nails used to crucify Christ. Essentially crucifying the church, the professor, as Christ, symbolically abandons it to search for a new spiritual home.

It is not just Catholicism that the film takes to task for being detached from lived experience and human interaction. As recorded through the flashback of a suspect student photographer describing his activities on the night of the crime to the carabinieri, one of the professor's students is an Indian woman (Amina Syed) who meets the professor in the library to discuss her thesis on female figures in major religions and how women can function as intermediaries of God's will. The professor, who, as evidenced by a lecture scene and his mentorship of this student, specializes in either philosophy or theology, challenges his student about her assertions of the importance of religion for her people. After telling her that religion has not made the world a better place, he points to the books around them and asks what good they have done. The professor then takes her hand and declares that there is more truth in the meeting of hands than in all the books in the world before he kisses her. The kiss incites the monsignor to angrily interrupt the flashback and the testimony, insisting that the photographer is lying because the professor recently confided in him his hope to enter the priesthood.

Although framed as a Christ-like figure and named Christ by the friends he makes when he retreats to the Po, the professor is far from an ideal character. He is plainly experiencing a mid-life crisis that has brought him to a reconsideration of every aspect of his life. Nailing precious books to the floor and kissing a student to teach the value of companionship are extreme reactions to a loss of his existential bearings before he decides to completely renounce his former life. The professor is not the director's *raisonneur*, but his choice to start his life completely anew in the countryside, in an attempt to connect to something authentic in his life, follows a path that Olmi sees as a route to saving humanity from its spiritual malaise and global environmental problems.

The morning following his crime, the professor speeds along the highway in his BMW, eluding the carabinieri, by stopping in a roadside café. At nightfall, the café owner sexually propositions him. Not looking to drown his uneasiness in a casual fling, the professor rejects the offer and heads back on the road without any fixed destination ahead. When he spots a large ship on the Po, near the town of Bagnolo San Vito, he stops in the middle of the highway, takes in the surroundings, and then ascends a bridge to stand directly above the river. The music and mise-en-scène imply that the professor contemplates suicide as he stares down into the water. But instead of killing himself, the professor decides to fake his own death. After taking

6. Christ and Religion According to an Aspiring Christian 173

money and a credit card out of his wallet, he throws it, a jacket, and his car keys into the river. He then grabs some basic necessities and a small bag from his car and spends the night sleeping outside next to the river.

Upon awaking the next morning, the professor commences a new life founded upon providing for his basic needs with what his surroundings offer, though he does not immediately put into practice his recently stated beliefs about the primacy of relationships in spirituality. Nearby the riverbank, he finds the ruins of a former house that he takes shelter in when a heavy rainstorm forces him to find cover. Intent on erasing his former identity, once inside he uses the house's fireplace to burn a copy of a forthcoming publication and warms himself next to the fire while he waits for the storm to pass. The small one-room house has been abandoned for many years. It has no running water or electricity, and shrubs overrun it, but part of its roof remains intact and the professor resolves to make it his home for his new life. After the storm clears, in the nearby village he finds a foldout bed and tools to clear the house and the lawn in front of it. In the town's market, he also has brief encounters with two future friends, a postman (Andrea Lanfredi) and a shy baker (Maria Grazia Guerrieri).

As evening arrives, the professor rigs a fishing line to a tree and ties it around its branches so when a fish takes the bait the resulting noise will wake him from sleep. The device works, and in the middle of the night the sound of a fish struggling to free itself from the line rouses the professor. However, before he can reach the line to pull in his catch, the fish pulls hard enough on it to break the branch and frees itself. As the fish swims away, Olmi cuts back to the library as the professor closes the gate after his crime and then the film returns to the professor's anxious attempts to sleep. Though puzzling at first, the fish's escape and the flashback take on meaning in the next scene and later on in the film when a villager brings the professor a container full of fish, a traditional symbol of Christ, as a gift.

The next morning as she delivers bread, the baker stops by the river when she spots the professor continuing his yard work. He accepts her offer to bring him some food after she tells him that she rides by the ruins every day. Soon after her departure, the postman, who explains that he also has worked as a mason, also stops and tells the professor that he too passes by the ruins daily and loves to greet his friends. In the middle of their conversation, calls of a pair of fishermen hauling in a large catfish shift their attention to the river. The postman tells the professor that this breed of foreign catfish has taken control of the river and destroyed it. The fish in the film are multivalent symbols that complement several ideas and themes, but at this juncture they point to the troubled professor's arrival in the village. He is an invader himself and has not yet integrated into the surrounding community. Although he has no stewardship over the village, the professor's presence unsettles and threatens his new environment as the colonel's does in *The Secret of the Old Woods*. However, because of the warmth of the community, rather than his own strength to follow his convictions, the professor finally puts into practice the amiable philosophy he previously expressed to his Indian student.

The carabinieri find the professor's car near the underpass and his wallet and jacket in the river, and assume that he committed suicide, although they continue their search for his corpse. Without the pursuit of law enforcement, the professor can interact freely with the locals without fear of being identified. At a riverside dance held on a patio, the baker invites the professor to join her on the floor. While the pair awkwardly chat and sway to the music, older patrons around the dance floor comment on the professor's resemblance to Jesus Christ (or at least traditional, Western depictions of him) and speculate where he has come from. The band at the dance performs "Non ti scordar di me" (Do not forget me), an Italian standard, out of tune. When the song concludes, the dancers stand still in the middle of the floor, hearing another, more melodious, rendition of the song in the distance. As they look to the Po, they see the same ship, playing the same song, on the river that passed when the professor found the area. In a strange, quasi-magical-realist moment, all of the villagers stand still to watch the ship pass by, as if acknowledging its turn in some unseen order of events set to take place. Unity pervades this Eden-like area where everything naturally corresponds with everything else. There is nothing sinister beneath the surface of this community, no type of political or religious authority pulling the strings behind the scenes. It is simply love that joins these people together.

The professor directly benefits from this spirit of amity when the postman and a group of elderly villagers help him fix his home by repairing the roof, boarding up the walls, and installing windows and doors. Afterward the men gather around a table outside and ask the professor, referring to him as Christ, if he can turn water into wine for them, as Christ does in the New Testament. Their jovial banter takes a reflective turn when one of the men asks the professor to retell the biblical version of the story.[44] The professor has told no one of his academic background, but the locals treat him as a religious authority. This respect stems, at first, from their jokes about his physical similarity to their interpretation of Christ. But once he begins to explain practical lessons from Christ's parables to them, they respect him for his wisdom. When he recites the miracle of the marriage at Cana and explains its purpose, he interprets the love and camaraderie that should exist when friends gather together as the source of Christ's wine, an explanation that the men identify with as they enjoy the drinks the professor has retrieved for them.

6. Christ and Religion According to an Aspiring Christian 175

On the banks of the Po river, the professor's (Raz Degan) friends await him so they can jokingly ask him to turn water into wine in *One Hundred Nails* (2007, Cinemaundici).

Hearing the professor's explanation of Christ's first miracle leaves a great impression on one of the men at the table and after a troubling dream of his son, he brings his wife along to visit the professor later, along with a container of cooked fish that faintly imply the villagers' acceptance of the professor as a Christ figure. The man asks the professor to recount a story, the parable of the prodigal son, he remembers from when he used to attend church.[45] In the professor's edition of the parable, he refrains from casting the son as a sinner, as in the Bible, emphasizing instead the joyful reunification with his father. For their spiritual needs, the inhabitants of the area do not seek out priests or churches but find comfort in one another and now through this mysterious stranger who they do not know is a professor. An internationally renowned scholar, the professor finds most of his background of little use when providing spiritual counsel to the locals. As an outsider, he enables them to review their experiences and to cherish themselves in spite of their personal hardships and unglamorous lives.

In this vein, *One Hundred Nails* reinterprets Christ's relationship with a Mary Magdalene figure as Olmi's *In the Summertime* also did. As with the earlier film's princess character, men actively pursue the baker but none of them offer her the type of love that fulfills her, which she describes as feeling "*abbracciata*," meaning "hugged" or "embraced." Attending a community get-together one evening at the riverside, the baker ardently fixes her gaze on the professor seated beside her and then places her head on his shoulder. He does not reciprocate her displays of affection, but he does not shun her advances either. The ship that played "Non ti scordar di me" earlier passes by again and, with her eyes closed, the baker imagines herself with the professor on the ship's deck dancing in formal evening wear. Even in this fantasy, the professor does not romantically commit himself to the baker, his face remaining expressionless, but not necessarily uncaring. In her imagination, she again lays her head on his shoulder with a warm, satisfied grin. Though perhaps not in the romantic mode she had wished for, the professor has made her feel loved simply by listening to her and treating her with respect, unlike the men in her village who greet her with sexually-charged jokes.

Beyond spiritual guidance and teaching the villagers how to accept themselves, the professor also endeavors to aid the locals when the government threatens to evict them from their makeshift riverside settlements. While not at their homes, the villagers spend most of their free time at an encampment where they eat, fish, write poetry, perform music or tell stories. These settlements essentially enable the community to exist as it does without institutional interference, to regenerate itself spiritually through close ties among its neighbors, its enjoyment of the river, and its environs. When they meet to form an appeal to the government's judgement, the professor urges the villagers to directly express what they feel entitles them to the land around the river. The elderly villagers cite their longstanding history with the Po, having occupied these spaces since they were children. Others give more poetic responses that illustrate the vitality and joy the river instills in them. These petitions do not impress the government, who not only dismiss the appeal but also charge a hefty twenty-seven thousand euro fine to the villagers for having already illegally occupied government lands. In his Christlike moment of self-sacrifice, the professor offers to pay the fine with a credit card, knowing that its use will raise a red flag for the authorities who pursue him.

Following his arrest, the professor's atonement also includes a trial by the powers that be, with the state, as represented by the police, and the pharisaical monsignor standing in for Pontius Pilate. When the carabinieri take custody of him, the professor rewords Christ's statements in John 14, which contains the promises that God will send the Holy Ghost after he has departed.[46] But in lieu of informing the villagers that the Holy Ghost will bring them peace, he wishes that they will continue to maintain the peace that comes from themselves and that they can remain at their encampment. Reframing Christ's discussion with Pilate over God's kingdom not being of this world, the professor additionally reminds his friends that those now in power have no true jurisdiction to evict the villagers from their settlements, adding that nature will ultimately reclaim its authority over itself from those now abusing it. In Olmi's films, nature has always doubled as God's temple, but in several of the films covered in this chapter, and specifically

6. Christ and Religion According to an Aspiring Christian 177

in *One Hundred Nails* through the professor's spiritual crisis, Olmi makes direct assertions that civilization has committed spiritual apostasy through its unchecked urbanization and the privatization of the environment and its resources. In his renewed search for God and an authentic moral center, the professor affirms, as he is arrested, that his spiritual ailments were cured by simply loving others and living by the Po amidst his new friends.

At the carabinieri station, officers immediately question the professor about the incident at the university library, for which he takes full responsibility but refuses to admit his guilt. He testifies that he committed the crime out of moral obligation. He continues to argue that in his position as a professor he could be considered a criminal or terrorist. When the carabinieri marshal (Carlo Beltrami) expresses bafflement with the professor's statements, confessions and his justifications for mutilating the books, the professor demonstrates his rationale for committing the crime by asking the marshal how many books he has read lately. The marshal replies that because his work requires so much from him, he has not found time to read any books recently, but he does admit to having read around ten during his life. Asked if he feels like he has missed anything by reading so little, the marshal replies that it never occurred to him that he needed to read more. This response validates the professor's reasoning, because, he argues, the marshal has lived a full life. In his own past, the professor only sees endless studying and research in an attempt to more fully comprehend the mysteries of God and existence, even though, as he discovered, what he sought from so much studying was a serenity that he could gain by much simpler means.

But books and learning are not really what the professor blames for the emptiness of his former life. In a flashback scene that follows the marshal's request for details of how the crime was committed, as the professor nails one of the books into the floor he reads a passage from it that kindles the idea to start anew from scratch and live off the land (something that likely runs through his mind as he contemplates killing himself on the bridge above the Po). This spark of inspiration counters the professor's earlier comments. Olmi does not address this contradiction except through the implication that the destruction of the books is a symbol that, through their association with the monsignor, condemns the staleness of institutional religion and academia. The professor's basis for evoking Christ's crucifixion by nailing the religious books to the floor is supported by his beliefs that despite the valuable knowledge and wisdom they contain, they mean nothing if their principles are not practiced.

Following the flashback, the monsignor accosts the professor in his cell at the carabinieri station. Angrily, he declares his love for the books that the professor destroyed, insisting on their sacred status as articulations of

God's will. The professor flinches at the mention of God, sparking a heated dispute with his former mentor about God's refusal to intercede and relieve the suffering in the world. His spiritual crisis derives not from doubts about God's existence but from the dearth of compassion and charity he sees from the God that the monsignor invokes and the religious institutions he represents. The virtual abandonment of Christ is symbolically articulated once the professor leaves jail. Confirming his conclusions about the merciless disposition of the monsignor and what he represents, upon release under house arrest the professor returns to the library as the priest pulls the nails out of the books. However, the monsignor rebuffs the professor's attempts at reconciliation and informs him he is no longer worthy of the library, insinuating the rejection of Christ and Christian love by purported Christian organizations.

As the film closes, Olmi proclaims that where Christ is welcome is in informal, loving communities like the village near the Po that welcomed the professor. The villagers prepare a feast for his return and finish covering his roof when they hear of his release. Following shots of the villagers seated together awaiting him, and the baker tearfully suspecting she may not see him again, the postman delivers an epilogue stating that the professor was never heard from. As the final credits roll, a boat sails down the Po. Brightly lit shots of the river throughout the film, especially during the closing credits, strongly contrast the heavy shadows of the moribund library. The river and the community around it is clearly where life and happiness are. At the conclusion, Olmi contends that instead of waiting for Christ's second coming to fulfill their desires of happiness, Christ's disciples should follow his example by relishing their friendships.

If *One Hundred Nails* would have been Olmi's final fictional work, as he originally intended it to be, its conclusion would have served as a potent closing statement, leaving his audience with his most fervent plea to consider how human society has lost its sense of purpose since the world's population left its community-bound, nature-based existence behind for unfettered and purposeless, material gain. Olmi's singular background (molded by his familiarity with the completeness of the lives of previous generations through his maternal family's farming background, his own unhappy experience working in an office job created by the new economy, and being on hand at Edisonvolta as Italy retooled itself to power the boom) informs the objective of his style: to question how we understand life and reality. This style is important to consider seriously because it demonstrates that we can look at the world, at our work, our sense of spirituality and/or God, and our relationships with families, friends and with the other, from a critical perspective that frees us to review reality based on our own experiences and intuition. While contemplating his films, we receive a sense of what was lost, and what can be regained, in humanity's renunciation of the ideals it previously held through its relationship with the natural world. In Olmi's cinema, nature is the ultimate muse and returning our gaze to it can save us from ourselves.

Chapter Notes

Introduction

1. Federico Fellini, *The Book of Dreams*, trans. Aaron Martin and David Stanton (New York: Rizzoli, 2008), 78.
2. Ermanno Olmi, interview by Daniela Padoan, *Ermanno Olmi: Il sentimento della realtà* [Ermanno Olmi: The feeling of reality] (Milan: Editrice San Raffaele, 2008), 56–57.
3. Derek Malcolm, review of *The Tree of Wooden Clogs*, The Guardian, September 2, 1999, https://www.theguardian.com/film/1999/sep/02/3.
4. Olmi, interview by Daniela Padoan, *Ermanno Olmi: Il sentimento della realtà*, 131–132.
5. Ni Zhen, *Memoirs from the Beijing Film Academy: The Genesis of China's Fifth Generation*, trans. Chris Berry (Durham, NC: Duke University Press, 2002), 102; Mike Leigh, "*Blow-Up*? It's a Pile of Pretentious Crap," *The Guardian*, October 26, 2015, https://www.theguardian.com/film/2015/oct/26/mike-leigh-blow-up-antonioni; Jonathan Rosenbaum, *Essential Cinema* (Baltimore: The Johns Hopkins University Press, 2004), 285.
6. Mark Shiel, *Italian Neorealism: Rebuilding the Cinematic City* (London: Wallflower Press, 2006), 1.
7. David Overbey, introduction to *Springtime in Italy*, ed. and trans. David Overbey (London: Talisman Books, 1978), 10.
8. Francesco Casetti, *Eye of the Century: Film, Experience, Modernity*, trans. Erin Larkin and Jennifer Pranolo (New York: Columbia University Press, 2008), 8.
9. André Bazin, "The Myth of Total Cinema," in *What Is Cinema?* vol. 1, ed. and trans. Hugh Gray (Berkeley: University of California Press, 1967), 17–22.
10. Stephen Prince, *The Warrior's Camera: The Cinema of Akira Kurosawa*, rev. ed. (Princeton: Princeton University Press, 1999), 159.
11. Tullio Kezich, *Il mestiere delle immagini, diario (in pubblico) di un amicizia* [The profession of images: a diary (in public) of a friendship] (Alessandria, Italy: Edizioni Falsopiano, 2004), 113–114.
12. Ermanno Olmi, interview by John Francis Lane, "A Conversation with John Francis Lane," *Sight and Sound* 39, no. 3 (1970): 150.
13. Ibid.
14. James Naremore, "Authorship," in *A Companion to Film Theory*, ed. Toby Miller and Robert Stam (Malden, MA: Blackwell Publishing, 2004), 23.
15. Marc Gervais, "Ermanno Olmi: Humanism in the Cinema," *Sight and Sound* 47, no. 4 (1978): 211.
16. For an excellent summary of environmentally related film studies, see Chapter 1 of Adam O'Brien, *Film and the natural Environment: Elements and Atmospheres* (London: Wallflower Press, 2018).
17. Paula Willoquet-Maricondi, "Shifting Paradigms: From Environmentalist Films to Ecocinema," in *Framing the World: Explorations in Ecocriticism and Film*, ed. Paula Willoquet-Maricondi (Charlottesville: University of Virginia Press, 2010), 45. With this definition, Willoquet-Maricondi seeks to distinguish ecocinema from "environmentalist" films.
18. Jonathan Watts, "We Have 12 Years to Limit Climate Change Catastrophe, Warns UN," *The Guardian*, October 8, 2018, https://www.theguardian.com/environ

ment/2018/oct/08/global-warming-must-not-exceed-15c-warns-landmark-un-report.

19. Richard James Havis, "Flashback: The Tree of Wooden Clogs—Ermanno Olmi's 1978 Tale of Poverty and Catholic Beliefs," review of *The Tree of Wooden Clogs*, *The South China Morning Post*, April 8, 2017, http://www.scmp.com/magazines/post-magazine/arts-music/article/2084406/flashback-tree-wooden-clogs-ermanno-olmis-1978.

A Brief Biography

1. Ermanno Olmi, interview by Charles Thomas Samuels, *Encountering Directors* (New York: Da Capo Press, 1987), 100.

2. Ermanno Olmi, *L'apocalisse è un lieto fine: storie della mia vita e del nostro futuro* [The apocalypse is a joyful conclusion: stories from my life and of our future] (Milan: RCS Libri, 2013), Kindle edition, chap.: La pianta di pomodori. Original Italian: "Questa è la mia vera data di nascita, e non è scritta su nessun documento. La mia vita è cominciata in quel loro primo lampo di sguardi."

3. *Ibid.*

4. Olmi, *L'apocalisse è un lieto fine*, chap.: La pianta di pomodori; Ermanno Olmi, interview by Charlie Owens, *Ermanno Olmi*. (Rome: Gremese, 2008), 9.

5. Olmi, *L'apocalisse è un lieto fine*, chap.: La pianta di pomodori.

6. Marco Manzoni, *Il primo sguardo* [The first glance] (Milan: Bompiani, 2015), Kindle edition, chap.: I documentari della sezione cinema della Edisonvolta.

7. Olmi, *L'apocalisse è un lieto fine*, O la scuola o il lavoro.

8. Olmi, interview by Charlie Owens, *Ermanno Olmi*, 10–12, 14.

9. Morando Morandini, *Ermanno Olmi* (Milan: Il Castro Cinema, 2009), 11.

10. Ermanno Olmi, interview by Sergio Toffetti, "Conversazione con Ermanno Olmi," in *I volti e le mani* [Faces and hands] (Milan: Feltrinelli Editore, 2008), 72–73.

11. *Ibid.*, 73.

12. Olmi, interview by Daniela Padoan, *Ermanno Olmi: Il sentimento della realtà*, 136.

13. Olmi, interview by Charlie Owens, *Ermanno Olmi*, 15. Although he does not specifically identify the work, Olmi describes the film as a work of German Expressionism.

14. Ermanno Olmi, interview by Emma Neri, "Conversazione con Ermanno Olmi," in AA. VV., *EuropaCinema '85*, n.p., quoted in Manzoni, *Il primo sguardo*, chap.: Dal piccolo all'universale: la poetica di Ermanno Olmi. Original Italian: "*Roma città aperta* fu la scoperta di un cinema che era la vita, che non divideva lo schermo dalla strada, ma proponeva una continuità per mezzo di quel mediatore ideale che è, o dovrebbe essere, il poeta. Il cinema, quindi, è stato il mio secondo amore.... La sberla che presi da *Roma città aperta* mi mise in un rapporto diverso con tutto il cinema che, da spettatore, frequentai. Cominciarono le prime cotte per Grierson, la grande scoperta di Flaherty. Mi resi conto che andavo al cinema non più per sognare, ma per capitare qualche cosa in più della vita."

15. Olmi, *L'apocalisse è un lieto fine*, chap.: Fare il teatro.

16. Kezich, *Il mestiere delle immagini, diario (in pubblico) di un amicizia*, 13.

17. Olmi, interview by Sergio Toffetti, "Conversazione con Ermanno Olmi," 75–76.

18. David Bruni, "I cortometraggi industriali," in *Ermanno Olmi. Il cinema, I film, la televisione, la scuola* [Ermanno Olmi: The cinema, the films, television, the school], ed. Adriano Aprà (Venice: Marsilio Editori, 2003), 119.

19. Paola Bonifazio, *Schooling in Modernity: The Politics of Sponsored Films in Postwar Italy* (Toronto: University of Toronto Press, 2014), 67.

20. *Ibid.*

21. Interestingly, Detto's character in *Il posto*, Antonietta, who also goes by the nickname "Magali," was likely named after an early love interest of Olmi's as a teenager. Olmi, *L'apocalisse è un lieto fine*, chap.: Favola e realtà.

22. Morandini, *Ermanno Olmi*, 41.

23. Manzoni, *Il primo sguardo*, chap.: Dal piccolo all'universale.

24. Ipotesi Cinema, "Lettera ai candidati per Ipotesi Cinema," in *Ermanno Olmi: L'esperienza di Ipotesi Cinema* [Ermanno Olmi: The experience of *Ipotesi cinema*], ed. Elisa Allegretti and Giancarlo Giraud (Bologna: Le Mani Editore, 2001), 185. Original Italian: "Non vogliamo che tu venga a

'Ipotesi Cinema' a cercare chi ti possa insegnare a fare il cinema ma a crearti tu stesso le opportunità di impararlo. Dipende solo da te."

25. "About Us," Slow Food, last modified, 2015. http://www.slowfood.com/about-us/.

26. Ermanno Olmi, interview by Marco Manzoni, *Il primo sguardo*, chap.: Il cinema dentro la vita: conversazione con Ermanno Olmi. Original Italian: "So che non finirò mai di essere acqua e luce. Perderò certamente la mia individualità, ma ho la speranza che non si disperderanno di me tutte quelle componenti che sono la vita."

27. Olmi, interview by Daniela Padoan, *Ermanno Olmi: Il sentimento della realtà*, 11. Original Italian: "Io amo più Cristo che Dio, amo più gli uomini che Dio, perché credo che, se da qualche parte è in giro nel cosmo, lui vuole questo."

Chapter 1

1. Giuliana Minghelli, "Haunted Frames: History and Landscape in Luchino Visconti's *Ossessione*," *Italica* 85, no. 2/3 (2008): 177. http://www.jstor.org/stable/40505801.

2. Peter Bondanella, *A History of Italian Cinema* (New York: Continuum, 2009), 227.

3. Ibid.

4. Edison has now made 15 of the films Olmi directed for the company available on their YouTube channel. They are collected in a playlist entitled "Archivio storico di Ermanno Olmi" that can be found at https://www.youtube.com/playlist?list=PLjV4jdWdzFfDCg5Q1vCtll7sWRp40Kl2W. In August 2008, the Italian publisher Feltrinelli also released a DVD, *Ermanno Olmi: gli anni Edison documentari e cortometraggi 1954-1958*, featuring seven of Olmi's Edison works. Four of these can also be found on the YouTube channel. Regrettably, English subtitles are not available on Edison's YouTube channel or on the DVD.

5. Sue Matheson, "The 'True Spirit' of Eating Raw Meat: London, Nietzsche, and Rousseau in Robert Flaherty's *Nanook of the North* (1922)," *Journal of Popular Film and Television* 39, no. 1 (2011): 18. https://doi.org/10.1080/01956051.2010.490074.

6. Aidan Arrowsmith, "Angles on Aran: Constructing Connection in the Work of J.M. Synge, Robert Flaherty and Sean Scully," *Textual Practice* 31 (2017): 16. http://dx.doi.org/10.1080/0950236X.2017.1314979.

7. Keith Beattie, *Documentary Screens: Non-Fiction Film and Television* (New York: Palgrave Macmillan, 2004), 31–32.

8. Bazin, *What Is Cinema?* vol. 1, 27.

9. In his essay on *Nanook of the North* for the Criterion Collection DVD of the film, Dean Duncan reviews the film's "faking and fudging in one form or another." Many of the scenes include simulations or recreations of traditional hunting or daily activities of the Inuit people that were not practiced at the time the film was made. Dean Duncan, "Nanook of the North," *The Criterion Collection*, last modified, 2017, https://www.criterion.com/current/posts/42-nanook-of-the-north.

10. Erik Barnouw, *Documentary: A History of the Non-fiction Film* (Oxford: Oxford University Press, 1974), 217.

11. John Grierson, "On Flaherty," *Reporter* 5, no. 8 (1951): 31–35, quoted in *Grierson on the Movies*, ed. Forsyth Hardy (London: Faber and Faber, 1981), 174.

12. Stephen G. Jones, *The British Labour Movement and Film, 1918–1939* (London: Routledge & Kegan Paul, 1987), 144.

13. Patricia Aufderheide, *Documentary: A Very Short Introduction* (Oxford: Oxford University Press, 2007), 35.

14. Andrew Sarris, "Film: The Illusion of Naturalism," *The Drama Review* 13, no. 2 (1968): 111. https://doi.org/10.2307/1144414.

15. Sam Rohdie, *The Passion of Pier Paolo Pasolini* (London: British Film Institute, 1995), 156.

16. A few of Olmi's Edison films (*Piccoli Calabresi*, *Michelino*, *Dialogo*, and *La Diga*) are discussed in detail in Bonifazio, *Schooling in Modernity: The Politics of Sponsored Films in Postwar Italy*, 67–76. These films, and the majority of Olmi's other documented Edison films, are covered here. *Grigio*, Olmi's second and final work with Pasolini, is the only other work, besides *Venezia città moderna*, I hoped to include but which I have not yet been able to view.

17. Unless otherwise indicated, my source of information regarding the background of the films discussed in this chapter is in the excellent annotated filmography written by Adriano Aprà, Laura Buffoni, and Stefania Carpiceci in Aprà, *Ermanno*

Olmi: Il cinema, i film, la televisione, la scuola, 327–332.

18. Olmi, *L'apocalisse è un lieto fine*, chap.: Apocalisse.

19. This film is a reconfiguration of *Sabbioni una diga a quota 2500* (Sabbioni, a Dam at 2500 m, 1952), which Edison made prior to the formation of the SCE.

20. Original Italian: "È una storia di tutti i giorni con eroi di tutti i giorni."

21. Jack Coogan, "Louisiana Story and an Ecology of the Imagination," *Wide Angle* 20, no. 2 (1998): 67. https://doi.org/10.1353/wan.1998.0013.

22. Olmi, interview by Sergio Toffetti, "Conversazione con Ermanno Olmi," 78–79.

23. Giovanni Cecchetti, introduction to *Operette morali* [Moral works], by Giacomo Leopardi, trans. Giovanni Cecchetti (Berkeley: University of California Press, 1982), 4.

24. Tag Gallagher, *The Adventures of Roberto Rossellini: His Life and Films* (New York: Da Capo Press, 1998), 408.

25. Chandak Sengoopta, "'The Universal Film for All of Us, Everywhere in the World': Satyajit Ray's *Pather Panchali* (1955) and the Shadow of Robert Flaherty," *Historical Journal of Film, Radio and Television* 29, no. 3 (2009): 283. https://doi.org/10.1080/01439680903145520.

26. This quote is included in the description of *La mia valle* on the official Edison YouTube channel. Edison's YouTube Channel page: *La mia valle*, published February 5, 2016, https://www.youtube.com/watch?v=TRfrZUtljMQ&list=PLjV4jdWdzFfDCg5Q1vCtll7sWRp40Kl2W&index=7. No source for the quote is given. Original Italian: "Inizio la lavorazione del film andando in cerca dei luoghi e delle persone. Queste ultime le cerco nell'ambiente in cui esse già vivono. Quando le trovo le riunisco e comincio a lavorare con loro... Il film viene fatto con una mia provocazione e con il loro coinvolgimento personale, il che consente di raccogliere una serie di contributi all'insaputa degli interpreti stessi."

27. John Woodhouse, *Gabriele d'Annunzio: Defiant Archangel* (Oxford: Oxford University Press, 2001), 208.

28. John David Rhodes, "The Eclipse of Place: Rome's EUR from Rossellini to Antonioni," in *Taking Place: Location and the Moving Image*, ed. John David Rhodes and Elena Gorfinkel (Minneapolis: University of Minnesota Press,, 2011), 33.

29. *EuropaCinema 85* (Rimini: Europa Cinema, 1985) quoted in "Olmi su Olmi," *Ermanno Olmi: l'esperienza di Ipotesi cinema*, 204. Original Italian: "Non in senso tecnico, ma di come l'autore deve porsi nei confronti della realtà."

30. Pier Paolo Pasolini, *Heretical Empiricism*, ed. by Louise Barnett, trans. Ben Lawton and Louise Barnett (Bloomington: Indiana University Press, 1988), 173.

31. André Bazin, *What Is Cinema?* vol. 2, ed. and trans. Hugh Gray (Berkeley: University of California Press, 1972), 87.

32. Pasolini, *Heretical Empiricism*, 177.

33. Naomi Greene, *Pier Paolo Pasolini: Cinema as Heresy* (Princeton: Princeton University Press, 1990), 43.

34. Morandini, *Ermanno Olmi*, 18. Original Italian: "Un'atmosfera fiabesca, quasi magica."

35. John Foot, "Migration and the 'Miracle' at Milan. The Neighbourhoods of Baggio, Barona, Bovisa and Comasina in the 1950s and 1960s," *Journal of Historical Sociology* 10, no. 2 (1997): 184. https://doi.org/10.1111/1467-6443.00036.

36. Bonifazio, *Schooling in Modernity: The Politics of Sponsored Films in Postwar Italy*, 73.

37. Kezich, *Ermanno Olmi: il mestiere delle immagini, diario (in pubblico) di un'amicizia*, 12. Original Italian: "Questo modo di fare il cinema significa scoprire un mondo."

Chapter 2

1. R.J.B. Bosworth, *Italy the Least of the Great Powers: Italian Foreign Policy Before the First World War* (Cambridge: Cambridge University Press, 1979), 9.

2. Paul Ginsborg, *A History of Contemporary Italy: Society and Politics 1943–1988* (New York: Palgrave Macmillan, 2003), 1.

3. For a thorough and clear description of the governmental decisions and general circumstances leading to the economic miracle, see the first two chapters of Donald Sassoon, *Contemporary Italy: Economy, Society, and Politics since 1945* (London: Longman Publishing, 1997).

4. John Foot, *Modern Italy* (New York: Palgrave Macmillan, 2003), 138.

5. Sassoon, *Contemporary Italy: Economy, Society, and Politics since 1945*, 125.
6. Morandini, *Ermanno Olmi*, 48–50.
7. Olmi, interview by Daniela Padoan, *Il sentimento della realtà*, 51.
8. Olmi, interview by Charlie Owens, *Ermanno Olmi*, 21. Elsewhere, Olmi has stated that Edisonvolta was hesitant to make feature films because the stockbrokers would feel too much money was being spent. Olmi, interview by Charles Thomas Samuels, *Encountering Directors*, 104.
9. Olmi, interview by Charlie Owens, *Ermanno Olmi*, 21.
10. Virgilio Fantuzzi, "Il cristiano muore ogni giorno e ogni giorno rinasce," in Aprà, *Ermanno Olmi: Il cinema, i film, la televisione, la scuola*, 39.
11. Scott MacDonald, "The Ecocinema Experience," in *Ecocinema Theory and Practice*, ed. Stephen Rust, Salma Monani, and Sean Cubitt (New York: Routledge, 2013), 20.
12. The day Salvetti departs coincidentally references an offshoot of Edisonvolta's cinema division, 22 Dicembre, that was probably added to the credits of *Time Stood Still* after the film received wider distribution rights. 22 Dicembre would later fund *I fidanzati* and eventually also produced *The Iron Age* when Roberto Rossellini could find no other support. See Gallagher, *The Adventures of Roberto Rossellini: His Life and Films*, 560.
13. Pasolini, *Heretical Empiricism*, 212–222. Pasolini gave a linguistic reading of the first eleven shots of the film in comparison with a scene from Bertolucci's *Prima della rivoluzione* (*Before the Revolution*, 1964). Reacting to Olmi's long shots detailing minute tasks, Pasolini states that if he had to reproduce the sequence "linguistically, by means of analogy" he would "put together a prose" composition in comparison with the poetry he would use for Bertolucci.
14. Marc Henri Piault, "Real with Fiction," *Visual Anthropology Review* 23, no. 1 (2007): 18. https://doi.org/10.1525/var.2007.23.1.16.
15. Clodagh Brook, "Beyond Dialogue: Speech-Silence, the Monologue, and Power in the Films of Ermanno Olmi," *The Italianist* 28, no. 2 (2008): 278. https://doi.org/10.1179/026143408x363569.
16. Natale is most likely reading a nationalistic, late nineteenth-century novel by Edmondo De Amicis that extolls traditional morals.
17. John Gillett, review of *Time Stood Still*, *Sight and Sound* 32, no. 2 (1963): 93–94.
18. Bosley Crowther, "Screen: A Clerk in Italy. 'Sound of Trumpets' at Two Theatres," review of *Il posto*, *New York Times*, October 23, 1963, https://www.nytimes.com/1963/10/23/archives/screen-a-clerk-in-italy-sound-of-trumpets-at-two-theaters.html.
19. Ernest Callenbach, review of *Il posto*, *Film Quarterly* 17, no. 4 (1964): 45. https://doi.org/10.2307/1210655.
20. See, for example, Millicent Marcus, *Italian Film in the Light of Neo-Realism* (Princeton: Princeton University Press, 1986), 219.
21. Bert Cardullo, "Married to the Job: Ermanno Olmi's *Il Posto* and *I fidanzati* Reconsidered," *The Cambridge Quarterly* 38, no. 2 (2009): 123. https://doi.org/10.7135/upo9781843313434.007.
22. "Reflecting Reality," *Il posto* (1961; New York: Criterion Collection, 2003), DVD.
23. David Bordwell, "Shot and Scene," in *The Classical Hollywood Cinema: Film Style and Mode of Production to 1960*, David Bordwell, Janet Staiger, and Kristin Thompson (London: Routledge, 2005), 64–71. Adobe eReader.
24. Elizabeth Alsop, "Neorealism in the Age of Mechanical Reproduction: Restoring the Aura in Olmi's *Il posto*," *Quarterly Review of Film and Video* 32, no. 2 (2015): 189. https://doi.org/10.1080/10509208.2013.811350.
25. Marcus, *Italian Film in the Light of Neo-Realism*, 212.
26. Bondanella, *A History of Italian Cinema*, 228.
27. Cardullo, "Married to the Job: Ermanno Olmi's *Il Posto* and *I Fidanzati* Reconsidered," 123.
28. Marcus, *Italian Film in the Light of Neo-Realism*, 220.
29. Amédée Ayfre, "Neo-Realism and Phenomenology," in *Cahiers du cinéma: The 1950s: Neo-Realism, Hollywood, New Wave*, ed. Jim Hillier (Cambridge, MA: Harvard University Press, 1985), 185.
30. "Mysteries of Life," *I fidanzati* (1963; New York: Criterion Collection, 2003), DVD.

31. The film did have its admirers. Jean-Luc Godard, to whom Olmi's film would have obvious allure, placed the film in a list of the top ten films ever made. See Kezich, *Ermanno Olmi: il mestiere delle immagini, diario (in pubblico) di un'amicizia*, 38–39.

32. Fernaldo di Giamatteo, "'Marienbadism' and the New Italian Directors," *Film Quarterly* 16, no. 2 (1962–1963): 20. https://doi.org/10.1525/fq.1962.16.2.04a00050.

33. András Kovács, *Screening Modernism: European Art Cinema, 1950–1980* (Chicago: The University of Chicago Press, 2007), 211. Kovács inaccurately suggests that *I fidanzati* is the only one of Olmi's works to feature fragmented form and non-linear time.

34. Olmi, interview by Charles Thomas Samuels, *Encountering Directors*, 112.

35. Emma Wilson, *Alain Resnais* (Manchester, UK: Manchester University Press, 2006), 5.

36. Kezich, *Ermanno Olmi: il mestiere delle immagini, diario (in pubblico) di un'amicizia*, 25. Original Italian: "La realtà e i ricordi, le esperienze e i sogni si confondono nella cronaca dell'esistenza di Giovanni." "Ha la superiore ambiguità della rappresentazioni totali, esaurenti."

37. The novel has been adapted several times for Italian cinema since the early twentieth century. At least three television versions have been made as well.

38. Rudolph M. Bell, *Fate and Honor, Family and Village: Demographic and Cultural Change in Rural Italy since 1800* (Chicago: University of Chicago Press, 1979), 5.

39. We can only presume the reasons for the setbacks in their relationship because the order of many of the events in the film are uncertain.

40. This scene was filmed at an actual Carnival festival in Paternò, northwest of Priolo, where most of the rest of the scenes in Sicily were shot. See Olmi, interview by Charlie Owens, *Ermanno Olmi*, 46.

41. For a summary of these arguments, and a rebuttal, see Jane and Peter Schneider, *Culture and Political Economy in Western Sicily* (New York: Academic Press, 1976), chap. 11.

42. John Foot, "Mass Cultures, Popular Cultures and the Working Class in Milan, 1950–70," *Social History* 24, no. 9 (1999): 137. https://doi.org/10.1080/03071029908568059.

43. Pier Paolo Pasolini, *Scritti corsari* [Corsair writings] (Milan: Garzanti, 1975), 45. Original Italian: "Il mondo contadino, dopo circa quattordici anni di vita, ha cessato di esistere praticamente di colpo."

44. Peter Brunette, *The Films of Michelangelo Antonioni* (Cambridge: Cambridge University Press, 1998), 31.

45. *Ibid.*

46. Olmi has spoken with interviewers several times about his prophecy that the rain required for this scene would fall despite a drought during the months they were shooting the film. One day during production, he prayed to his deceased grandmother for rain and then dreamed of her that evening presiding over him filming in the rain. The next morning when he awoke to clear skies, he instructed a baffled crew to prepare themselves for the rain shots. See Olmi, interview by Charles Thomas Samuels, *Encountering Directors*, 109–110 and Olmi, interview by Charlie Owens, *Ermanno Olmi*, 49.

47. Bazin, *What Is Cinema?*, Vol. 2, 67.

48. *Ibid.*, 66.

Chapter 3

1. Sidney Tarrow, *Democracy and Disorder: Protest and Politics in Italy 1965–1975* (Oxford: Oxford University Press, 1989), 51.

2. Richard Drake, "Italy in the 1960s: A Legacy of Terrorism and Liberation," *South Central Review* 16–17, no. 4–1 (1999–2000): 63. https://doi.org/10.2307/3190077.

3. Alan O'Leary, "Italian cinema and the *anni di piombo*," *Journal of European Studies* 40, no. 3 (2010): 244–245. https://doi.org/10.1177/0047244110371912. There are exceptions. Several of Elio Petri's films of the 1970s (e.g. *La classe operaia va in paradiso* [*Lulu the Tool*, 1971], and *Todo modo* [*One Way or Another*,1976]) were engaged in concurrent Italian events. Later, Bertolucci would depict three complacent youths at the outset of the French counterpart to Italy's 1968 student protests in *The Dreamers* (2003) and Marco Bellocchio returned to the Moro kidnapping case in *Buongiorno, notte* (*Good Morning, Night*, 2003).

4. Roberto Rossellini, "A Panorama of

History," in *My Method: Writings and Interviews*, ed. Adriano Aprà, trans. Annapaola Cancogni (New York: Marsilio Publishers, 1992), 179. Also see Michael Cramer, "Rossellini's History Lessons," *New Left Review* 78 (2012). Cramer provides a thorough background of Rossellini's ambitious project and its utopian aspirations.

4. Manzoni, *Il primo sguardo*, chap.: *Un certo giorno*.

5. John Francis Lane, "Ermanno Olmi: Camera of Concern," in *Movies of the Seventies*, ed. Ann Lloyd (London: Orbis Publishing, 1984), 138.

6. Olmi, interview by Charlie Owens, *Ermanno Olmi*, 65.

7. Basil Wright, *The Long View* (New York: Alfred A. Knopf, 1974), 528.

8. See Olmi, interview by Charlie Owens, *Ermanno Olmi*, 64–65. Olmi shares that this incident was unfortunately based on a firsthand experience. His friend, who was driving the car, also hit a road-side worker who died two days after the collision. Olmi saw the driver years later and sensed that the man did not want to speak of the accident. However, his friend eventually confessed that he was unable to put the event behind him and that it had changed his life.

9. The carabinieri is one of Italy's national police forces.

10. "Intervista a Ermanno Olmi," *Un certo giorno* (1968; Dolmen Home Video, 2009). DVD.

11. Jean-Paul Sartre, *No Exit and Three Other Plays*, trans. Stuart Gilbert (New York: Vintage Books, 1976), 45.

12. Olmi, interview by Charlie Owens, *Ermanno Olmi*, 61. Original Italian: "Una sorta di delitto."

13. Pierre Leprohon, *The Italian Cinema*, trans. Roger Graves and Oliver Stallybrass (New York: Praeger Publishers, 1972), 201.

14. Anat Pick, "Three Worlds: Dwelling and Worldhood on Screen," in *Screening Nature: Cinema Beyond the Human*, ed. Anat Pick and Guinevere Narraway (New York: Berghahn Books, 2013), 31.

15. Richard Roud, "Roman Summer," *Sight and Sound* 40, no. 4 (1971): 202.

16. Olmi, interview by Charlie Owens, *Ermanno Olmi*, 78.

17. Luca Finatti, *Stupore e mistero nel cinema di Ermanno Olmi* [Stupor and mystery in the cinema of Ermanno Olmi] (Rome: Associazione Nazionale Circoli Cinematografici Italiani, 2000), 139–140. Finatti also follows Olmi's lead in categorizing the film as one of the director's parables. However, due to its contemporary setting, and its political subtext, I have grouped the film together with *One Fine Day* and *The Circumstance*. Also see Olmi, interview by Charles Thomas Samuels, *Encountering Directors*, 114, for the director's admission that he based the film on the Gospels of the New Testament.

18. David Thompson, *The New Biographical Dictionary of Film*, 5th ed. (New York: Alfred A. Knopf, 2010), 724.

19. Wright, *The Long View*, 529.

20. Olmi, interview by Charles Thomas Samuels, *Encountering Directors*, 114.

21. Olmi, interview by Daniela Padoan, *Il sentimento della realtà*, 12–13. Original Italian: "La raccomandazione di Cristo non è tanto osservare le regole, come precetto, ma è ama il tuo prossimo come te stesso." "In un certo senso è proprio la disobbedienza ciò che ci porta al Cristo uomo, uno come noi, che possiamo ancora incontrare in un qualsiasi giorno della nostra esistenza, in qualsiasi tempo e luogo."

22. Charles Maland, *City Lights* (London: British Film Institute, 2007), 77.

23. See Alsop, "Neorealism in the Age of Mechanical Reproduction: Restoring the Aura in Olmi's *Il Posto*," 180. Alsop argues that the final scene of Olmi's second feature conveys a Benjaminian philosophy that appears throughout Olmi's work. She describes the scene as expressing "an anxiety about decreasing veneration not only for the 'work of art,' but for more mundane human works, the kinds of unexceptional activity regularly and often reverently depicted in his films."

24. Walter Benjamin, "The Work of Art in the Age of Mechanical Reproduction" in *Illuminations: Essays and Reflections*, ed. Hannah Arendt, trans. Harry Zohn (New York: Schocken Books, 2007), 223.

25. William Rothman, *The 'I' of the Camera: Essays in Film Criticism, History, and Aesthetics* (Cambridge: Cambridge University Press, 2004), 54.

26. Morandini, *Ermanno Olmi*, 56. Among the film's supporters was Bertolucci who complimented Olmi on the film's gentleness.

27. Simona de Iulio and Carlo Vinti, "The Americanization of Italian Advertising During the 1950s and the 1960s: Mediations, Conflicts, and Appropriations," *Journal of Historical Research in Marketing* 1, no. 2 (2009): 286–287. https://doi.org/10.1108/17557500910974613.

28. *Ibid.*, 288.

29. Olmi, interview by Charlie Owens, *Ermanno Olmi*, 87.

30. "Intervista a Ermanno Olmi," *La circostanza* (1973; Milan: Dolmen Home Video, 2009). DVD.

31. Chris Fujiwara, "One Fine Filmmaker: The uncertain idealism of Ermanno Olmi," *The Boston Phoenix*, August 1–8, 2002, accessed January 4, 2014, boston phoenix.com. (site discontinued).

32. I base my assumption about this scene's chronology on Laura's clothing as she enters the house. She wears the same outfit seen at the hospital in an earlier scene.

33. Sassoon, *Contemporary Italy: Economy, Society and Politics Since 1945*, 126.

34. Finatti, *Stupore e mistero nel cinema di Ermanno Olmi*, 59. Original Italian: "L'unico personaggio positivo." "La sua presenza nel racconto è incolore, senza spessore drammaturgico, un bozzetto mal riuscito."

35. Olmi feels uneasy about this final scene because Tommaso's counterpart from the family the film is based on died after overtaking a vehicle on the highway. In an interview on the film's DVD, he expresses responsibility for somehow foreshadowing the tragedy. "In reality, there are precise signs that, in some way or another, preconstitute an idea of destiny" adding that he feels he "stole part of their soul. "Intervista a Ermanno Olmi," *La circostanza*.

36. Finatti, *Stupore e mistero nel cinema di Ermanno Olmi*, 59.

37. Leger Grindon, *Shadows on the Past: Studies in the Historical Fiction Film* (Philadelphia: Temple University Press, 1994), 5.

Chapter 4

1. Simonetta Falasca-Zamponi, *Fascist Spectacle: The Aesthetics of Power in Mussolini's Italy* (Berkeley: University of California Press, 1997), 90–95.

2. Marcia Landy, "The Subject of History: Italian Filmmakers as Historians," in *A Companion to the Historical Film*, ed. Robert A. Rosenstone and Constantin Parvulescu (Chichester, UK: Wiley-Blackwell, 2013), 133–134.

3. Robert Rosenstone, *Visions of the Past: The Challenge of Film to Our Idea of History* (Cambridge, MA: Harvard University Press, 1995), 63.

4. Cristina Piccino, "Ermanno Olmi gira un film sulla Grande guerra," *Il manifesto*, January 22, 2014, https://ilmanifesto.it/ermanno-olmi-gira-un-film-sulla-grande-guerra/.

5. Kezich, *Ermanno Olmi: il mestiere delle immagini, diario (in pubblico) di un'amicizia*, 32.

6. *Ibid.*

7. *Ibid.*, 31.

8. See Mario Rigoni Stern, interview by Felix Siddell, "'Sette volte bosco, sette volte prato': An Interview with Mario Rigoni Stern," *Modern Language Notes* 113, no. 1 (1998): 232. https://doi.org/10.1353/mln.1998.0015. Stern would develop a similar story about scavengers for war relics, set between the two world wars, in his 1995 novel, *Le stagioni di Giacomo [Giacomo's Seasons]*.

9. Stern was also a soldier in Russia during World War II and *Sergeant in the Snow* memorialized his own journey back to Italy following the war.

10. Roy Armes, "Family Resemblances: A Note on Ermanno Olmi," *London Magazine*, June 1, 1971, 109.

11. This is the same song Lunardi sang to Olmi, Stern, and Kezich when they first encountered him at the inn.

12. Morandini, *Ermanno Olmi*, 53. Original Italian: "Ma quando entra in scena il vecchio Du… il film diventa sua storia."

13. Finatti, *Stupore e mistero nel cinema di Ermanno Olmi*, 39. Original Italian: "La semplice visione di questi corpi morti si fa quindi 'rivelazione' misteriosa, epifania che interpella la coscienza di chi guarda e lo inviata a cambiare vita."

14. Kezich, *Ermanno Olmi: il mestiere delle immagini, diario (in pubblico) di un'amicizia*, 39.

15. *Ibid.*, 40.

16. Deborah Young, "On Earth as It Is in Heaven," *Film Comment* 37, no. 2 (2001): 60.

17. Mike Leigh, interview with Mark Monahan, "Film makers on Film: Mike

Leigh," *The Telegraph*, October 19, 2002. https://www.telegraph.co.uk/culture/film/3584402/Film-makers-on-film-Mike-Leigh.html.

18. Jonathan Keates, "In the Cascina," *Sight and Sound* 58, no. 1 (1988): 27.

19. Alberto Moravia, "Ora basta, disse il cavallo" *L'espresso*, October 22, 1978, 154–156. Original Italian: "L'ideologia di 'L'albero degli zoccoli' è invece quella manzoniana, cioè quella di chi guarda alla cultura contadina come ad un modello, con ammirazione ed approvazione, cercando di adottarne la visione del mondo."

20. M.A Hall, "Cinema Paradiso: Re-Picturing the Medieval Cult of Saints," *Peregrinations: Journal of Medieval Art and Architecture* 2, no. 1 (2005): n.p. http://digital.kenyon.edu/perejournal/vol2/iss1/6.

21. The scenes in Milan were actually shot in Pavia, which had changed very little in the seventy-eight years since the setting of the film.

22. Martin Walsh, "Ermanno Olmi: The Ethic of Individual Responsibility," *Monogram* 1, no. 2 (1978): 25.

23. Charlie Owens, "il mestiere delle armi" in *Ermanno Olmi* (Rome: Gremese, 2008), 145.

24. Kezich, *Ermanno Olmi: il mestiere delle immagini, diario (in pubblico) di un'amicizia*, 163.

25. See Olaf Möller, "A Specter Called Knowledge," *Film Comment* 39, no. 6 (2003): 62. Möller reports that when the film showed in Cannes, attendees left the film in droves due to its challenging style.

26. Christopher Hibbert, *The House of Medici: Its Rise and Fall* (New York: William Morrow and Company, 1975), 69–72.

27. See James Cleugh, *The Medici: A Tale of Fifteen Generations* (New York: Dorset Press, 1990), 239. Many historians skip over Giovanni dalle Bande Nere to focus on his son, Cosimo. Cleugh is an exception among recent Medici historians. He is one of the few to provide any detailed information at all about Giovanni, his personality, and his fearsome reputation.

28. Ibid., 241–243.

29. Ibid., 239, 248–249.

30. Ibid., 240.

31. Stephanie Pappas, "Tomb of Renaissance Warrior Reveals Mystery Amputation," *Live Science*, November 21, 2012, https://www.livescience.com/24981-renaissance-tomb-reveals-mystery-injury.html.

32. Cleugh, *The Medici: A Tale of Fifteen Generations*, 251, 254.

33. Hibbert, *The House of Medici: Its Rise and Fall*, 242.

34. There have been many theories regarding the actual cause of Giovanni's death. Some speculate that he was poisoned while he was being treated for his wound. Others suggest he may have been the victim of a political plot. The historically accepted cause of death is gangrene. After *The Profession of Arms* was completed, a group of scientists participated in The Medici Project from 2004–2007. The project consisted of exhuming the bodies of the Medici family entombed in the San Lorenzo church in Florence. However, after examining Giovanni's body, researchers were still unable to determine the exact cause of his death. See Gino Fornaciari, et al., "A Great Enigma of the Italian Renaissance: Paleopathological Study on the Death of Giovanni dalle Bande Nere (1498–1526) and Historical Relevance of a Leg Amputation," *BMC Musculoskeletal Disorders* 15, no. 301 (2014): 1–7. https://doi.org/10.1186/1471-2474-15-301.

35. There are at least three other films about Giovanni dalle Bande Nere. A silent film, *Giovanni dalle Bande Nere*, was released in 1910. In 1956 Vittorio Gassman starred in *Giovanni dalle Bande Nere (The Violent Patriot)*. And in 1937, *Condottieri* was commissioned by the fascist government. Cristelle Baskins details how the film was meant to promote patriotism but debunks the idea that it can simply be understood as a fascist allegory. See Cristelle Baskins, "A Storm of Images: Italian Renaissance Art in Luis Trenker's *Condottieri* (1937)," *The Italianist* 31, no. 2 (2011): 181–204. https://doi.org/10.1179/026143411x13051090964596.

36. Daniel Leisawitz, "*Il mestiere delle armi*: Renaissance Technology and the Cinema," in *New Worlds and the Italian Renaissance*, ed. Andrea Moudarres and Christiana Purdy Moudarres (Leiden, Netherlands: Brill, 2012), 99.

37. Several of Olmi's recent feature length documentaries, *Terra madre* and *Rupi del vino*, have also been produced by *Ipotesi Cinema*.

38. Manzoni, *Il primo sguardo*, chap.: *Torneranno I prati*.

39. A literal English translation of the Italian title would be "the fields will return."

40. Original Italian: "La guerra è una brutta bestia che gira il mondo e non si ferma mai."

41. John R. Schindler, *Isonzo: The Forgotten Sacrifice of the Great War* (Westport: Praeger, 2001), xii.

42. Mark Thompson, *The White War: Life and Death on the Italian Front* (New York: Basic Books, 2008), 18.

43. *Ibid.*, 17.

44. *Ibid.*, 149.

45. Schindler, *Isonzo: The Forgotten Sacrifice of the Great War*, 109.

46. Thompson, *The White War: Life and Death on the Italian Front*, 1–2.

47. Alessandro Zaccuri, "Grande guerra, Olmi porta Giobbe in trincea," *Avvenire*, November 4, 2014. https://www.avvenire.it/agora/pagine/olmi-.

48. Kristian Moen, *Film and Fairy Tales: The Birth of Modern Fantasy* (London: I.B. Tauris, 2013), xv.

Chapter 5

1. Jack Zipes, "The Great Cultural Tsunami of Fairy Tale Films," in *Fairy-Tale Films Beyond Disney: International Perspectives*, ed. Jack Zipes, Pauline Greenhill, and Kendra Magnus-Johnston (New York: Routledge, 2016), 1–17.

2. *Ibid.*, 6.

3. Finatti, *Stupore e mistero nel cinema di Ermanno Olmi*, 154. Original Italian: "… Danno la possibilità al regista di proporre in qualche modo 'modelli' di umanità… dare forma a ideali, forse utopie."

4. Olmi, interview by Charles Thomas Samuels, *Encountering Directors*, 104.

5. Ermanno Olmi, interview by Luca Pellegrini, "Ottimista per disperazione," *L'osservatore Romano*, September 4, 2008. http://www.vatican.va/news_services/or/or_quo/interviste/2008/206q05a1.html. Original Italian: "Perché le favole sono come le parabole. La favole sono un modo per capire la realtà estraendola dal suo contesto e rendendo tutto emblematico. Nelle favole si condensano tutti i nodi, le trame, tutto ciò che è nascosto nella vita reale. Le favole, come le parabole, sono formate da realtà esemplari."

6. Manzoni, *Il primo sguardo*, chap.: Dal piccolo all'universale.

7. Goffredo Fofi, Introduction to *Il ragazzo della Bovisa* [The boy from Bovisa], by Ermanno Olmi. (Milan: Oscar Mondadori, 2004), v.

8. Olmi, interview by Charlie Owens, *Ermanno Olmi*, 109–110.

9. *Ibid.*, 110, 115.

10. Morandini, *Ermanno Olmi*, 68.

11. The castle of the film is actually Castel Ivano, around an hour away from Olmi's home in Asiago. Olmi, interview by Charlie Owens, *Ermanno Olmi*, 115.

12. Marcia Landy, *Italian Film* (Cambridge: Cambridge University Press, 2000), 149–153, 161–164. Landy considers *The Tree of Wooden Clogs* a Gramscian work, alongside other films from Visconti, Bertolucci, Monicelli, Pasolini, and the Taviani brothers. She suggests that "the name of Antonio Gramsci is as important for cinema as it is for Italian political thought" in her argument that these works probe "the immersion of the subaltern classes in a way of life and thinking."

13. David Shipman, "Cinema: A Quarterly Review," *Contemporary Review*, April 1, 1988, 208.

14. For example, *The Phantom of Liberty* has an infamous sequence in which a group of dinner guests lower their underwear and pants before sitting on toilets placed around a table and then formally chat about excrement and urine.

15. Melanie A. Kimball, "From Folktales to Fiction: Orphan Characters in Children's Literature," *Library Trends* 47, no. 3 (1999): 559.

16. See, for example, Anna Wierzbicka's explanation of this interpretation of Christ's commandment to "be perfect." Anna Wierzbicka, *What Did Jesus Mean?: Explaining the Sermon on the Mount and the Parables in Simple and Universal Human Concepts* (Oxford: Oxford University Press, 2001), 115.

17. Morandini, *Ermanno Olmi*, 70–71.

18. Olmi, interview by Charlie Owens, *Ermanno Olmi*, 117. Tullio Kezich's wife, Lalla, who died before the project was completed, recommended Olmi direct the film.

19. *Ibid.*, 134. Spinotti had worked as an assistant camera operator on *A Man Named John* and had just began working in Hollywood when he accepted a position on Olmi's film.

20. David Bronsen, "Austrian Versus

Jew: The Torn Identity of Joseph Roth," *The Leo Baeck Institute Year Book* 18, no. 1 (1973): 224–225. https://doi.org/10.1093/leobaeck/18.1.220.

21. In the English audio version, the main actors in the film speak in English, with the voices of the original cast, while many of the minor characters communicate in French and occasionally in English. This was Olmi's first feature with a language other than Italian, or one of its dialects, as the major spoken language of the film.

22. Thomas Nevin, *Thérèse of Lisieux: God's Gentle Warrior* (Oxford: Oxford University Press, 2006), 288, 293. Nevin claims that *Thérèse* had a spiritual crisis before her early death, which led her to conclude that there was no heaven. He sees her commitment to make earth her heaven as a result of this turning point in her belief system.

23. Barbara Corrado Pope, "A Heroine Without Heroics: The Little Flower of Jesus and Her Times," *Church History: Studies in Christianity and Culture* 57, no. 1 (1988): 48–50.

24. Joseph Roth, *Right and Left & Legend of the Holy Drinker*, trans. Michael Hoffmann (Woodstock, NY: Overlook Press, 1992), 287.

25. Finatti, *Stupore e mistero nel cinema di Ermanno Olmi*, 97.

26. Willoquet-Maricondi, "Shifting Paradigms: From Environmentalist Films to Ecocinema," in *Framing the World: Explorations in Ecocriticism and Film*, 45.

27. Olmi, interview by Charlie Owens, *Ermanno Olmi*, 128.

28. Olmi, interview by Charlie Owens, *Ermanno Olmi*, 128; "Intervista a Ermanno Olmi," *Il segreto del bosco vecchio* (1993; Medusa Video, 2010). DVD.

29. Bondanella, *A History of Italian Cinema*, 212.

30. Olmi, interview by Charlie Owens, *Ermanno Olmi*, 131. No trees were harmed for the film's production. The tree the lumberjacks saw down in the film was in a protected park and a forest ranger already marked it for removal to ensure the survival of surrounding trees.

31. Morandini, *Ermanno Olmi*, 76.

32. I am using the pinyin rendition of 郑 (zhèng), the widow's last name. She is also known as widow (or madame) Ching, or Ching Shi.

33. Morandini, *Ermanno Olmi*, 87.

34. Jay Weissberg, "Singing Behind Screens," *Variety*, October 23, 2003. http://variety.com/2003/film/reviews/singing-behind-screens-1200538428/.

35. Kezich, *Ermanno Olmi: il mestiere delle immagini, diario (in pubblico) di un'amicizia*, 169.

36. "Il maestro e la favola," *Cantando dietro i paraventi* (2003; 01 Distribution, 2006). DVD.

37. Kezich, *Ermanno Olmi: il mestiere delle immagini, diario (in pubblico) di un'amicizia*, 197.

38. See Olga Kourelou, "'Put the Blame on ... Mei': Zhang Ziyi and the Politics of Global Stardom" in *The Femme Fatale: Images, Histories, Contexts*, ed. Helen Hanson and Catherine O'Rawe (London: Palgrave Macmillan, 2010), 113–126. Kourelou discusses the accusations thrown at one of the stars, Zhang Ziyi, of both betraying and misrepresenting her country for appearing in transnational films.

39. Bertolt Brecht, "On Chinese Acting," trans. Eric Bently, *The Tulane Drama Review* 6, no. 1 (1961): 130. https://doi.org/10.2307/1125011.

40. The widow also appears, in a small role, in the third installment of the *Pirates of the Caribbean* franchise, *Pirates of the Caribbean: At World's End* (2007), as one of the nine pirate lords.

41. Wenshang Wan, *White Lotus Rebels and South China Pirates: Crisis and Reform in the Qing Empire* (Cambridge, MA: Harvard University Press, 2014), 86.

42. Brecht, "On Chinese Acting," 131.

43. In this instance, the mixing of Asian cultural traditions (*seppuku* is a Japanese tradition, not a Chinese one) is not an original invention of Olmi's sandbox vision of China, but an incident adapted from Borges' short story.

44. Olmi, interview with Daniela Padoan, *Ermanno Olmi: Il sentimento della realtà*, 95. Part of a longer quote in the original Italian: "Se la donna ha, da protagonista, il compito di rigenerare, se è la carne in cui ci si incarna, lo stesso primato ce l'ha nella conoscenza dell'amore, secondo un sapere che gli uomini, intesi come maschi, non hanno. Questo è il motive per cui, nei momenti di difficoltà della storia, è la donna a farsi protagonista."

45. Antonella Molinaro, "Speciale evento: Ermanno Olmi gira a Bari,"

Cinemio, last modified 2017. http://cinemio.it/film-italiani/il-villaggio-di-cartone-ermanno-olmi/7161/.

46. Manzoni, *Il primo sguardo*, chap.: *Il villaggio di cartone*.

47. Molinaro, "Speciale evento: Ermanno Olmi gira a Bari," *Cinemio*.

48. "*Il villaggio di cartone*: Ermanno Olmi gira il suo nuovo film a Bari" Apulia Film Commission, accessed November 3, 2017, http://www.apuliafilmcommission.it/news/il-villaggio-di-cartone-ermanno-olmi-gira-il-suo-nuovo-film-a-bari.

49. Robert Bresson, *Notes on Cinematography*, trans. Jonathan Griffin (New York: Urizen Books, 1975), 24.

50. Paul Schrader, *Transcendental Style in Film* (New York: Da Capo Press, 1972), 65.

51. During a conversation when one of the refugees calls the mother of a friend who fell overboard during the journey, it is revealed that they departed from Gore, which could refer to a city in either Chad or Ethiopia. No further context is provided to indicate whether Gore is their hometown or if it was just a stop on their way to Europe.

52. Ermanno Olmi, interview by Paolo Rumiz, "Ritorno alla terra," *La Repubblica*, April 28, 2009. http://ricerca.repubblica.it/repubblica/archivio/repubblica/2009/04/28/ritorno-alla-terra.html. Original Italian: "tornare all'essenza, alla verità dei bisogni."

53. Elliot Stein, "Outsider Providence," *The Village Voice*, March 21–March 27, 2001. https://www.villagevoice.com/2001/03/20/outsider-providence/.

Chapter 6

1. See Chapter 4 of this book.
2. Young, "On Earth as It Is in Heaven," *Film Comment*, 57.
3. Ermanno Olmi, interview by Marco Manzoni, *Il primo sguardo*, chap.: Il cinema dentro la vita: conversazione con Ermanno Olmi. Original Italian: "Aspirante cristiano."
4. Olmi, interview with Daniela Padoan, *Ermanno Olmi: Il sentimento della realtà*, 8. Original Italian: "Non sono mai stato un uomo di fede, nel senso che non ho potuto raggiungere una condizione in cui poter dire, 'bene, da adesso credo, e nulla più verrà a incrinare questa mia condizione.' Non è stato così, e non è ancora così. Sono costantemente in cerca di fede. Ogni tano afferro dei bagliori in cui provo il brivido di una fede totale, ma un momento dopo mi ritrovo in quello che è un continuo rimuginare."
5. Molinaro, "Speciale evento: Ermanno Olmi gira a Bari," *Cinemio*.
6. Olmi, interview with Daniela Padoan, *Ermanno Olmi: Il sentimento della realtà*, 7. Original Italian: "Ho sempre sentito Cristo come qualcuno che mi stava col fiato sul collo."
7. Ermanno Olmi, *Lettera a una chiesa che ha dimenticato Gesù* [Letter to a church that has forgotten Jesus] (Milan: Edizioni Piemme, 2013), 9. Original Italian: "Quel Gesù di Nazareth, falegname e maestro, col suo esempio può farci ancora ritrovare la gioia di come spendere il bene prezioso della nostra esistenza. Invece tu, vecchia chiesa che hai innalzato tanti altari di Cristo, sembri averlo dimenticato."
8. Olmi, interview by Marco Manzoni, *Il primo sguardo*, chap.: Il cinema dentro la vita: conversazione con Ermanno Olmi.
9. Olmi, interview with Charlie Owens, *Ermanno Olmi*, 53.
10. *Ibid.*, 55.
11. *A Man Named John* was released in the same year Celi played a Bond villain in *Thunderball* (1965).
12. Olmi, interview with Charles Thomas Samuels, *Encountering Directors*, 104.
13. Pamela Grace, *The Religious Film* (Chichester: Wiley-Blackwell, 2009), 1.
14. Greg Tobin, *The Good Pope: The Making of a Saint and the Remaking of the Church—The Story of John XXIII and Vatican II* (New York: Harper Collins, 2012), EPUB edition, chap. 2.
16. *Ibid.*
15. For a more thorough description of the historical context of this event, see John Pollard, *Catholicism in Modern Italy: Religion, Society, and Politics Since 1861* (New York: Routledge, 2008), 61–65.
16. Olmi, interview with Charlie Owens, *Ermanno Olmi*, 105.
17. Brent Landau, *Revelation of the Magi: The Lost Tale of the Wise Men's Journey to Bethlehem* (New York: Harper Collins, 2010), 3.
18. Harlan Kennedy, "Searching for the Star Child: Ermanno Olmi and *Cam-*

minacammina," *Film Comment* 20, no. 5 (1984): 62.

19. When referring to the names of people and places in the film, I will utilize the biblical proper nouns.

20. John Francis Lane, "Olmi in Volterra," *Sight and Sound* 50, no. 1 (1980), 7.

21. Finatti, *Stupore e mistero nel cinema di Ermanno Olmi*, 65.

22. Ibid., 66.

23. Dean Duncan, *Stories of Childhood: Evolving Portrayals in Books and Films* (Jefferson, NC: McFarland & Company, 2015), Kindle edition, chap. 5: The Problem with Perfection and Ways Forward.

24. The Sermon on the Mount can be found in Matt. 5–7 (King James Version) and Christ's response to the question "which is the great commandment in the law" can be found in Matt. 22: 36–40 (King James Version).

25. Finatti, *Stupore e mistero nel cinema di Ermanno Olmi*: 65–101. Finatti applies Gianfranco Bettetini's concept of "textual temporality" to *Keep Walking* and *Legend of the Holy Drinker* in a comparison of the differences in the two films' stylistic representations of time.

26. *Ibid.*,78. Original Italian: "…Una frammentazione del racconto stesso in tanti episodi, slegandoli da una dimensione temporale di successione lineare e causale."

27. Ibid., 84. Original Italian: "…Struttura epifanica."

28. Milly Buonanno, *Italian TV Drama and Beyond: Stories from the Soil, Stories from the Sea* (Bristol, UK: Intellect Books, 2012), 184.

29. Olmi, interview with Charlie Owens, *Ermanno Olmi*, 137.

32. The voice of British actor, Paul Scofield, replaces Antonutti's in the English language version.

30. Buonanno, *Italian TV Drama and Beyond: Stories from the Soil, Stories from the Sea*, 284.

31. Adele Reinhartz, *Bible and Cinema: An Introduction* (New York: Routledge, 2013), 22.

32. Augustine, *The City of God*, trans. Marcus Dods (New York: Modern Library, 2000), 423.

33. Olmi, interview with Charles Thomas Samuels, *Encountering Directors*, 105.

34. Morandini, *Ermanno Olmi*, 89.

35. Olmi, interview by Daniela Padoan, *Ermanno Olmi: il sentimento della realtà*, 16.

36. "Intervista ad Ermanno Olmi." *Centochiodi* (2007; Alba, Italy: Multimedia San Paolo Srl, 2007), DVD.

37. *Ibid.*

38. Morandini, *Ermanno Olmi*, 73.

39. Ermanno Olmi, interview by Marco Vitale, "Centochiodi: Ermanno Olmi alla scuola normale di Pisa," *Celluloidportraits.com*, accessed January 10, 2017, http://www.celluloidportraits.com/schedaintervista.php?id=56.

40. *Ibid.*

41. This event can be found in John 2: 1–11 (King James Version).

42. Christ tells the parable of the prodigal son in Luke 15: 11–32 (King James Version).

43. John 14: 16–18 (King James Version).

Bibliography

Alsop, Elizabeth. "Neorealism in the Age of Mechanical Reproduction: Restoring the Aura in Olmi's *Il posto*." *Quarterly Review of Film and Video* 32, no. 2 (2015): 179–191. https://doi.org/10.1080/10509208.2013.811350.

Aprà, Adriano, ed. *Ermanno Olmi: Il cinema, i film, la televisione, la scuola* [Ermanno Olmi: The cinema, the films, television, the school]. Venice, Italy: Marsilio Editori, 2003.

Aprà, Adriano, Laura Buffoni, and Stefania Carpiceci. "Filmografia." In Aprà, *Ermanno Olmi: Il cinema, i film, la televisione, la scuola*, 327–332.

Apulia Film Commission. "*Il villaggio di cartone*: Ermanno Olmi gira il suo nuovo film a Bari." Accessed November 3, 2017. http://www.apuliafilmcommission.it/news/il-villaggio-di-cartone-ermanno-olmi-gira-il-suo-nuovo-film-a-bari.

Armes, Roy. "Family Resemblances: A Note on Ermanno Olmi." *London Magazine*, June 1, 1971.

Arrowsmith, Aidan. "Angles on Aran: Constructing Connection in the Work of J.M. Synge, Robert Flaherty and Sean Scully." *Textual Practice* 31 (2017): 1–26. http://dx.doi.org/10.1080/0950236X.2017.1314979.

Aufderheide, Patricia. *Documentary: A Very Short Introduction*. Oxford: Oxford University Press, 2007.

Augustine. *The City of God*. Translated by Marcus Dods. New York: Modern Library, 2000.

Ayfre, Amédée. "Neo-Realism and Phenomenology." In *Cahiers du cinéma: The 1950s: Neo-Realism, Hollywood, New Wave*, edited by Jim Hillier, 182–191. Cambridge, MA: Harvard University Press, 1985.

Barnouw, Erik. *Documentary: A History of the Non-fiction Film*. Oxford: Oxford University Press, 1974.

Baskins, Cristelle. "A Storm of Images: Italian Renaissance Art in Luis Trenker's *Condottieri* (1937)." *The Italianist* 31, no. 2 (2011): 181–204. https://doi.org/10.1179/026143411x13051090964596.

Bazin, André. *What Is Cinema?* Edited and Translated by Hugh Gray. Vol. 1. Berkeley: University of California Press, 1967.

———. *What Is Cinema?* Edited and Translated by Hugh Gray. Vol. 2. Berkeley: University of California Press, 1972.

Beattie, Keith. *Documentary Screens: Non-Fiction Film and Television*. New York: Palgrave Macmillan, 2004.

Bell, Rudolph M. *Fate and Honor, Family and Village: Demographic and Cultural Change in Rural Italy since 1800*. Chicago: University of Chicago Press, 1979.

Benjamin, Walter. "The Work of Art in the Age of Mechanical Reproduction." In *Illuminations: Essays and Reflections*. Edited by Hannah Arendt. Translated by Harry Zohn. New York: Schocken Books, 2007.

Bondanella, Peter. *A History of Italian Cinema*. New York: Continuum, 2009.

Bonifazio, Paola. *Schooling in Modernity: The Politics of Sponsored Films in Postwar Italy*. Toronto: University of Toronto Press, 2014.

Bordwell, David. "Shot and Scene." In *The Classical Hollywood Cinema: Film Style and Mode of Production to 1960*, David Bordwell, Janet Staiger, and Kristin Thompson, 64–71. London: Routledge, 2005. Adobe eReader.

Bosworth, R.J.B. *Italy the Least of the Great Powers: Italian Foreign Policy Before the*

First World War. Cambridge: Cambridge University Press, 1979.

Brecht, Bertolt. "On Chinese Acting." Translated by Eric Bently. *The Tulane Drama Review* 6, no. 1 (1961): 130–136. https://doi.org/10.2307/1125011.

Bresson, Robert. *Notes on Cinematography*. Translated by Jonathan Griffin. New York: Urizen Books, 1975.

Bronsen, David. "Austrian Versus Jew: The Torn Identity of Joseph Roth." *The Leo Baeck Institute Year Book* 18, no. 1 (1973): 220–226. https://doi.org/10.1093/leobaeck/18.1.220.

Brook, Clodagh. "Beyond Dialogue: Speech-Silence, the Monologue, and Power in the Films of Ermanno Olmi." *The Italianist* 28, no. 2 (2008): 268–280. https://doi.org/10.1179/026143408x363569.

Brunette, Peter. *The Films of Michelangelo Antonioni*. Cambridge: Cambridge University Press, 1998.

Bruni, David. "I cortometraggi industriali." In Aprà, *Ermanno Olmi. Il cinema, I film, la televisione, la scuola*, 119–131.

Buonanno, Milly. *Italian TV Drama and Beyond: Stories from the Soil, Stories from the Sea*. Bristol, UK: Intellect Books, 2012.

Callenbach, Ernest. Review of *Il posto*. *Film Quarterly* 17, no. 4 (1964): 44–45. https://doi.org/10.2307/1210655.

Cardullo, Bert. "Married to the Job: Ermanno Olmi's *Il Posto* and *I fidanzati* Reconsidered." *The Cambridge Quarterly* 38, no. 2 (2009): 89–98. https://doi.org/10.7135/upo9781843313434.007.

Casetti, Francesco. *Eye of the Century: Film, Experience, Modernity*. Translated by Erin Larkin and Jennifer Pranolo. New York: Columbia University Press, 2008.

Cecchetti, Giovanni. Introduction to *Operette Morali* [Moral works], by Giacomo Leopardi, 1–18. Translated by Giovanni Cecchetti. Berkeley: University of California Press, 1982.

Cleugh, James. *The Medici: A Tale of Fifteen Generations*. New York: Dorset Press, 1990.

Coogan, Jack. "Louisiana Story and an Ecology of the Imagination." *Wide Angle* 20, no. 2 (1998): 58–69. https://doi.org/10.1353/wan.1998.0013.

Cramer, Michael. "Rossellini's History Lessons." *New Left Review* 78 (2012): 115–134.

Crowther, Bosley. "Screen: A Clerk in Italy. '*Sound of Trumpets*' at Two Theatres." Review of *Il posto*. *New York Times*, October 23, 1963. https://www.nytimes.com/1963/10/23/archives/screen-a-clerk-in-italy-sound-of-trumpets-at-two-theaters.html.

De Iulio, Simona, and Carlo Vinti. "The Americanization of Italian Advertising During the 1950s and the 1960s: Mediations, Conflicts, and Appropriations." *Journal of Historical Research in Marketing* 1, no. 2 (2009): 270–294. https://doi.org/10.1108/17557500910974613.

Di Giamatteo, Fernaldo. "'Marienbadism' and the New Italian Directors." *Film Quarterly* 16, no. 2 (1962–1963): 20–25. https://doi.org/10.1525/fq.1962.16.2.04a00050.

Drake, Richard. "Italy in the 1960s: A Legacy of Terrorism and Liberation." *South Central Review* 16–17, no. 4–1 (1999–2000): 62–76. https://doi.org/10.2307/3190077.

Duncan, Dean. "Nanook of the North." *The Criterion Collection*. Last modified, 2017. https://www.criterion.com/current/posts/42-nanook-of-the-north.

———. *Stories of Childhood: Evolving Portrayals in Books and Films*. Jefferson, NC: McFarland, 2015. Kindle edition.

Edison's YouTube channel page: *La mia valle*. Published February 5, 2016. https://www.youtube.com/watch?v=TRfrZUtljMQ&list=PLjV4jdWdzFfDCg5Q1vCtll7sWRp40Kl2W&index=7.

Edwards, Gwynne. *A Companion to Luis Buñuel*. Rochester, NY: Tamesis, 2005.

EuropaCinema 85. Rimini, Italy: Europa Cinema, 1985. Quoted in "Olmi su Olmi," *Ermanno Olmi: l'esperienza di Ipotesi cinema*.

Falasca-Zamponi, Simonetta. *Fascist Spectacle: The Aesthetics of Power in Mussolini's Italy*. Berkeley: University of California Press, 1997.

Fantuzzi, Virgilio. "Il cristiano muore ogni giorno e ogni giorno rinasce." In Aprà, *Ermanno Olmi: Il cinema, i film, la televisione, la scuola*, 38–69.

Fellini, Federico. *The Book of Dreams*. Translated by Aaron Martin and David Stanton. New York: Rizzoli, 2008.

Finatti, Luca. *Stupore e mistero nel cinema di Ermanno Olmi* [Stupor and mystery in the cinema of Ermanno Olmi]. Rome:

Associazione Nazionale Circoli Cinematografici Italiani, 2000.

Fofi, Goffredo. Introduction to *Il ragazzo della Bovisa* [The boy from Bovisa], by Ermanno Olmi, v-x. Milan: Oscar Mondadori, 2004.

Foot, John. "Mass Cultures, Popular Cultures and the Working Class in Milan, 1950-70." *Social History* 24, no. 9 (1999): 134-157. https://doi.org/10.1080/0307 1029908568059.

———. "Migration and the 'Miracle' at Milan. The Neighbourhoods of Baggio, Barona, Bovisa and Comasina in the 1950s and 1960s." *Journal of Historical Sociology* 10, no. 2 (1997): 184-213. https://doi.org/10.1111/1467-6443.00036.

———. *Modern Italy*. New York: Palgrave Macmillan, 2003.

Fornaciari, Gino, Pietro Bartolozzi, Carlo Bartolozzi, Barbara Rossi, Ilario Menchi, and Andrea Piccioli. "A Great Enigma of the Italian Renaissance: Paleopathological Study on the Death of Giovanni dalle Bande Nere (1498-1526) and Historical Relevance of a Leg Amputation." *BMC Musculoskeletal Disorders* 15, no. 301 (2014): 1-7. https://doi.org/10.1186/1471-2474-15-301.

Fujiwara, Chris. "One Fine Filmmaker: The Uncertain Idealism of Ermanno Olmi." *The Boston Phoenix*, August 1-8, 2002. Accessed January 4, 2014. bostonphoenix.com (site discontinued).

Gallagher, Tag. *The Adventures of Roberto Rossellini: His Life and Films*. New York: Da Capo Press, 1998.

Gervais, Marc. "Ermanno Olmi: Humanism in the Cinema." *Sight and Sound* 47, no. 4 (1978): 210-215.

Gillett, John. Review of *Time Stood Still*. *Sight and Sound* 32, no. 2 (1963): 93-94.

Ginsborg, Paul. *A History of Contemporary Italy: Society and Politics 1943-1988*. New York: Palgrave Macmillan, 2003.

Grace, Pamela. *The Religious Film*. Chichester, UK: Wiley-Blackwell, 2009.

Greene, Naomi. *Pier Paolo Pasolini: Cinema as Heresy*. Princeton: Princeton University Press, 1990.

Grierson, John. "On Flaherty." *Reporter* 5, no. 8 (1951): 31-35. Quoted in *Grierson on the Movies*. Edited by Forsyth Hardy. London: Faber & Faber, 1981.

Grindon, Leger. *Shadows on the Past: Studies in the Historical Fiction Film*. Philadelphia: Temple University Press, 1994.

Hall, M.A. "Cinema Paradiso: Re-Picturing the Medieval Cult of Saints." *Peregrinations: Journal of Medieval Art and Architecture* 2, no. 1 (2005): n.p. http://digital.kenyon.edu/perejournal/vol2/iss1/6.

Havis, Richard James. "Flashback: The Tree of Wooden Clogs—Ermanno Olmi's 1978 Tale of Poverty and Catholic Beliefs." Review of *The Tree of Wooden Clogs*. *The South China Morning Post*, April 8, 2017, http://www.scmp.com/magazines/post-magazine/arts-music/article/2084406/flashback-tree-wooden-clogs-ermanno-olmis-1978.

Hibbert, Christopher. *The House of Medici: Its Rise and Fall*. New York: William Morrow and Company, 1975.

"Il maestro e la favola." *Cantando dietro i paraventi*. 2003; 01 Distribution, 2006. DVD.

"Intervista a Ermanno Olmi." *Centochiodi*. 2007; Alba, Italy: Multimedia San Paolo Srl, 2007. DVD.

———. *Il segreto del bosco vecchio*. 1993; Rome: Medusa Video, 2010. DVD.

"Intervista a Ermanno Olmi," *La circostanza*. 1973; Milan: Dolmen Home Video, 2009. DVD.

"Intervista a Ermanno Olmi." *Un certo giorno*. 1968; Milan: Dolmen Home Video, 2009. DVD.

Ipotesi Cinema. "Lettera ai candidati per Ipotesi Cinema." In *Ermanno Olmi: L'esperienza di Ipotesi Cinema* [Ermanno Olmi: The experience of Ipotesi cinema], edited by Elisa Allegretti and Giancarlo Giraud, 181-185. Bologna: Le Mani Editore, 2001.

Jones, Stephen G. *The British Labour Movement and Film, 1918-1939*. London: Routledge & Kegan Paul, 1987.

Keates, Jonathan. "In the Cascina," *Sight and Sound* 58, no. 1 (1988): 27-30.

Kennedy, Harlan. "Searching for the Star Child: Ermanno Olmi and *Camminacammina*." *Film Comment* 20, no. 5 (1984): 58-63.

Kezich, Tullio. *Ermanno Olmi: il mestiere delle immagini, diario (in pubblico) di un'amicizia* [The profession of images: a diary (in public) of a friendship]. Alessandria, Italy: Edizioni Falsopiano, 2004.

Kimball, Melanie A. "From Folktales to Fiction: Orphan Characters in Children's

Literature." *Library Trends* 47, no. 3 (1999): 558–578.

Kourelou, Olga. "'Put the Blame on ... Mei': Zhang Ziyi and the Politics of Global Stardom." In *The Femme Fatale: Images, Histories, Contexts*, edited by Helen Hanson and Catherine O'Rawe, 113–126. London: Palgrave Macmillan, 2010.

Kovács, András. *Screening Modernism: European Art Cinema, 1950–1980*. Chicago: The University of Chicago Press, 2007.

Landau, Brent. *Revelation of the Magi: The Lost Tale of the Wise Men's Journey to Bethlehem*. New York: HarperCollins, 2010.

Landy, Marcia. *Italian Film*. Cambridge: Cambridge University Press, 2000.

———. "The Subject of History: Italian Filmmakers as Historians." In *A Companion to the Historical Film*, edited by Robert A. Rosenstone and Constantin Parvulescu, 133–153. Chichester, UK: Wiley-Blackwell, 2013.

Lane, John Francis. "Ermanno Olmi: Camera of Concern." In *Movies of the Seventies*, edited by Ann Lloyd, 137–139. London: Orbis Publishing, 1984.

———. "Olmi in Volterra." *Sight and Sound* 50, no. 1 (1980).

Leigh, Mike. "*Blow-Up*? It's a Pile of Pretentious Crap." *The Guardian*, October 26, 2015. https://www.theguardian.com/film/2015/oct/26/mike-leigh-blow-up-antonioni.

———. Interview with Mark Monahan. "Film makers on Film: Mike Leigh." *The Telegraph*, October 19, 2002. https://www.telegraph.co.uk/culture/film/3584402/Film-makers-on-film-Mike-Leigh.html.

Leisawitz, Daniel. "*Il mestiere delle armi*: Renaissance Technology and the Cinema." In *New Worlds and the Italian Renaissance*, edited by Andrea Moudarres and Christiana Purdy Moudarres, 87–121. Leiden, Netherlands: Brill, 2012.

Leprohon, Pierre. *The Italian Cinema*. Translated by Roger Graves and Oliver Stallybrass. New York: Praeger Publishers, 1972.

MacDonald, Scott. "The Ecocinema Experience." In *Ecocinema Theory and Practice*, edited by Stephen Rust, Salma Monani, and Sean Cubitt, 17–41. New York: Routledge, 2013.

Maland, Charles. *City Lights*. London: British Film Institute, 2007.

Malcom, Derek. Review of *The Tree of Wooden Clogs*. *The Guardian*, September 2, 1999. https://www.theguardian.com/film/1999/sep/02/3.

Manzoni, Marco. *Il primo sguardo* [The first glance]. Milan: Bompiani, 2015. Kindle edition.

Marcus, Millicent. *Italian Film in the Light of Neo-Realism*. Princeton: Princeton University Press, 1986.

Matheson, Sue. "The 'True Spirit' of Eating Raw Meat: London, Nietzsche, and Rousseau in Robert Flaherty's *Nanook of the North* (1922)." *Journal of Popular Film and Television* 39, no. 1 (2011): 12–19. https://doi.org/10.1080/01956051.2010.490074.

Minghelli, Giuliana. "Haunted Frames: History and Landscape in Luchino Visconti's *Ossessione*." *Italica* 85, no. 2/3 (2008): 173–196. http://www.jstor.org/stable/40505801.

Moen, Kristian. *Film and Fairy Tales: The Birth of Modern Fantasy*. London: I.B. Tauris, 2013.

Molinaro, Antonella. "Speciale evento: Ermanno Olmi gira a Bari." *Cinemio*. Last modified 2017. http://cinemio.it/film-italiani/il-villaggio-di-cartone-ermanno-olmi/7161/.

Möller, Olaf. "A Specter Called Knowledge." *Film Comment* 39, no. 6 (2003): 62–64.

Morandini, Morando. *Ermanno Olmi*. Milan: Il Castro Cinema, 2009.

Moravia, Alberto. "Ora basta, disse il cavallo," *L'espresso*, October 22, 1978.

"Mysteries of Life." *I fidanzati*. 1963; New York: Criterion Collection, 2003. DVD.

Naremore, James. "Authorship." In *A Companion to Film Theory*, edited by Toby Miller and Robert Stam, 9–24. Malden, MA: Blackwell Publishing, 2004.

Nevin, Thomas. *Thérèse of Lisieux: God's Gentle Warrior*. Oxford: Oxford University Press, 2006.

Ni, Zhen. *Memoirs from the Beijing Film Academy: The Genesis of China's Fifth Generation*. Translated by Chris Berry. Durham, NC: Duke University Press, 2002.

O'Brien, Adam. *Film and the Natural Environment: Elements and Atmospheres*. London: Wallflower Press, 2018.

O'Leary, Alan. "Italian cinema and the *anni*

di piombo." *Journal of European Studies* 40, no. 3 (2010): 243–257. https://doi.org/10.1177/0047244110371912.
Olmi, Ermanno. Interview by Charles Thomas Samuels, *Encountering Directors*, 99–115. New York: Da Capo Press, 1987.
_____. Interview by Charlie Owens. *Ermanno Olmi*. Rome: Gremese, 2008.
_____. Interview by Daniela Padoan. *Ermanno Olmi: Il sentimento della realtà* [Ermanno Olmi: The feeling of reality]. Milan: Editrice San Raffaele, 2008.
_____. Interview by Emma Neri. "Conversazione con Ermanno Olmi." In AA. VV., *EuropaCinema '85*. (1985). Quoted in Manzoni, Marco. *Il primo sguardo*. Milan: Bompiani, 2015. Kindle edition.
_____. Interview by John Francis Lane. "A Conversation with John Francis Lane." *Sight and Sound* 39, no. 3 (1970): 148–152.
_____. Interview by Luca Pellegrini. "Ottimista per disperazione." *L'osservatore Romano*, September 4, 2008. http://www.vatican.va/news_services/or/or_quo/interviste/2008/206q05a1.html.
_____. Interview by Marco Manzoni. *Il primo sguardo*.
_____. Interview by Marco Vitale. "Centochiodi: Ermanno Olmi alla scuola normale di Pisa." *Celluloidportraits.com*. Accessed January 10, 2017, http://www.celluloidportraits.com/schedaintervista.php?id=56.
_____. Interview by Paolo Rumiz. "Ritorno alla terra." *La Repubblica*, April 28, 2009. http://ricerca.repubblica.it/repubblica/archivio/repubblica/2009/04/28/ritorno-alla-terra.html.
_____. Interview by Sergio Toffetti. "Conversazione con Ermanno Olmi." In *I volti e le mani* [Faces and hands], 71–86. Milan: Feltrinelli editore, 2008.
_____. *L'apocalisse è un lieto fine: storie della mia vita e del nostro future* [The apocalypse is a joyful conclusion: stories from my life and of our future]. Milan: RCS Libri, 2013. Kindle edition.
_____. *Lettera a una chiesa che ha dimenticato Gesù* [Letter to a church that has forgotten Jesus]. Milan: Edizioni Piemme, 2013.
Overbey, David. Introduction to *Springtime in Italy*. Edited and translated by David Overbey. London: Talisman Books, 1978.
Pappas, Stephanie. "Tomb of Renaissance Warrior Reveals Mystery Amputation." *Live Science*, November 21, 2012. https://www.livescience.com/24981-renaissance-tomb-reveals-mystery-injury.html.
Pasolini, Pier Paolo. *Heretical Empiricism*. Edited by Louise Barnett. Translated by Ben Lawton and Louise Barnett. Bloomington: Indiana University Press, 1988.
_____. *Scritti corsari* [Corsair writings]. Milan: Garzanti, 1975.
Piault, Marc Henri. "Real with Fiction." *Visual Anthropology Review* 23, no. 1 (2007): 16–25. https://doi.org/10.1525/var.2007.23.1.16.
Piccino, Cristina. "Ermanno Olmi gira un film sulla Grande guerra." *Il manifesto*, January 22, 2014. https://ilmanifesto.it/ermanno-olmi-gira-un-film-sulla-grande-guerra/.
Pick, Anat. "Three Worlds: Dwelling and Worldhood on Screen." In *Screening Nature: Cinema Beyond the Human*, edited by Anat Pick and Guinevere Narraway, 21–36. New York: Berghahn Books, 2013.
Pollard, John. *Catholicism in Modern Italy: Religion, Society, and Politics Since 1861*. New York: Routledge, 2008.
Pope, Barbara Corrado. "A Heroine Without Heroics: The Little Flower of Jesus and Her Times." *Church History: Studies in Christianity and Culture* 57, no. 1 (1988): 46–60.
Prince, Stephen. *The Warrior's Camera: The Cinema of Akira Kurosawa*. Revised ed. Princeton: Princeton University Press, 1999.
"Reflecting Reality." *Il posto*. 1961; New York: Criterion Collection, 2003. DVD.
Reinhartz, Adele. *Bible and Cinema: An Introduction*. New York: Routledge, 2013.
Rhodes, John David. "The Eclipse of Place: Rome's EUR from Rossellini to Antonioni." In *Taking Place: Location and the Moving Image*, edited by John David Rhodes and Elena Gorfinkel, 31–54. Minneapolis: University of Minnesota Press, 2011.
Rohdie, Sam. *The Passion of Pier Paolo Pasolini*. London: British Film Institute, 1995.
Rosenbaum, Jonathan. *Essential Cinema*. Baltimore: The Johns Hopkins University Press, 2004.
Rosenstone, Robert. *Visions of the Past: The Challenge of Film to Our Idea of History*.

Cambridge, MA: Harvard University Press, 1995.

Rossellini, Roberto. "A Panorama of History." In *My Method: Writings and Interviews*, edited by Adriano Aprà, translated by Annapaola Cancogni, 179–212. New York: Marsilio Publishers, 1992.

Roth, Joseph. *Right and Left & Legend of the Holy Drinker*. Translated by Michael Hoffmann. Woodstock, NY: Overlook Press, 1992.

Rothman, William. *The 'I' of the Camera: Essays in Film Criticism, History, and Aesthetics*. Cambridge: Cambridge University Press, 2004.

Roud, Richard. "Roman Summer." *Sight and Sound* 40, no. 4 (1971): 197–202.

Sarris, Andrew. "Film: The Illusion of Naturalism." *The Drama Review* 13, no. 2 (1968): 108–112. https://doi.org/10.2307/1144414.

Sartre, Jean-Paul. *No Exit and Three Other Plays*. Translated by Stuart Gilbert. New York: Vintage Books, 1976.

Sassoon, Donald. *Contemporary Italy: Economy, Society, and Politics since 1945*. London: Longman Publishing, 1997.

Schindler, John R. *Isonzo: The Forgotten Sacrifice of the Great War*. Westport, CT: Praeger, 2001.

Schneider, Jane, and Peter. *Culture and Political Economy in Western Sicily*. New York: Academic Press, 1976.

Schrader, Paul. *Transcendental Style in Film*. New York: Da Capo Press, 1972.

Sengoopta, Chandak. "'The Universal Film for All of Us, Everywhere in the World': Satyajit Ray's *Pather Panchali* (1955) and the Shadow of Robert Flaherty." *Historical Journal of Film, Radio and Television* 29, no. 3 (2009): 277–293. https://doi.org/10.1080/01439680903145520.

Shiel, Mark. *Italian Neorealism: Rebuilding the Cinematic City*. London: Wallflower Press, 2006.

Shipman, David. "Cinema: A Quarterly Review." *Contemporary Review*, April 1, 1988.

Slow Food. "About Us." Last modified, 2015. http://www.slowfood.com/about-us/.

Stein, Elliot. "Outsider Providence." *The Village Voice*, March 21–March 27, 2001. https://www.villagevoice.com/2001/03/20/outsider-providence/.

Stern, Mario Rigoni. Interview by Felix Siddell. "'Sette volte bosco, sette volte prato': An Interview with Mario Rigoni Stern." *Modern Language Notes* 113, no. 1 (1998): 231–243. https://doi.org/10.1353/mln.1998.0015.

Tarrow, Sidney. *Democracy and Disorder: Protest and Politics in Italy 1965–1975*. Oxford: Oxford University Press, 1989.

Thompson, David. *The New Biographical Dictionary of Film*. 5th ed. New York: Alfred A. Knopf, 2010.

Thompson, Mark. *The White War: Life and Death on the Italian Front*. New York: Basic Books, 2008.

Tobin, Greg. *The Good Pope: The Making of a Saint and the Remaking of the Church—the Story of John XXIII and Vatican II*. New York: HarperCollins, 2012.

Walsh, Martin. "Ermanno Olmi: The Ethic of Individual Responsibility." *Monogram* 1, no. 2 (1978): 25–30.

Wan, Wenshang. *White Lotus Rebels and South China Pirates: Crisis and Reform in the Qing Empire*. Cambridge, MA: Harvard University Press, 2014.

Watts, Jonathan. "We Have 12 Years to Limit Climate Change Catastrophe, Warns UN." *The Guardian*, October 8, 2018. https://www.theguardian.com/environment/2018/oct/08/global-warming-must-not-exceed-15c-warns-landmark-un-report.

Weissberg, Jay. Review of *Singing Behind Screens*. *Variety*, October 23, 2003. http://variety.com/2003/film/reviews/singing-behind-screens-1200538428/.

Wierzbicka, Anna. *What Did Jesus Mean?: Explaining the Sermon on the Mount and the Parables in Simple and Universal Human Concepts*. Oxford: Oxford University Press, 2001.

Willoquet-Maricondi, Paula. "Shifting Paradigms: From Environmentalist Films to Ecocinema." In *Framing the World: Explorations in Ecocriticism and Film*, edited by Paula Willoquet-Maricondi, 43–61. Charlottesville: University of Virginia Press, 2010.

Wilson, Emma. *Alain Resnais*. Manchester, UK: Manchester University Press, 2006.

Woodhouse, John. *Gabriele d'Annunzio: Defiant Archangel*. Oxford: Oxford University Press, 2001.

Wright, Basil. *The Long View*. New York: Alfred A. Knopf, 1974.

Young, Deborah. "On Earth as It Is in

Heaven." *Film Comment* 37, no. 2 (2001): 56–62.

Zaccuri, Alessandro. "Grande guerra, Olmi porta Giobbe in trincea." *Avvenire*, November 4, 2014. https://www.avvenire.it/agora/pagine/olmi-.

Zipes, Jack. "The Great Cultural Tsunami of Fairy Tale Films." In *Fairy-Tale Films Beyond Disney: International Perspectives*, edited by Jack Zipes, Pauline Greenhill, and Kendra Magnus-Johnston, 1–17. New York: Routledge, 2016.

Index

Abel 167–168
Adam 165–167
Aesop 114
L'albero degli zoccoli (*The Tree of Wooden Clogs*) 3, 6, 10, 17–18, 24, 45–46, 55, 80, 83, 90–100, 110, 112, 148, 151–152, 155, 166, 169
Allen, Woody 122
Al-Masudi 156
Alsop, Elizabeth 47–48
El ángel exterminador (*The Exterminating Angel*) 117
L'année dernière à Marienbad (*Last Year at Marienbad*) 52
gli anni di piombo 9, 61, 63, 70–71, 76–77, 79, 90
Antonioni, Michelangelo 4, 17, 57, 62
Antonutti, Omero 133, 163, 165
Aretino, Pietro 101–102, 106
Armes, Roy 85
Arrowsmith, Aidan 23
Aufderheide, Patricia 25
Avvenire 110
L'avventura (*The adventure*) 57
Aziz, Sabir 166

Bach, Johann Sebastian 92
Barnouw, Erik 24
Bazin, André 5, 23–24, 33, 50, 59–60, 68, 114
Beattie, Keith 23
The Beijing Film Academy 4
Belatreche, Dalila 126
Belelli, Giancarlo 103
Bell, Rudolph M. 54
La bella corsara (*The Beautiful Corsair*) 136–137
Beltrami, Carlo 177
Benetti, Domenico 109
Benigni, Roberto 129
Benjamin, Walter 74
Bergman, Ingrid 89
Bernabei, Ettore 163
Bertocchi, Antonio 152
Bertocchi, Rita 151
Bertolucci, Bernardo 4, 61, 83, 91

Bianchi, Raffaella 77
Bondanella, Peter 22, 48, 129
Bonifazio, Paola 15, 36
"the boom" *see* "economic miracle"
Bordwell, David 47
Borges, Jorge Luis 135
Brecht, Bertolt 136–138
Brescianini, Teresa 95
Bresson, Robert 4, 142
Brignoli, Giuseppe 94
Brignoli, Mario 93
Brignoli, Omar 92
British Film Institute 17, 45
Brogi, Giulio 131
Brook, Clodagh 41
Brunette, Peter 57
Buñuel, Luis 4, 117–118
Buonanno, Milly 163
Buongiorno natura (Hello nature) 32
Burnett, Charles 4
Buzzati, Dino 129

"Ça c'est Paris" 122
Cabrini, Carlo 53
Cadorna, Luigi 107
Cain 167–168
Callegari, Rosanna 70
Callenbach, Ernest 45
Camminacammina (*Keep Walking*) 10, 114, 155–164
Cannes Film Festival 4, 17, 52, 91, 100, 156
Cantando dietro i paraventi (*Singing Behind Screens*) 10, 135–141
Cantiere d'inverno (A worksite in winter) 32–33, 40
Canzi, Anna 53
Cardullo. Bert 48
Carli, Andreino 85
Carosello (*Carousel*) 76–77, 90
Casetti, Francesco 5
Cavour 38
Ceccarelli, Sandra 105
Cecchetti, Giovanni 29
Celi, Adolfo 150

Index

Centochiodi (*One Hundred Nails*) 10, 71, 141, 170–178
Ceresa, Giovanna 62
Un certo giorno (One Fine Day) 8–9, 11, 39, 62–68
Chanet, Jean-Maurice 125
Chaplin, Charlie 69, 76
Le charme discret de la bourgeoisie (*The Discreet Charm of the Bourgeoisie*) 117
Chen, Xuwu 139
Cherrill, Virginia 76
Christ 10, 19, 44, 69, 71, 73, 98, 104, 116, 135, 141–144, 146–147, 149, 152, 154, 156–163, 169, 170–178
A Christmas Carol 126
Chung Kuo-Cina (Chung Kuo-China) 62
Cicutto, Roberto 121
Cinemaundici 107
La circostanza (*The Circumstance*) 9, 17, 77–82, 90
City Lights 69, 72, 76
Cold War 39
commedia dell'arte 62
Coogan, Jack 28
Costruzioni meccaniche Riva (Mechanical constructions Riva) 26
La cotta (*The Crush*) 39
The Criterion Collection 3
Crosignani, Maria 66
Crowther, Bosley 45
Cucciarrè, Antonio 156
Cuore (*Heart*) 42–43
Cusastro, Matteo 103

dalle Bande Nere, Giovanni or Giovanni de' Medici or Lodovico de' Medici 10, 84, 100–106, 110
Damioli, Vitaliano 62
d'Annunzio, Gabriele 31
Dao ma zei (*The Horse Thief*) 4
De Francovich, Massimo 145
Degan, Raz 171, 175
della Rovere, Francesco Maria I 101–104
del Vita, Brunetto 62
de' Medici, Cosimo I 106
de' Medici, Giovanni *see* dalle Bande Nere, Giovanni
de' Medici, Giovanni di Bicci 100
de' Medici, Giovanni di Pierfrancesco 100
de' Medici, Lodovico *see* dalle Bande Nere, Giovanni
de' Medici, Lucrezia Maria Romola 101
De Medina, Joseph 124
de Roberto, Federico 107
De Sica, Vittorio 4–5, 21–22, 33, 60
d'este, Alfonso 103
Detto, Loredana 17, 46, 84
Dialogo di un venditore di almanacchi e di un passeggiere (Dialogue between an almanac seller and a passerby) 28–30, 35

Di Antonio, Andrea Iacopo 106
Dickens, Charles 126
La diga del ghiacciaio (The glacier's dam) 26–27
di Giamatteo, Fernaldo 52
La dolce vita (The sweet life) 17, 21
Dragonetti, Davide 136
Drake, Richard 61
Dreyer, Carl Theodor 71
The Drifters 25
Dumas, Sandrine 122, 126
Duncan, Dean 158
Durante l'estate (*In the Summertime*, a.k.a. *During the Summer*) 9, 18, 69–76, 175

E venne un uomo (*A Man Named John*) 7, 10, 17, 135, 149–155, 166
"economic miracle" or "the boom" 8, 21, 29, 35–36, 38–40, 42–43, 46, 48, 51, 54–55, 68–69, 71, 90, 131, 168, 178
Edisonvolta 4–5, 7–9, 13–16, 21–37, 40, 42, 45, 55, 68, 114, 133, 166, 178
8½ 52
Eisenstein, Sergei 25
Empire Marketing Board 24
environmental film studies (and/or eco-cinema studies) 7, 68–69, 129–130
Esposito, Marco 114
Eve 165–167

Faconti, Piero 35
Le fantôme de la liberté (The Phantom of Liberty) 117
Fellini, Federico 3–4, 17, 21, 23, 33, 52, 83, 118
Fiat 16
I fidanzati (*The Fiances*) 3, 5, 7, 9, 17, 26, 52–60, 90, 102, 145, 150–151, 166
Film Quarterly 45
Finatti, Luca 69, 81–82, 89, 113, 128, 159
Flaherty, Robert 8, 15, 22–25, 28, 30–31, 34, 37, 40–41, 60, 92
Fontanesi, Gabriele 72
Foot, John 38
Forman, Miloš 48
Formichetti, Francesco 109
Francescato, Alberto 119
Francesco, giullare di Dio (*The Flowers of Saint Francis*) 92
French New Wave 59
Fujiwara, Chris 77–78
Fumagalli, Alberto 156, 161
Fuortes, Lidia 62

Gallagher, Tag 30
Garibaldi, Giuseppe 38
Il gattopardo (*The Leopard*) 52
General Lautrec 98
General Post Office 24
Genesi: la creazione e il diluvio (*Genesis: The Creation and the Flood*) 10–11, 163–170

Germania anno zero (*Germany Year Zero*) 52
Gillett, John 44
Ginsborg, Paul 38
Il giornale dell'anima (*Journal of a Soul*) 149
Giubbani, Fabio 103
Giustiniani, Micaela 131
Godard, Jean-Luc 4, 48, 59
Gonzaga, Federico II 101, 103, 105
Gonzaga, Loyso 101, 104
Grace, Pamela 150
Grammatico, Sergio 102
Gramsci, Antonio 117
Le grand barrage (The great barrier) 26
La grande illusion (*Grand Illusion*) 108
Il grande paese d'acciaio (The great land of steel) 36, 55
Greene, Naomi 34
Grierson, John 8, 15, 22, 24–25, 27, 29, 37, 60
Grindon, Leger 83
Guadrubbi, Paolo 40
Guerrieri, Maria Grazia 170
Guillain-Barré syndrome 10, 18, 114, 156

Hall, M.A. 95
Hauer, Rutger 121–122, 125, 142
Havis, Richard James 10
Haydn, Joseph 170
Herod the Great 161–163
High Hopes 4
Hiroshima mon amour (Hiroshima my love) 52
Historia universal de la infamia (*Universal History of Infamy*) 135
Hong xiang (*The Red Elephant*) 4

Ichikawa, Jun 136, 140
Ipotesi Cinema (Hypothesis cinema) 18, 112
Italian War of 1521–1526 101

Jackson, Peter 108
Jivkov, Christo 101
Job 110
Judas Iscariot 144
Jung, Carl 35

Kafka, Franz 45, 115
Keates, Jonathan 91
Keaton, Buster 45
Kezich, Tullio 37, 53, 84
Killer of Sheep 4
Kimball, Melanie A. 120
Klibansky, Raymond 171
Ko, Carlene 136
Kobayashi, Makoto 137
Kovács, András 52
Kubrick, Stanley 167

Ladri di biciclette (*Bicycle Thieves*) 52, 85
Lamech 168

Landau, Brent 156
Landy, Marcia 83, 117
Lanfredi, Andrea 173
Lang, Fritz 15
Lazzaro felice (*Happy as Lazzaro*) 18
La leggenda del santo bevitore (*The Legend of the Holy Drinker*) 10–11, 121–129, 145
Leigh, Mike 4, 91
Leisawitz, Daniel 102
Leone, Sergio 76
Leopardi, Giacomo 28–29
Leprohon, Pierre 68
Levinas, Emmanuel 144
Li, Xiangyang 139
Lonsdale, Michael 142
Lorrain, Claude 92
Louisiana Story 24, 28, 31
Lunardi, Toni 85–86
Lunga vita alla signora! (*Long Live the Lady*) 7, 10, 113–121
Lungo il fiume (Along the river) 170
Lux Vide 163

Magagna, Paolo 102
Magdalene, Mary 72, 175
Maland, Charles 72
Malcolm, Derek 4
Malick, Terrence 4
Manon Finestra 2 (Manon window 2) 33–34, 40, 44
Manzoni, Alessandro 53, 91
Manzoni, Marco 19
Marcus, Millicent 48–49
Marshall Plan 39
Massari, Lea 57
Mastroianni, Marcello 129
Matheson, Sue 23
Matteotti, Giacomo 86
Memoirs of a Geisha 136
Il mestiere delle armi (*The Profession of Arms*) 10, 83–84, 100–107, 110, 112, 135
Un metro lungo cinque (One meter is as long as five) 36, 68
La mia valle (My valley) 30–31
Michelino 1º B 35
Midnight in Paris 122
Minghelli, Giuliana 21
Modugno, Raffaele 63
Moen, Kristian 113
Morandini, Morando 35, 86, 135
Moras, Nikolaus 102
Moravia, Alberto 91, 99–100, 148
Moriggi, Francesca 92
Moro, Aldo 61
Morricone, Ennio 166
Mozart, Wolfgang Amadeus 94
Mussolini, Benito 83

Nanook of the North 23, 31, 34
Naremore, James 6

Index

National Syndicate of Italian Film Journalists 45
Neo-Realism 5, 8, 9, 17, 21–22, 29, 31, 33–34, 37, 48, 50, 52, 59–61, 85
Nevin, Thomas R. 123
New York Film Critic's Circle 45, 91
New York Times 45
Die Nibelungen (The Nibelungs) 15
Nicholson, Jack 4
1900 91
No Exit 64
Noah 10, 168–170
Le notti di Cabiria (*Nights of Cabiria*) 21

Olivetti 16
Olmi, Andrea 17, 84
Olmi, Elisabetta 17–18, 84
Olmi, Fabio 17, 84. 107
Olmi, Giambattista 13–14, 27, 84, 107
Olmi, Luciano 14
Olmi, Maddalena Teresa 13–15, 27
Omarov, Sultan Temir 139
Operette morali (moral works) 28–29
Ordet 71
Ornaghi, Luigi 92
Oshima, Nagisa 48
Othello 15
Our Town 15
Overbey, David 5

Panseri, Sandro 45
Paracchi, Renato 69
Parise, Goffredo 35
Pasolini, Pier Paolo 4, 8, 15, 17, 22–23, 25, 33–34, 37, 57, 61
Pasqualino, Fortunato 69
The Passenger 62
Pather Panchali 31
La pattuglia del passo San Giacomo (The patrol of the San Giacomo passage) 13, 27–28
La Paura (*Fear*) 107
Il pensionato (The pensioner) 35–36
peripheral figures 9, 27–30, 40, 46–48, 52, 54, 57, 81, 111
Pezzoli, Lucia 93
Pezzuto, Barbara 77
Il pianeta che ci ospita (*Our Host Planet*) 19
Piault, Marc Henri 41
Piccoli calabresi sul Lago Maggiore: nuovi ospiti alla colonia di Suna (Little Calabrians on lake Maggiore: new guests at Suna's summer camp) 15, 26–27
Pick, Anat 68
Pilate, Pontius 176
Pilenga, Franco 93
Pinon, Dominique 122, 127
Pirates of the Caribbean 137
Polo, Marco 156
Pontecorvo, Gillo 76
Pope Benedict XVI 19, 149, 171

Pope Clement VII 101, 103–104
Pope Francis 149
Pope John XXIII or Angelo Giuseppe Roncalli 7, 10, 17, 62, 149–155
Pope Leo X 101
Pope Pius IX 153
Porro, Gaetano 77
Il posto (*The Job*, a.k.a. *The Sound of Trumpets*) 3, 5, 9, 14, 17, 23, 35, 39, 44–52, 62–63, 69, 90, 114–115, 119, 121, 145
Prince, Stephen 6
I promessi sposi (*The Betrothed*) 53–54
Pudovkin, Vsevolod 25

Quayle, Anthony 122–123

Racconti di giovani amori (Stories of young love) 39
Il racconto della Stura (The story of the Stura) 32
Radini-Tedeschi, Giacomo 151, 154
Il ragazzo della Bovisa (The boy from Bovisa) 18, 114
RAI (Radiotelevisione Italiana) 17–18, 35, 39, 68, 69, 76, 84, 90, 155, 163
RAI Cinema 107
Ray, Nicholas 31
Ray, Satyajit 31
Read, Mary 136
I recuperanti (*The Scavengers*) 10–11, 17, 55, 68, 83–90, 107, 112, 131
Red Brigades 61
Reinhertz, Adele 164
Renoir, Jean 108
Resnais, Alain 9, 52–53, 59
Rhodes, John David 32
Ritorno al paese (*Returning to the village*) 68, 84
Rohdie, Sam 25
Rohrwacher, Alice 18
Roma: città aperta (*Rome: Open City*) 15
Roncaglia, Giorgio 80
Roncalli, Angelo Giuseppe *see* Pope John XXIII
Rosenstone, Robert 84
Rosi, Francesco 17
Rossellini, Roberto 4–5, 15, 17, 21–23, 29–30, 33, 37, 60–61, 83–84, 89, 91–92, 100
Rossi, Alberto 153
Rossi, Fabrisio 152
Rossi, Natale 40
Roth, Joseph 121–122, 124
Rothman, William 76
Run for Cover 31
Rye, Preben Lerdorff 71

Sabbatini, Sandra 115
Sack of Rome 100–107
Saint Augustine 166
Saint Joseph 158, 162

Index

Sainte Thérèse of Lisieux 123–128
Saltzman, Harry 17, 149–150
Salviati, Maria 101–102, 104–106
Samuels, Charles Thomas 13, 52
Sánchez, José Padilla 122
Sanders, George 30
Santamaria, Claudio 109
Sardi, Walter 63
Sarris, Andrew 25
Sartre, Jean-Paul 64
Sassoon, Donald 39, 80
Savelli, Ada 77
SCE (*Sezione Cinema Edisonvolta*) [Edisonvolta Cinema Division] 15, 22, 26
Schrader, Paul 142
Das Schloss (*The Castle*) 115
Segalen, Sophie 125
Il segreto del bosco vecchio (*The Secret of the Old Woods*) 7, 10, 122, 129–135, 174
Sengoopta, Chandak 31
Senni, Niccolò 111
Il sergente nella neve (*The Sergeant in the Snow*) 84
Seveso, Roberto 40
Shiel, Mark 5
Shipman, David 117
Sight and Sound 44
Silva, Carmelo 92
Sireci, Mario 77
Slow Food movement 18, 146
Spencer, Bud 136
Sperduti, Alessandro 109
Spielberg, Steven 108
Spinotti, Dante 122, 133
Standard Oil 24
Steiger, Rod 17, 122, 135, 149
Stern, Mario Rigoni 68, 84
Stravinsky, Igor 122, 125, 140
Syed, Amina 172

Tabak, Massimo 77
Tarkovsky, Andrei 4
Il tempo si è fermato (*Time Stood Still*) 3, 6, 9, 16, 28, 40–45, 68, 86
Tenekedjieva, Dessy 102
Terra madre 18, 146
They Shall Not Grow Old 108
Thompson, David 69
Thoreau, Henry David 86
three wise men 155–163
Tian, Zhuangzhuang 4
Tibullus, Albius 101
time-shifting editing 5–6, 9, 13–14, 26, 28, 33, 40, 52–53, 55, 58–59, 65–67, 69–70, 77–79, 81, 100–107, 116, 123–126, 128, 145, 159, 164, 171
Tobin, Greg 153
Tolstoy, Leo 4

Torneranno i prati (*Greenery Will Bloom Again*) 10, 13, 18, 83, 107–112
Toscano, Aldo 102
Totò 76
Tre fili fino a Milano (Three cables all the way to Milan) 34–35
Trevaini, Battista 92
2001: A Space Odyssey 167

Umberto D. 21
The United Nations' Intergovernmental Panel on Climate Change 8

Valmarana, Paolo 18
Van Gogh, Vincent 92
Venice International Film Festival 15, 44–45, 76
Verdi, Giuseppe 15
Vertov, Dziga 25
Viaggio in Italia (*Journey to Italy*) 21, 29–30, 89
Vidotto, Giovanna 119
The Village Voice 148
Il villaggio di cartone (*The Cardboard Village*) 10, 141–147
Villaggio, Paolo 129
Virgin Mary 143, 158, 162
Visconti, Luchino 4–5, 21, 52, 83
von Frundsberg, Georg 101–103
Vulicevic, Sasa 101

Walsh, Martin 98
War Horse 108
Whitman, Walt 87
widow Zheng *see* Zheng Yi Sao
Wilder, Thornton 15
Willoquet-Maricondi, Paula 7, 129
Wilson, Emma 53
Winnie the Pooh 144
Woodhouse, John 31
World War I 14, 84, 86–89, 107–112, 154
World War II 5, 15–16, 27, 32, 37–38, 61, 83, 85, 88, 90–91, 114, 154–155
Wright, Basil 62, 69

Xie, Xiaojing 4

Young, Deborah 148
Yuan, Yung-Lun 135

Zabriskie Point 62
Zandonella, Luciano 131
Zannantonio, Riccardo 130
Zattara, Michele 102, 171
Zheng, Yi 137–138
Zheng, Yisao or the widow Zheng 135–141
Zipes, Jack 113
Zoubida, Haddou 165–167

www.ingramcontent.com/pod-product-compliance
Lightning Source LLC
Chambersburg PA
CBHW020836020526
44114CB00040B/1225